Keynes, Keynesians, and Monetarists

By the Same Author

Price Theory (1949)

Income and Employment Analysis (1951)

An Approach to the Theory of Income Distribution (1958)

Forest Service Price and Appraisal Policies (1958)

A General Theory of the Price Level (1959)

Classical Keynesianism, Monetary Theory, and the Price Level (1961)

Some Aspects of Wage Theory and Policy (1963)

Intermediate Price Theory (1964)

Growth Without Inflation in India (1965)

A Keynesian Theory of Employment and Income Distribution (1966)

Keynes and the Monetarists, and Other Essays (1973)

Income Inequality (Editor, 1973)

Incomes Policy for Full Employment Without Inflation in Canada (1976)

Modern Economic Thought (Editor, 1976)

Capitalism's Inflation and Unemployment Crises (1978)

Keynes, Keynesians and Monetarists

SIDNEY WEINTRAUB

With Co-authors:

Paul Davidson   Hamid Habibagahi

Henry Wallich   E. Roy Weintraub

UNIVERSITY OF PENNSYLVANIA PRESS / 1978

Copyright © 1973 by Rutgers University, the State University of
New Jersey

Copyright © 1978 by Sidney Weintraub

Parts of this book originally appeared as *Keynes and the Monetarists*.
Acknowledgments for permission to reproduce chapters 1, 2, 3, 5, 6, 7,
8, 9, 10, 11, 12, 13, 14, 15, 16, Appendix 1, Appendix 2, and Appendix
3 will be found on pages ix and x.

Library of Congress Cataloging in Publication Data

Weintraub, Sidney, 1914-
   Keynes, Keynesians, and Monetarists.

   Parts of this book originally appeared as
"Keynes and the Monetarists."
   Includes bibliographical references and index.
   1. Economics—Addresses, essays, lectures.
2. Keynesian economics—Addresses, essays, lectures.
3. Money—Addresses, essays, lectures. I. Title.
HB171.W34   330.15′6   77-20307
ISBN 0-8122-7741-4

In Appreciation of
DR. JUAN APONTE
Gifted Student and Esteemed Friend

Contents

Acknowledgments

Permission to reproduce articles has been generously granted by the original copyright holders listed below.

"Keynes and the Monetarists," *Canadian Journal of Economics* (February 1971).

"The Keynesian Light That Failed," *Nebraska Journal of Economics and Business* (Autumn 1975).

"Keynes and the Quantity Theory Elasticities," *Nebraska Journal of Economics and Business* (Spring 1971), co-author Hamid Habibagahi.

"The Full Employment Model: A Critique," *Kyklos* (Fasc. 1, 1972), co-author E. Roy Weintraub.

"Revision and Recantation in Hicksian Economics," *Journal of Economic Issues* (Sept. 1976).

"Money Supplies and Price-Output Indeterminateness: The Friedman Puzzle," *Journal of Economic Issues* (June 1972), co-author Hamid Habibagahi.

"Money As Cause and Effect," *Economic Journal* (December 1973), co-author Paul Davidson. Permission by Cambridge University Press.

"A Theory of Monetary Policy Under Wage Inflation," *University of Queensland* (July 12, 1974). Research lecture, auspices of Australia and New Zealand Banking Group Ltd.

"The Price Level in the Open Economy," *Kyklos* (Fasc. 1, 1977).

"A Macro Theory of Pricing, Income Distribution, and Employment," *Weltwirtschaftliches Archiv* (March 1969).

"Marginal Productivity and Macrodistribution Theory," *Western Economic Journal* (March 1972).

"Rising Demand Curves in Price Level Theory," *Oxford Economic Papers* (March 1971).

"Cost Inflation and the State of Economic Theory: A Comment," *Economic Journal* (June 1974).

"New Books on Keynes," *Journal of Economic Literature* (March 1977).

"A Tax-Based Incomes Policy," *Journal of Economic Issues* (June 1971), co-author Henry Wallich.

"In Defense of Wage-Price Guideposts . . . Plus," *Prices: Issues In Theory, Practice and Public Policy* (University of Pennsylvania Press, 1968), Almarin Phillips and O. E. Williamson, editors.

"An Incomes Policy to Stop Inflation," *Lloyds Bank Review* (January 1971).

"Solow and Stiglitz on Employment and Distribution: A New Romance with An Old Model," *Quarterly Journal of Economics* (February 1970).

Preface

I am extremely grateful to Dean Juan Aponte for inviting me to deliver an inaugural series of lectures to mark the launching of an M.B.A. program at the University of Puerto Rico in February, 1971, and for his friendly insistence that the talks be published. The assembled essays remain substantially in form and content as they were given. I have included one article that was referred to but not then presented, and two other selections are attached as appendices on the recommendation of readers for the University Press.

My work on the various writings had begun earlier. Considering their independent origin there is an inevitable overlap and duplication—economists repeat themselves and I am no exception. Some redundancy has been eliminated but pieces once published seem to possess a life of their own and so, forsaking the substantial revision which might alter the original themes, I have let the reiteration stay.

The issues developed go deep, involving inflation, full employment, income distribution, and monetary policy. Even when economists appear to be talking of other matters they quickly find themselves focusing on these topics. So, in my work, I repeat myself consciously in analyzing these themes.

I am indebted to my associates not only for their initial participation but for their permission to reproduce the writings here. Coauthorship is acknowledged where appropriate. I must also thank the several journals which acquiesced to the reprinting of the published items.

Besides the hospitality and encouragement of Dean Aponte, I also recall with gratitude the favors tendered during my stay in

Puerto Rico by Professor Carlos E. Toro Vizcarrondo, program director, and Professor Manuel Siquenza.

Most of the manuscripts were prepared by Mrs. Donna O'Brecht, at the University of Waterloo. It is overdue that I acknowledge her many labors on my behalf.

SIDNEY WEINTRAUB

Philadelphia
February 1973

Preface to the New Edition

The re-issue of *Keynes and the Monetarists and Other Essays* allows me to amend the title to identify the contents with reasonable accuracy and to include later writings that blend in rather naturally with the original series. Some make new points, others extract shaded nuances of the older themes.

Injecting "Keynesians" into the title reflects my long belief that the doctrines that flourished under his name were at some odds with his thoughts. Currently the more gross impostors have been exposed. Elsewhere I have characterized the model that attached Keynes' name as *Hicksianism,* for it was the design of Sir John Hicks which was widely expounded and manipulated for policy orientation.* Hicks has sought, on at least two occasions, to edge away from this line of thought. Thus:

> "The 'Keynesian revolution' went off at half-cock. . . . The [general] equilibrists . . . thought that what Keynes has said could be absorbed into their equilibrium systems."

> "I must say . . . [the IS-LM] diagram is now much less popular with me than . . . with many other people. It reduces *The General Theory* to equilibrium economics; it is not really [a theory of an economy moving] in time."

> "It is my own opinion that it [steady state growth economics] has been rather a curse . . . maybe it will be one of the (few) advantages of the present economic crisis that it will teach us to get over it . . . [for] it has encouraged economists to waste their time

---

* For specific criticism see "Hicksian Keynesianism: Early Dominance and Later Decline," in my edited volume on *Modern Economic Thought* (Philadelphia: University of Pennsylvania Press, 1977).

upon constructions . . . of great intellectual complexity but . . .
so much out of time, and out of history, as to be practically futile
and indeed misleading."° °

On "in-time" analysis Joan Robinson has often tried to remind
us that Keynes was always tending to move away from the blackboard and out into a time dimension. In mind were the blackboard scribbles of timeless plane diagrams, whether of supply
and demand, or an investment or a propensity to consume
function.

Hicks' remarks constitute a remarkable act of candor, for the
distinguished Nobel Laureate has been responsible not only for
so much of the Keynesian lore but for the modern revival of
mathematical general equilibrium theory and some neater phases
of steady state growthmanship. Undoubtedly it will take time for
his disclaimers to filter down into the professional consciousness
and change the face of the technical and textbook literature.
Nonetheless, his departure from the Keynesian ranks should
mark a giant step forward in releasing superfluous baggage that
has befogged the macro-theory perspective.

The problems that occupied the *Keynes and the Monetarist*
volume were more important practically than doctrinally, though
the latter is the handmaiden of the former; professional disputes
could be relegated to the realm of philosophic aesthetics unless
they spill over into the world of affairs. Keynes, in his magnificent
peroration, reminded us that in economics ideas, whether right or
wrong, ultimately dominate other vested interests. Thus, not
unrelated to what I regarded as wrong ideas, the anguish of
inflation and unemployment intensified since the original publication date in 1973. Stagflation (and slumpflation in the United
Kingdom) became far more pronounced thereafter.

Surely, by this time, it should be apparent that something is
missing. The elemental and conspicuous lack (to me) has been
the absence of a feasible Incomes Policy, implemented in a

** Sir John Hicks, "Some Questions of Time in Economics," in *Evolution,
Welfare, and Time in Economics: Essays In Honor of Nicholas Georgescu-
Roegen*, A. M. Tang, F. M. Westfield, J. S. Worley, eds. (Lexington Books,
1976), pp. 140–143.

manner compatible with a market economy relying on price-cost incentives (and deterrents) to accomplish the necessary production and resource-use functions for human well-being.

Thought in this area moves at the proverbial snail's pace. History must judge us severely for not acting sooner to correct the blight in practical affairs. Economists have too long condoned the insult to our intelligence in the assaults on the laws of arithmetic where general money income advances have leaped ahead by 8, 10, 15, . . . 25 percent (depending on the country) while production has been inching ahead by a meager 2 and 3 per cent.

September 1977   SIDNEY WEINTRAUB

Introduction

PERSPECTIVES ON MONEY WAGES

Economists are as prone as foreign secretaries to admit that their theories and their policy prescriptions are mistaken.[1] When events ensuing from policies are disappointing, the normal reaction is to plead for more time and patience, to insist that the intellectual model is not really in error. Not infrequently, this rationalization is persuasive, for in our subject a conclusive proof of the irrelevance of a set of doctrines is rare. When an intellectual position is at stake, those who have been committed to a point of view are predictably tenacious in insisting on its validity. In principle, we are committed to the search for truth, for valid answers; in practice, the human trait is to be bound to one's intellectual past even when it is no longer tenable. When a set of views has become widely accepted and conventional, transmitted to disciples and then disseminated to a new generation of students, there is an even stronger vested interest in affirming that they are correct.

Yet events are stronger than words in resolving issues and attaching credibility to an alternate set of views. Where logic is wasted, the failure of policies to realize the intended results will quickly arouse skepticism until the views are finally toppled by their practical bankruptcy. Something of this nature has at last happened on the pervasive issue of inflation, embodying major implications for full employment. The theory of money may thereby be in for a revision nearly as important for well-being as the overall reconsideration that ensued from Keynes's criticism based on the unemployment blight of the Great Depression which upset the economist's faith in the prevailing orthodoxy.[2]

1

Within the decade we have witnessed the irrelevance of one school on the inflation issue, and we are now observing the demise of another. Decisively rejected are the Keynesians. They taught originally that inflation and full employment were mutually exclusive so that policies could be neatly symmetrical: increase aggregate demand to cope with unemployment and reduce aggregate demand to prevent inflation. At the optimal aggregate demand position there would be full employment without inflation.[3]

Curiously, although this was the doctrine of the Keynesian school it was never the view of Keynes; the slip in interpretation has led Joan Robinson to denounce the set of ideas as *Bastard Keynesianism.* Largely, it was a development confined to American Keynesians and never promulgated by prominent English disciples of Keynes.

Keynesianism simply failed on the inflation issue. Any cognizance of the facts outside of the United States during the period when it was the ascendant theory should have carried a warning of its inadequacy; even while it was taught, much of the world was suffering from simultaneous inflation *and* unemployment, so that its favorite recipes for price stability and full employment could not have been executed. In recent years this theory of inflation has quietly vanished because of its utter inapplicability to events. On a correct reading of Keynes the incongruity should have been foreseen earlier.

Yet Keynesianism, as practiced under the Kennedy and Johnson years, must be credited for leading the economy on to higher levels of employment and nearly eight years of consecutive output and employment expansion. The ideas on aggregate demand demonstrated that we could, as a practical matter, eradicate the business cycle. Over this period, for several reasons, the record on inflation was reasonably acceptable. But beginning in 1968, as Keynesians led us within sight of the promised land of full employment, in an overdose of caution they recommended tax measures to prevent "overheating." The taxes were designed to stop us just short of full employment and thus, to Keynesian thinking, to avert inflation by creating some unemployment. Of course, with unemployment they could then feel comfortable in denouncing economic stagnation and recommending full employment policies once again! In sight of the goal they counseled retreat before a renewed advance—and retreat again.

The surtax failed to halt the inflation. But it did slow up output and employment. Despite optimistic predictions on how inflation would be checked, the events confirmed that the Keynesian school had no proper theory of inflation nor an adequate appreciation of policies to achieve simultaneous price stability and full employment.

There was also an anti-Keynes element in the thinking of the Keynesian school; the attachment to Phillips curves was designed to show the *incompatibility* of full employment and price stability; proponents then suggested that we must learn to live in a world that denied our aspirations; we had to be resigned to either inflation or unemployment, or to live with an overdose of each. Their medicine could cure kidney disease but induce heart ailments.

Keynesian failures, plus the remarkable energy and persuasiveness of Professor Friedman, established an era of Monetarist ascendancy. The inadequacies of Keynesianism on the inflation front were obvious despite rationalizations that taxes were neither high enough nor increases imposed early enough. Monetarists argued, to the lamentable Nixon administration and a public anxious to believe that a simple and costless remedy would be effective, that stability could be achieved by minor changes in the conduct of monetary policy. The theory was that inflation was due to excesses committed by the central bank, the Federal Reserve. If the Fed would only pursue a steady monetary course, and limit the annual growth in the money supply—variously defined—to the annual output growth rate, then the economy would be stabilized, i.e., it would, after a reasonable time lag, achieve simultaneous full employment and price level stability. Whatever unemployment would occur would be "natural," neither unreasonably high nor abnormal judged by past years. (Those recommending the policies, obviously, would not be unemployed so it was not objectionable on that score!)

While the policy was not followed with quite the meticulous precision that Monetarists would regard as a conclusive test of their opinions, it is a fact that they were privileged to design and conduct a rare and vast laboratory experiment in the American economy to give scope to their ideas. Few schools of thought have been equally fortunate—or unfortunate. Pursuing Monetarists' doctrines between early 1969 and middle 1971 the Nixon administration succeeded in increasing the unemployment rolls by some 2.5 millions while observing with consternation that the price level rose by about 15 per cent. So Monetarism, at the moment of enormous popular and professional acclaim, was overturned by events. Fate was indeed cruel to the theoretical preconceptions.

At the policy level the demise of Monetarism was pronounced in mid-August, 1971, when President Nixon, in a dramatic telecast, implemented a program of price and wage controls in a display of his flexible "principles." The impeachable president who had often pledged "never" to controls, succumbed to pronounce "now." The money wage was recognized as crucial for inflation. Logically, the fatal flaw for a continued adherence to Monetarism at that time was obvious to practical men. If the President was to reduce inflation, according to Monetarist advice, he had to sponsor a policy of tight money. If he was to pursue a policy of full employment, he had to embrace easy money. Unlike the economist without public responsibility, and willing to counsel more time and patience—and more unemployment-inflation sacrifices of others—the dilemma was apparent to the politician. The 1972 election loomed on the horizon, and a disgruntled electorate had to be faced.

While the pathology of simultaneous inflation and unemployment had evolved earlier, the theoretical belief was formulated that this was "temporary," and that if the policy of Monetarist steadiness was pursued, the economy would right itself. This was the "game plan," the football analogy that persuaded a President who enjoyed his spectator sports on Sundays. The game plan of "gradualism," by which the economy would restore itself, given time, finally disintegrated; a new Phase I and Phase II set of plays was installed thereafter. Money wages were recognized as the crucial inflationary factor.

POSTSCRIPT: 1977

The foregoing introduction (of vintage mid-1972, with a few slight verbal changes for this edition) has, I think, survived the passage of time: practically all eleven essays of the original edition were written between late 1969 and early 1971.

Inflation and unemployment, in tandem, grew more rampant and agonizing in the years after publication, especially after the Nixon dismantlement of Phase III in January 1973 as the Nixon advisors, with the election safely won, again revealed their abiding faith in the efficacy of monetary policy. Double-digit price leaps and alarming job layoff trends occurred in the United States in 1974. Superimposed on top of the political trauma the Nixon-Ford years thus faced an immanent crisis of capitalism, with the market economy torpedoed by the double strain of simultaneous inflation and unemployment. While the worst of the storm subsided thereafter—temporarily?—the primal disorders promise to become chronic without some institutional innovation. Yet Monetarists and Keynesians too often cling to their traditional models and labelled prescriptions, pretending that the stagflation events will yield to the conventional remedies.

Figure 1 traces the graphics of the index movements of the consumer price level and the unemployment rate since 1967 to mid-year 1977. The United Kingdom would paint a more horrendous picture, with inflation rates of 25 percent inflicting its anguish in accompanying even greater surges in the unemployment rate than in the United States. Australia has been buffeted almost as badly by the dual blows. Canada, in some desperation and in what is likely to prove another futile and temporary exercise, invoked price and wage controls in October 1975 under a principle of successive de-escalation that guarantees price lunges and excessive unemployment under government auspices. In England, through a series of dodges and inflated rhetorical flourishes about a 'Social Compact,' unions have agreed to bide their wage demands for the pledge of welfare legislation. Even these porous cathedral ceilings threaten to be breached as unions rumble about seceding from the stipulations in favor of muscle-

	Consumer Price Index 1967 = 100	Unemployment Rate %
1967	100.0	3.8
1968	104.2	3.6
1969	109.8	3.5
1970	116.3	4.9
1971	121.3	5.9
1972	125.3	5.6
1973	133.1	4.9
1974	147.7	5.6
1975	161.2	8.7
1976	170.5	7.7
1977	182	6.9

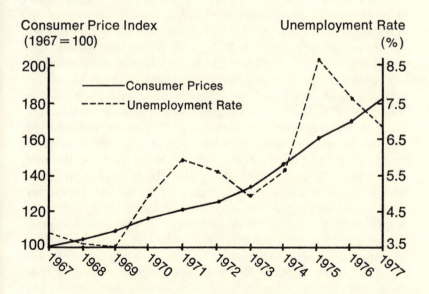

Figure 1.   Consumer Price Index and Unemployment Rate,
United States, 1967-1977

flexing collective bargaining ventures that must surely launch a renewed wage-price spiral and job miseries in that beleagured, though historically enlightened, land of political and economic moderation.

So far (August 1977) the Carter administration· has done nothing to tackle the price ills apart from acting as a tolerant bystander to the monotonous turns of the monetary screws by a Federal Reserve that still retains undiluted faith in its monetary inflation theology despite a history of abject failure. Mainly there seems a wish for an act of God—as in the Ford years—to quench the inflation fires. Policy-wise the Carter administration has been slightly more vigorous (at a creepy tempo) about terminating the unemployment obscenities. It is being pressured to do more.

KEYNES AND THE MONETARISTS

The following essays, though primarily theoretical, deal with precisely this major set of public issues. Running through them consistently, in the theory as in the concrete policy recommendations, is an emphasis on money wages relative to labor productivity as governing the course and force of inflation and, with money supplies, controlling employment/unemployment.

The initial essay was written during the period when Monetarist doctrines were most pervasive and uncritically embraced. Other than making the point, in the interest of historical accuracy of Keynes's life-long concern with money and a smooth monetary mechanism, the article explores the nature of Monetarist thinking. There is the recognition of money linked, after some lag, to money income rather than to prices, the latter being the older quantity theory. There is some skepticism on the Monetarists' account of money supply increases, as if these occurred exogenously and independently of changing *demands* for money resulting from higher money wages. There is a (fruitless) search for "where" and "how" money wages enter into the Monetarist version of the economic process and into the gestation of inflation.

The essay deals at some length with the *two* theories in Keynes: his P-theory of the price level and his N-theory of employment.

Keynesians, unfortunately, concentrated so much on the latter that they overlooked the former. For the price level, the money wage is the linchpin. A critique of Keynesianism appears in the second chapter.

At the policy level Professor Friedman has himself been an authority on the choices open to us, whether (1) to stabilize the quantity of money, or (2) to stabilize factor incomes, or (3) to stabilize the price level. His familiar "rule" has the last objective; it is not the stable money supply that is sought but a stable price level.

Yet, if any of these policies is to succeed it is apparent that an *incomes policy* is a prerequisite, either through conscious attempts to bring money wages into balance, or indirectly, after significant and persistent unemployment.

Assessed in this way, the differences in attitudes become less distinct. An incomes policy could supplement monetary policy, though Monetarists—or so many of them—are often resistant to *any* suggestion of an institutional modification. My own view is that none of their policies can accomplish the full stability that is our mutual goal without a conscious policy on incomes, unless fortuitous and propitious labor market behavior renders conscious policy superfluous.

Closing out the lead article there is the serious question that Monetarists never bother with: suppose they are mistaken? What then? What is their contingency plan? Surely we cannot adhere permanently to their program regardless of cost or consequence. An army draws up a contingency plan in warfare. Why not in economics? We are likely to have more faith in Monetarist prescriptions if we are told of a fallback strategy that may be invoked if the main campaign falters. A nation cannot undertake a policy and, if it is unsuccessful, merely shrug it off without devising an alternative approach.

The Keynesian Light that Failed distinguishes more sharply between Keynes and the doctrines taught under his name. There is now more clarity and agreement on this subject than when I originally attempted to make the anomaly patent, in 1961 in *Classical Keynesianism*. However, even Axel Leijonhuvfud, who has done so much to isolate the Keynes-Keynesian split personality, has gone too far in fostering Walrasian images for Keynes, and has underplayed the pivotal role of Keynes' wage-unit. These facets must be rectified before an accurate perception allows the best in Keynes's analysis to be purely distilled.

MORE ON KEYNES

Friedman himself is the authority for describing his theory as one of *money income,* and admitting that it is not particularly illuminating on the relation of money to price movements or to output movements. Keynes did concern himself with these separate strands in his theory. This part of Keynes's work has been neglected even though Keynes's concepts are readily quantifiable as analytic grist in this day of econometric mulling.

Interestingly, Chapter 3, *Keynes and the Quantity Theory Elasticities,* reveals Keynes's unremitting stress on the money wage for inflation. The contrast is sharp and strong, a reminder of the neglect by Friedman and the Keynesians.

Keynes was dubious of the transfer of the concept of "derived demand" from value theory to what is now known as macroeconomics (Chapter 4). Curiously, this concept, so crucial to the marginal utility revolutionaries—Jevons, Menger, and Walras, and then Marshall—is largely unappreciated today; although it has not disappeared from our textbooks it is not given its due prominence (to judge by examination results!).

Yet it is decisive on critical matters. For if one argues that money operates directly (or by minor detour) on prices, then to control prices by controlled money emissions would be sufficient to control wages. This alone can make sense of those arguments, all too frequent, which suggest that we control the money supply to make prices behave, and forget about an incomes policy. This elemental argument *does* rest on *the theory of derived demand* even though the theoretical linkage is overlooked by many advocates of the policy. Keynes thought that this reasoning chain was mistaken, that the causal path was rather the reverse, that it ran primarily from money wages to prices: it was wages that settled the price dimensions of our economy.

So far as *real* demand goes, there *may* be merit in the theory of derived demand. But this is not the issue; our concern is with *price* formation and not with real demand. The essay undertakes a brief excursion into the history of economic thought, concentrating on the essentials of the doctrine.

FULL EMPLOYMENT AND THE IS-LM MODELS

Not wholly original to Patinkin, but reaching its apogee in his work, has been a tendency to charactize Keynes' unemployment theory as being a "disequilibrium" or "dynamic" theory, with a full employment model being charactized as an "equilibrium" model. But Keynes witnessed an enduring period of unemployment from the early 1920s to the mid-1930s, with no automatic tendency of the economy to right itself. Very properly, then, on an empiric judgment, an unemployment equilibrium prevailed. Keynes' method, too, if assessed closely, was the method of Marshall in analyzing an equilibrium state. Chapter 5 elaborates an underemployment equilibrium interpretation of Keynes, on any reasonable use of these words.

It is thus possible to identify a variety of models, some of which pay lip-service to Keynes, that are by assumption anti-Keynes. For example, there is now a fascination with general equilibrium models in the spirit of Walras. Invariably, the critical assumption is made that "labor demand is equal to labor supply."

Once this is injected it is easy to "prove" that full employment must emerge, and that Keynes was "wrong" in challenging orthodox theory, or in expounding unemployment, or underemployment, equilibria. But to judge by obvious and persistent facts, unemployment is a prevalent and enduring phenomenon, in our own economy and elsewhere; the onus of proof for the relevance of full employment models must be on those who use them.

The point has been overlooked too long: when one writes "labor demand equals labor supply," other model equations are superfluous to demonstrate that full employment will be forthcoming; the elaborate analytic superstructure describing the full employment equilibrium forces becomes a spurious exercise. Yet this kind of analysis is once again in fashion, as if Keynes had never lived, as if unemployment seldom appeared, or Keynes's analysis was no longer germane. It is the full employment model that is devoid of realism, not Keynes. General equilibrium models with "labor demand equals labor supply" provide a mental block to understanding our world. Keynes's insights were meaningful, however untidy the inequality mathematics of labor demand *less than* labor supply may be.

One further point. The demonstration of the full employment outcome is invariably based on balancing the *real*-wage demanded with that offered. A mythical market process is used in proof, showing that as money wages go up and the price level holds firm, a reduction in employment ensues.

This is to ignore Keynes's vital argument that there was no way for labor to bargain in real terms in a money economy, for whenever money wages went up the price level, barring technical improvements, would rise proportionately. On this, Keynes's arguments appear validated by events. Yet it is commonplace to find the "proof" that as money wages go up, real wages go up, while prices hold firm! There is implicit an utter blind spot, conveying complete darkness, on the money wage-price level nexus. This aspect of "full employment" model theorizing should be discarded in the interest of understanding the actual economy.

Hicks has gone further, as noted in the preface, to disassociate himself from his original work on the IS-LM model that pervaded Keynesian economics. In his *Crisis in Keynesian Economics* (reviewed in Chapter 6) it was my view that his revisionism had not gone far enough, and that the fault of original obscurity could not be legitimately charged to Keynes. Despite Hicks' twice-told disclaimer, the IS-LM mechanics (which I have long deplored) continue to be taught, thereby serving as a foundation for illicit policy prescriptions.

Some may want to read, at this point, the short Chapter 15 containing a review of two recent, and worthwhile, books on Keynes.

MONEY, MONETARY POLICY, AND THE OPEN ECONOMY

Professor Friedman has been unduly laconic on the theory of

money wages, yet, for the success of his brand of Monetarism, there is the need for wage levels to approximate productivity norms. He seems to think that this will occur automatically. There is the gnawing doubt: if not, what then? Persistent, permanent unemployment? What policies would he recommend if labor markets did not behave nicely, sensitively, and reasonably, in accordance with his mental construct?

For those non-Monetarists who emphasize the key importance of money wages for the price level, it becomes imperative to explain how money enters and affects the system.

Given any exogenous change in the average level of the money wage—or really *any* changes in money wages (to avoid an interminable debate over the chicken and the egg)—it follows that merely to hold the output and employment level constant (under stationary productivity circumstances), the money supply will ordinarily have to be enlarged.

Essentially, this involves a partial restoration of *Banking Principle* doctrine: in the event of a money wage rise, more money is necessary to meet the needs of trade. The Banking Principle thereby acquires a new respectability in the long doctrinal dispute.[4] It is natural, on this basis, to regard changes in the money supply, once money wages move up, as endogenous, as being *forced* on monetary authorities merely to maintain the prevailing level of output and employment.[5]

Scope for the Currency Principle, involving the causal incidence of money, can be retained with respect to output and employment, and only somewhat indirectly on the level of prices.

If the theory of the price level argued herein is substantially correct, there will be the need for a reconsideration of much of current monetary theory.

In passing, a great deal of modern work stresses equilibrium cash balances corresponding to the "desired" amount of money. Unfortunately, this concentration obscures the essential fact that in using money we are rarely in an equilibrium state; money expenditures are always being adjusted to income receipts in an interminable movement toward the elusive equilibrium. The money equilibrium concept is concerned almost entirely with money "sitting," whereas the typical problems of monetary theory are with "money on the wing," as Dennis Robertson once so felicitously described it.[6]

The essay also offers some resolution of the puzzle that Friedman confesses has evaded his methods, namely, the separable effect of money on prices and on output. In my essay it is argued that money is causal for output but accommodates itself to prices. Obviously, this simple declaration conceals issues of profound importance for theory and policy.

The glaring indeterminateness of monetarism, which is little short of *a lack of a theory of price level variations over time*, and thus a theory of inflation, is better perceived since the time Chapter 7 was originally written. Professor Lawrence Ritter, for one, has poked fun at the monetarist revisionism, which after so long claiming that the important subtleties involved M, money, that they now centered instead around Q, output. Confronted with the "muddle-in-the-middle" of the theory—and skepticism over the stability of the money demand function—the doctrinaire monetarist theory has lost its former strident bounce, professionally if not publicly.

Money As Cause and Effect (Chapter 8), with coauthor Paul Davidson, attempts to place money, and its potency for good or ill, in a perspective more akin to the tone and spirit of Keynes' life-long writing on the subject as against the Quantity theory shadings of monetarism. Its clock-time sequences try to delineate the complications facing the monetary authorities in the real world "in-time" phenomena, as Hicks has aptly named it, in which the policy maneuvers operate. The analysis, too, is in harmony with the older techniques of D. H. Robertson, the modern Swedish school descendents of Wicksell, and even the "disequilibrium-time" models. The argument points up that money wages enter spontaneously, alongside of exogenous money supply changes and productivity developments, either induced or autonomous.

The monetarist money income indeterminativeness is analyzed at more length in Chapter 9, with an elaboration of the WCM solution of their problem. Monetary policy is shown capable of leading real output into a rising growth path, a flat sidewise trend, or into recession. The classification of possibilities details prospects of what, on orthodox quantity theory analyses, are "impossible" juxtapositions of events—which have been only too possible in the real world state of affairs. The limits, and the consequences of monetary policy, in an era of wage excesses, are thereby exposed.

Money market participants seek to divine the future from each central bank money market sneeze. Yet the basic theory taught is of the *independence* of money supply and demand. There is a strong interaction, or interdependence of the two. A brief analysis appears in Chapter 15, reviewing the new books on Keynes. The importance of the point far surpasses the brevity of the discussion.[7]

As part of this grouping of chapters, monetary policy is constrained to operate in an open economy subject to world prices and import-export flows. It is possible, I think, to simplify the theory enormously despite the prolix discussions that are commonly encountered. Chapter 10 aims to close the theoretical gap and shows the rather small modification necessary on at least the formal plane. The conclusion is that it is an act of undue pessimism to blame "world inflation" as responsible for domestic inflation: the affluent trading nations *can* control their own price level fortunes.

INCOME DISTRIBUTION

Income distribution has, for many years, been treated as a fairly neglected stepchild in economic theory; marginal productivity doctrines held sway, being taught by professors who could never explain how they would go about measuring their own marginal product. Recently, the renewed concern over poverty, welfare reform, and in response to hardened human aspirations for acquisition of more material goods, plus the impact of disaffected electorates on political candidates, the issue has come to prominence, more often in descriptions than in analytic studies.

Chapter 11 (and 12) deals with the relation of income distribution, savings propensities, the employment level, and the rate of growth. Income distribution, as a macroeconomic happening, had been relegated to the background in the Keynesian literature. Drawing on the new Cambridge (England) theories, these papers do something, perhaps, to restore the balance. Income shifts to, or from, wage earners can have potent macroeconomic effects. Further, the essay shows the profound penetrating power of the hypothesis that "wage earners spend all, capitalists save all." Necessary qualifications tend to leave their essence undisturbed.

Chapter 12 suggests that the marginal productivity theory is a relic of a nonexistent barter, competitive, stationary, commodity world that never existed, and surely does not exist now. It is thus time to examine the new macrodistributive theories sketched by Mrs. Robinson, Kaldor, Kalecki, and others. A sympathetic approval seems overdue; their concepts lend themselves to quantification and prediction; resistance to them, in this age of econometrics, is hard to fathom. Profit theory especially should be benefitted as it is rescued from a collection of banalities. Others may be encouraged to press forward on the new lines.

The implications for economic growth and development are substantial. The cracks in the old theory, and a skepticism of the pseudo macroeconomics evolving on Cobb-Douglas lines, are apparent in some perceptive recent writings by Professor Franklin Fisher.[8] He surmises that the success of Cobb-Douglas functions in prediction is attributable to the implicit hypothesis of a constant wage share. The constancy of the wage share becomes the essential fact, rather than the other attributes of Cobb-Douglas, such as the "homogeneous" capital aggregate, or the more nebulous derivation of labor's "marginal product," as if physical commodities alone were produced in our economy—and under pure competition!—without any change, over time, in the nature of the composite commodity.

Perhaps fewer of these mystical mathematical calculations will be made once Fisher's important articles are digested. Considering the vested intellectual interests in the concepts, they may continue a lingering, if meaningless, life. Acceptance of the fact of the constancy of the wage share has been basic to my price level argument. Future theoretical work must explain not its constancy—any explanation can serve when a ratio does not change—but how the ratio got stuck at its constant value sometime in the past.

THE CONSUMER PRICE LEVEL

The consumer price level is important to all of us as the other shoe determining our personal *real* income when matched against earnings. *Rising Demand Curves in Price Level Theory*, Chapter 13, should have some theoretical appeal. The argument abandons the absurd assumption (in the name of Keynes!) that the money supply is (?)—should be(?)—constant regardless of output and employment variations. It is particularly stultifying for it hypothecates what seldom is—or never was—an on-going fact. The article stresses the parametric importance of money wages in affecting *both* product demand and product supply curves. In macroeconomics, we stress the *interdependence* of aggregate demand and supply. Too often, however, we forget that for price level theory the Marshallian microeconomic treatment of demand and supply *independence* is inapplicable.

While money wages are held constant in tracing D and S in this paper, Chapter 14 goes the rest of the way in imparting more prominence to the money wage as the consumer price-level maker. This analysis, it should be underscored, starts entirely from *demand* aspects; nonetheless it elicits money wages as instrumental in demand-pull inflation. For consumer markets, the segregation of "demand-pull" from "cost-push" theories is an obstruction that confuses thought. A clearer perception is that in consumer markets both demand and costs dangle from the same marionette strings. It takes only a slight manipulation to apply the same techniques to any consumer sector price level, e.g., for food and energy.[9]

INCOMES POLICY

If money wages are causal for the price level, and if they cannot be affected through monetary policy except at an intolerable cost in unemployment and after a protracted time lag, both the economics and the politics of the matter—noting Keynes's dictum that in the long run we are all dead—impel us to seek a conscious method for insuring prompt and reasonable confluence of money wage and productivity trends.

It is too late in the day for economists merely to chant "Incomes Policy." The best plan that I have been able to devise is included below, involving a joint effort with Dr. Henry Wallich; both of us had arrived independently at much the same approach, namely, of using the corporate income tax mechanism to deter firms from acquiescing in undue wage settlements with unions.

Some minor differences arose in the pleasant collaboration of (then Professor, now Federal Reserve Governor) Wallich and myself. Originally, I favored a simple wage and salary average to dominate the implementation. Governor Wallich favors a *weighted* average as more meaningful. The issue is whether the extra efficiency of the latter is not overshadowed by its complexity. This deserves more study in empirical instances. Neither of us is wholly committed to either conception; both of us, however, believe that of the alternatives currently available the proposed policy, because of its market orientation involving minimal interference in our economy, and tied to familiar tax practices, will inflict the least damage on our economy. Perhaps the proposal will stimulate a search for better methods, compatible with our institutions, for curbing inflation.

A word on the importance of stopping inflation: Some Keynesians are willing to forget the price level and just forge ahead to full employment.

This would be a disaster in practice and it would throw our science into disrepute. Inflation imposes inequities that are not subject to easy evaluation or correction. A society that tolerates inequities has one strike against it; we should not opt for results that we know are unfair, especially when elderly citizens, or unadaptable members of the labor force, are involved. Further, so long as the view prevails that inflation *does* matter, and unless we have an incomes policy to combat it, the attack on inflation will be pursued by monetary and fiscal action. Unemployment will be the predictable outcome. Therefore, to secure the full employment goal we must persist in the battle against inflation. Checking inflation is likely to be the surest means of facilitating our full employment aims.

A successful and feasible incomes policy thus becomes one of the major unfinished tasks. Not only price stability but also full employment depends on it.

Appendix 2 contains my initial elaboration of TIP. It may have its use in its shading of some nuances of the proposal.

APPENDIX ESSAYS

The essay *In Defense of Wage-Price Guideposts . . . Plus* indicates a long concern with incomes policy. Written in 1966 (other writings go back to 1959), it is reprinted at the urging of a referee that it contains a few considerations ignored in the other articles.

Following my initial TIP publication, the final article in this volume deals with recent novelties introduced into macroeconomics by Professors Solow and Stiglitz. Naturally, I am pleased that almost a decade after his critical review, Professor Solow has embraced some key features of the model which he found objectionable earlier.

A FINAL WORD

The 1973 edition opened this final section by saying that "anyone persisting in his views can do so only in the belief that his position is substantially correct." Events in our economy, and in almost all market economies, together with the Keynesian crumbling and the Monetarist flounces on a "suddenly" discovered instability in rates of money velocity, their haziness on price-output variations, the exogeneity inherent in their recognition of "expectations of inflation" on money wages, and on their succumbing to indexation remedies, persuade me at least of the comparative advantages of my approach. So, the new essays, along with the old, "persist."

Challenges, and opportunities, abound in the realm of thought, and particularly about policy, to minister to the writhing market economies in their struggle to achieve a more optimal performance so as to preserve their virtues while suppressing their defects. While I continue to hold that Keynes was most nearly right in identifying the main elements of the macrotheory of inflation and unemployment, especially on the part played by money wages, the future promises a major post-Keynesian revision. Egregious fresh elements of complexity have surfaced. They include the hardened human aspirations for more real income, the quantum leaps in technology, the altered size of the private and public sector, the threatened energy shortfall, and above all the gigantic puff-up in economic magnitudes that record the transformation of the system, and making for incommensurate dimensions of the economic problems since the Great Depression era in which he wrote.

Much economic analysis and associated policy implications will have to be repaired, and other parts withdrawn, as Hicks concedes for Keynesianism and as Monetarists ill conceal for their own models. Economic theory remains an unfinished subject even though some respected figures disseminate the self-serving idea—as defective now as Jevons discerned for his day—that the art is in a settled state based on their own work.

Perhaps the next generation will indulge the suspicion that whenever there is a shortfall from optimal performance in the economy there *may* be a valid presumption that the theory is remiss. This "heretical" thought is at least always worth checking out.

NOTES

1. Hicks, as the quotation in the new preface above reveals, must be counted as the major exception at the current date.

2. On the evils of a "despotic calm" in science, and dependence on "authority," W. S. Jevons' peroration still remains fresh and recommended reading. See *The Theory of Political Economy*, 5th ed. (New York: Augustus Kelley, 1965, reprint), pp. 275–277.

3. Cf. my "Classical Keynesianism: A Plea for Its Abandonment," in *Classical Keynesianism, Monetary Theory, and the Price Level* (Philadelphia: Chilton Book Co., 1961).

4. Cf. Joan Robinson, *Economic Heresies* (New York: Basic Books, 1971).

5. Cf. Nicholas Kaldor, "The New Monetarism," *Lloyds Bank Reveiw*, July 1970.

6. D. H. Robertson, *Money* (New York: Harcourt, Brace and Co., 1927), pp. 37–40.

7. I have tried to do more in my *Capitalism's Inflation and Unemployment Crisis* (Reading, Mass.: Addison-Wesley, 1978).

8. See Franklin M. Fisher, "Aggregate Production Functions and the Explanation of Wages: A Simulation Experiment," *Review of Economics and Statistics*, November 1971, and "The Existence of Aggregate Production Functions," *Econometrica*, 1969.

9. See my *Capitalism's Inflation and Unemployment Crisis.*

1 Keynes and the Monetarists

Now, as I have often pointed out to my students, some of whom have been brought up in sporting circles, high-brow opinion is like a hunted hare; if you stand in the same place . . . it can be relied upon to come round to you in circle. D. H. Robertson, *Economic Commentaries* (London: Staples Press Ltd., 1956), p. 81.

Undoubtedly the late Sir Dennis Robertson, and Keynes himself, would have approved the modern Monetarist inscription that "money matters." Both might be astonished to learn that any economist thought otherwise. Near death, Keynes was engrossed in plans for guiding the world banks toward establishing a viable international monetary order; the man who gave currency to the concept of monetary management can hardly be accused of ignoring monetary influences.[1]

In the light of modern controversy it is of some importance to examine how and where money enters into Keynes's system in contrast with the views of Milton Friedman, the most prominent Monetarist. This should permit a judgment on the possible rapprochement of ideas or the identification of any impassable chasm. It will prove convenient to commence with Friedman's Monetarist doctrines, for their directness should afford ready contrast with the "two theories" that can be demarcated in Keynes.

The Friedman Monetarist View

In his exposition of monetary phenomena Professor Friedman usually connects the changes in the money aggregate to changes in money *income,* thereby transforming the old into the new quantity theory of money.[2] In the hands of Jean Bodin, John Locke, Richard Cantillon, and the two Davids, Hume and Ricardo, changes in the money stock compelled changes in the price level (P) with due recognition of transitional effects on output (Q) and employment (N).

While the predictive superiority of models is not under review here, Professor Friedman has deployed income models of the following nature which convey his thinking on the pervasive influence of money supplies: [3]

$$\Delta Y = V'\Delta M \tag{1}$$

$$d \log Y(T)/d \log M(T) = f(y_p, \delta, \hat{w}) \tag{2}$$

where Y = money income; M = money supply; V' = marginal income velocity of money; y_p = permanent income; δ = other variables; $\hat{w}$ = elasticity of price level to money income.

From the above, and in the analytic statement which is erected firmly on a modernized version of the Cambridge demand function for money (embodying several of Keynes's liquidity-preference ingredients), Friedman espouses his rules for monetary policy to achieve steadier growth in the economy without inflation.[4] Although conceding that the past record discloses some feedback tendencies tracking the other way, Professor Friedman extracts as the main lesson that of the governing power of money; he traces the causal train running from $\Delta M \rightarrow \Delta P$ and, in conditions of unemployment either under cyclical recession or labor force growth, from $\Delta M \rightarrow \Delta Q$, with a variable time lag historically as low as four months and as high as twenty-nine months.[5]

Reflecting on his inductive studies, Professor Friedman concludes, nonetheless, that the money income split between $Q\Delta P$ and $P\Delta Q$ subsequent upon ΔM is obscure: [6] "The general subject of the division of changes in money income between prices and quantity badly needs more investigation." Also: "none of our leading economic theories has much to say about it."

Despite the inability of his statistical techniques to isolate the precise ΔP impact, Professor Friedman insists on the "close link between money changes" and macro phenomena so that "if you want to control prices and incomes," money supplies provide the lever.[7]

A Monetarist Version of Inflation

In the title essay of his recent collection of writings Friedman invites us to visualize a helicopter dropping dollar bills over an economy in settled equilibrium, to double the existing cash holdings.[8] Through his M_d equation of money-demand, with each individual seeking to maintain his representative real holdings, the doubled expenditure will double prices and nominal income: with Q unchanged P must yield.

This is a revival of David Hume's parable of imagining each Englishman awakening to find an extra £5 note "slipt into his pocket." Hume also recounts that P will ascend to reflect the greater money supply.[9] Professor Friedman includes repeated helicopter "raids": P will rise at the same pace as M, with proper reservations for anticipations and uncertainty.

Over time, barring only the other determinants of M_d—the expectation of inflation especially—and the Q-changes, P responds to M; inflation is inherently a monetary phenomenon. The system "gets out of order" when M "behaves erratically, when either its rate of increase is sharply stepped up—which will mean price inflation, or sharply contracted—which will mean economic depression. . . ."[10]

Money Wages

In the Monetarist doctrine full employment ensues from the automatic market forces establishing appropriate prices and factor incomes reflecting the ultimate real relations regardless of the size of M.[11] Missing in the usual Monetarist version of inflation is any stress on average money wages (w).[12] But this lack is not inadvertent for there are other passages in which the wage-price spiral is either rejected or denounced as of no significance.[13] The reasoning seems to be based on the contemplation of a system in general equilibrium, in which once M is fixed, through an implicit stipulation of the velocity of money (V), MV governs Y.

With Y settled, given the demand and cost phenomena, product prices are resolved. Adjusted simultaneously are factor prices. To "explain" factor prices the system is opened, and the "partial" equilibrium theory generally utilized invokes the principle of "derived-demand," to wit, that product prices determine factor prices.[14]

Disorderly Labor Markets?

In the Monetarist vision then, once M is introduced and supplemented by the real forces, full equilibrium will be established and the endogenous P-Y-Q-w-N-r variables will be ordered.

Suppose that in this tranquil Walrasian image there is an increase in w, sponsored by a new sentiment that permits this to happen. Union leaders propose and business leaders defer. Clearly, with M (and V) rigid then P *must* rise, and Q and N *must* drop: unemployment will occur as the demand for nominal money balances increases because of the price rise, and interest rates rise, depressing investment. This is scarcely a novel conclusion; non-Keynesians long ago concluded that Keynes's unemployment theory was erected on wage rigidity.[15]

We shall return to the implications of this analysis shortly for it is just at this point that the Monetarist position is faced with the ultimate hard implication of espousing unemployment on the presumption that the wage level will right itself mechanistically without any direct intervention in the form of incomes or wage policy. Conceptually, the wage level may be resistant to this self-correcting dependence so that the outcome partakes of features of the worst of both worlds, of unacceptable rates of inflation with persistent wage hikes and excessive unemployment, as in the United States in 1957-9 and 1969-70.

Further, the dilemma cannot be escaped by arguing that over time improvements in labor productivity will simply neutralize the wage gains. For the facts are likely to be such that the progress of the calendar will also report new wage increases so that the same issues remain though with altered impacts, depending on the size of the wage-productivity ingredients in the new mix of relations.

The P- and Q-Theories of Keynes

With minor qualification the Monetarist position rests on the causal relation of $\Delta M \to \Delta Y$ with an intervening time lag. Noting:

$$dY = PdQ + QdP, \qquad (3a)$$

$$\text{or} \quad dY/Y = dQ/Q + dP/P \qquad (3b)$$

Professor Friedman admits to some obscurity surrounding the magnitude of the respective $P\Delta Q$ and $Q\Delta P$ portions of the ΔY variation ensuing upon an exogenous ΔM change.

Despite some failures in subsequent interpretations of his work, Keynes was concerned with this very issue.[16] Two core themes are distinguishable in *The General Theory*. One, of course, delineates the employment-output determinants: this is the N (or Q)-theory. The other is Keynes's price level theory, a P-theory. Of these two facets of Keynesianism the Q-theory has achieved far greater prominence in exposition and application than the P-theory. Our account will reverse this practice. Although the elaboration of each theory will be brief, some attempt will be made to explore the monetary implications of each theory for evidence of agreement with and dissent from the Monetarist point of view.

The Q-Theory

In the Great Depression it was inevitable that Keynes's N-precepts were spotlighted. The message was codified and transferred to the textbooks by means of the 45° diagram of Hansen and Samuelson, with further generalization in Hicks's *IS-LM* interpretation: this Q-distillation bears the "Keynesian" label.[17]

These models are so commonplace that there is no need to dwell on them. They run in terms of real output and thus assume, implicitly, a constant price level—at least until "full employment." Inflation is thus effectively precluded. So far as their monetary implications go, barring the absolute liquidity preferences that would mark only the special circumstances of the 1930s which discouraged Keynes's faith in monetary policy, we would have:

$$(\partial Q/\partial I)\,(\partial I/\partial r)\,(dr/dM) > 0, \text{with} \qquad (4a)$$

$$\partial Q/\partial I > 0 \text{ and } \partial I/\partial r < 0 > dr/dM \qquad (4b)$$

where I = real investment, r = the level of interest rates.

More money would thus yield more output in amount related to the investment function and the multiplier. For Keynes, the "laws of return" would also be a factor for there could be some price level perturbations, say, under diminishing returns. For the money increment to match up with the output increment, and any associated price eruption to evoke the output, we would have:

$$V\Delta M + M\Delta V + \Delta V\Delta M = P\Delta Q + Q\Delta P + \Delta P\Delta Q. \quad (5a)$$

If $\Delta V = 0$, and availing ourselves of the truism $V = PQ/M$, then:

$$(Q\Delta M/M\Delta Q) = 1 + (Q\Delta P/P\Delta Q) + \Delta P/P. \qquad (5b)$$

Writing E_{mq} for the elasticity on the left side, *though viewing money as the independent variable for policy,* and recognizing the right side parentheses as the reciprocal of the (aggregate) supply elasticity (E_s), we have:

$$E_{mq} = 1 + (1 + \Delta Q/Q)/E_s. \qquad (5c)$$

In equation 5c, by working in constant dollars so long as there is unemployment, Keynesians really view $E_s = \infty$, so that a one per cent money variation has an output *potential* of one per cent, with the precise outcome hinging on the investment and liquidity functions (and thus, implicitly, on the ΔV variation). Monetarists would generally share this view, but with an appropriate ΔV qualifier being more central and explicit. Keynes, on the other hand, would also give attention to the "laws of return," and some latent price perturbations accompanying the output flow after a money injection—even with money wages (the "wage-unit") constant. To Keynes, E_s would be neither zero nor infinite; its magnitude would depend on the productivity of the available labor and the state of idle equipment. "Diminishing-returns inflation," while not normally a serious phenomenon in an employment upswing, could not be summarily precluded.

Nonetheless, in the overall monetary implications of equation 5a there is nothing *in principle* to separate Keynes from either Keynesians or Monetarists: more money is generally indispensable for higher output-employment levels. The money increment in equation 5a, whose exact amount is imperfectly predictable because of changes in the average velocity of money (which Keynes thought would vary because of volatility in the speculative motive), is causal, as in the Monetarist view. The money injection required to budge Q in amount ΔQ can be described as the *stimulative* aspect of monetary policy. In older terminology it has its analogue in the Currency Principle which viewed money as transmitting a causal influence in governing macroeconomic phenomena.

There can be little serious dispute then, so far as the Q-theory goes, in identifying Keynes with the Monetarists under conditions of unemployment and interest rate-investment sensitivity to larger money supplies, with wages rigid *and constant returns* under pure competition so that price movements were precluded. In this Keynesian model that has largely dominated the literature the P-aspects were effectively suppressed; the mitigating factor was that nobody suspected that cumulative inflation would mar the post-war scene. Through Keynesian insights, unemployment has been *nearly* eradicated. Inflation is our new devil. Hence Keynes must now be appraised in the perspective of inflation theory.

Keynesian Caricatures: the "Symmetrical" Theory

Keynes's inflation ideas have been badly caricatured, even by dedicated Keynesians.[18] For whereas Keynes deliberately chose wage-units as his "deflator," Keynesians blithely made the translation in *real* terms—"constant dollars"—despite his admonitions.[19] For Q-theory this probably made no difference; for the P-theory it does. Working in real terms Keynesians evolved a neat—albeit erroneous—symmetry, with unemployment on one side of the full employment equilibrium and inflation on the other.[20] Overlooked entirely was the obvious fact that most of the postwar world suffered concomitant unemployment *and* inflation. There was also the analytical anomaly of expounding inflation in a model of constant prices.

Phillips Curve as Anti-Keynes

Lately, with the Phillips curve grafted on to the Keynesian apparatus a plausible theory of inflation has emerged. The Q-determinants (with labor force) transmit simultaneously the unemployment forces; unemployment rates thereupon govern the wage *increments* which impel P-perturbations.

Phillips curves, with their trade-off fixation, imbed some complacency into modern Keynesianism. Technically, proponents are apt to overlook Phillips's empirical curve-fittings in an analytic leap toward smooth functions which suppress an immanent range of indeterminateness. Philosophically, Phillips curve addiction perpetrates a cruel hoax on Keynes in its invitation to abide *some* unemployment and *some* inflation; it has led some Keynesians to abdicate the promised land of full employment for the comfort of vague but possible price damping.[21] It has led others to brush off inflation as unimportant. Keynes's entire intellectual commitment was to use reason to eradicate economic ailments rather than to "trade-off" one ill for another.[22]

Keynes on Wages and Prices: the P-Theory

Once Keynes assumes a given wage unit—interpreted here as an average money wage level and structure—only his Q- or N-theory really surfaces. Given w, P is determinate: while P may rise as N advances because of some diminishing returns, or some rise in monopoly power accompanying shifts in the consumption function or the investment level, the P-perturbations are probably small. For the Q-theory, therefore, "constant-dollar" Keynesianism is amply representative of Keynes.

Once w alters, the conventional Keynesianism fails; nothing really happens either under the 45° approach or the *IS-LM* coverage. Of course, this dichotomization of Keynes into two isolated and independent core theories need not arise; a unified approach would serve both ends for there are some indubitable interactions between w, P, r, Q, and N. Keynes himself, in his neglected chapters on w and P interdependence (*The General Theory*, chaps. 19–21), sketched in his own masterly way the key consequences of a general cut in wages. Noting that wage cuts were frequently recommended as the remedy for unemployment, Keynes concluded that lowering w would compel a (nearly) proportionate fall in P.[23] Employment might increase, *if the nominal money supply was unchanged,* because the curtailed demand for money at the lower P would depress r: a general fall in w was thus revealed to be a roundabout method of expanding *real* cash balances and reducing r; the ends of monetary policy would thereby be accomplished through trade union acquiescence. In the prevailing moods of the Great Depression the N-effects would be minimal. This is one of the more percipient analyses of *The General Theory*.

Prices and Unit Wage Costs

The price level in Keynes depends substantially on the relation of w to the average productivity of labor (A).[24] A relative rise in w would raise unit labor costs and spur a higher P. Monopoly power is also admitted while *expectations of the future enter through user costs;* the Monetarist stress on "inflationary expectations" could cite Keynes's priority. With minor latitude Keynes's P-theory can be transcribed as $P = kw/A$, where $k =$ the markup of prices over unit labor costs or the reciprocal of the wage share. With k "nearly" constant, unit labor costs dominate the P-outcome.

Monetary Aspects

The monetary implications of Keynes's P-theory follow readily. Lowering w and thus P, with Q unchanged, r may fall if M is fixed. The r-reduction may stimulate I, and thus Q and N. A higher w would spark the opposite sequence. To offset any unemployment incidence the M-total would have to expand. Keynes *always* advocated action to increase M and reduce r so long as unemployment prevailed, the state of liquidity preferences permitting. There can be little question on this, or on his view that, with an increase of employment, and M constant, that interest rates would edge upward. To reverse the argument and make it at least partially relevant to contemporary inflation, with higher wage and price levels we would have (when output growth has been retarded)

$$\Delta(MV) = Q\Delta P \text{ or } (P\Delta M/M\Delta P) = 1, \text{ if } \Delta V = \Delta Q = 0. \quad (6)$$

For Keynes, once a wage movement had occurred through trade union success at the bargaining table, the money supply would have to be enlarged to avert unemployment following a higher demand for money and higher interest rates if M is unchanged. The causal impetus, however, resides in the ΔP advance (following Δw). Monetary action which is geared to maintain the Q-level might be described as performing a *sustaining* function, or merely "meeting the needs of trade" in the language of the older Banking School.[25]

It is with respect to the execution of the "sustaining" function that Keynes's analysis deviates from the Monetarist position. The money increment is not a causal factor; it is an effect of "business conditions" which Friedman acknowledges as occurring empirically—but not assigned by him the form of an inflation anticlimax, as the foregoing interpretation of Keynes would have it. Further, for Keynes the demand for more money implicit in equation 6 tends to *compel* sustaining operations on the part of the monetary authorities. Thus increments in the money supply are not envisaged as descending from a helicopter but as reflecting:

(1) the higher wage and price levels, which (2) induce an increased demand for nominal money quantities, which (3) is then relieved by the monetary authorities acknowledging the unpalatable political, social, and economic facts of unemployment in the midst of an inflation about which they are practically impotent. On the inflation front, rather than indicting their actions in expanding the money supply as causing the unwanted price phenomena, the monetary authorities are instead engaged in scotching the other ailment, that of unemployment; in the generation of inflation they are neither culpable agents nor willing accomplices.

Liquidity-Preference Proper

Even these brief remarks stamp Keynes as a Monetarist, cognizant that "money matters." Keynes's Monetarism would also lean to the provision of more money to sate the speculative-demand for cash balances whenever "liquidity-preference proper" threatened to lift the r-structure and impede full employment. Whenever individuals (or institutions) wanted green cheese (money), the green cheese factory—the central bank—had to produce such objects of fancy (*The General Theory*, p. 235). Only more money could check a Q-N deterioration; an unresponsive M would indeed matter. In a Monetarist version these aspects of a greater demand for money would be subsumed, presumably, in a change in money velocity (ΔV) at higher interest rates. Keynes's monetary analysis sought out the source or cause of such variations; velocity changes were the necessary accompaniment of the behavioral relations described.

The Friedman Monetarist Rules

The spirit and feasibility of a theory can often be tested in its strategy for policy. Professor Friedman has listed three alternative proposals; all of them are a throwback to discussions in the 1930s. He writes: [26] ". . . I have always emphasized that a *steady* and known rate of increase in the quantity of money is more important than the precise numerical value of the rate of increase."

Let us consider his monetary prescriptions. In all cases we shall enunciate the rule and then comment on the M, P, and w path. The t-subscript will denote the year, with t-n referring to the date at which the policy commences.[27]

Rule 1. A Constant M. The first proposal involves holding M constant. Friedman declares this policy would accomplish "a decline in prices of about 4 to 5 per cent a year, if the real demand for money continues to rise with real income as it has on the average of the past century" (p. 46).

Rule 1: $M_t = M_{t-1} = M_{t-2} = M_{t-3} = \cdots = M_{t-n};$

P-series: $P_t = 0.95P_{t-1} = 0.95^2P_{t-2} = \cdots = 0.95^nP_{t-n};$

w-series: $w_t = (1 - e)w_{t-1} = (1 - e)^2w_{t-2}$
$$= \cdots (1 - e)^nw_{t-n}.$$

On rule 1 the money wage level would fall at a rate (approximately) equal to the growth of the labor force (e), with e in the 1 per cent–2 per cent range. Reflecting on the path of w is enough to dispel confidence in the immediate implementation of rule 1. Even if full employment could proceed under P-deflation, the requisite of a falling w would presage severe union strife, for it is a program to secure labor's assent to falling money wages.

Rule 2. Constant w. Retaining rule 1 as a "long-run" objective, but "too drastic" for the near future, Friedman announces "a more limited policy objective might be to stabilize the price of factor services" (p. 46). On his estimates of unitary income elasticity of demand for real cash balances "this would require for the United States a rise in the quantity of money of about 1 per cent per year, to match the growth in population and labor force." For a somewhat higher elasticity, a 2 per cent money increment would be in order.

Rule 2: $w_t = w_{t-1} = w_{t-2} = \cdots w_{t-n}$;

M-*series:* $M_t = 1.02M_{t-1} = (1.02)^2M_{t-2} = \cdots = (1.02)^nM_{t-n}$;

P-*series:* $P_t = 0.97P_{t-1} = (0.97)^2P_{t-2} = \cdots = (0.97)^nP_{t-n}$.

Friedman appears reticent about specifying money wages and, instead, talks of the prices of "factor services." Surely wages *must* be paramount.[28] The P-series assumes that technological factors raise output by about 3 per cent per annum. Unquestionably this rule imposes a powerful discipline on labor, to forego, on average, increases in money wages.

Rule 3. A Constant M-*Growth.* Because of the recent tendencies of P to rise by some 3 per cent to 5 per cent per annum, Professor Friedman renounces rule 2 as involving "serious transitional costs." Despite his attachment to rule 2, as a concession to tradition and "a near-consensus in the profession, that a stable level of prices of final products was a desirable policy objective," he recommends a 4 to 5 per cent annual increase in the monetary total (of currency outside the banks plus all commercial bank demand *and* time deposits) as the most appropriate rule for current implementation (pp. 47–8).

Rule 3: $M_t = 1.05M_{t-1} = (1.05)^2M_{t-2} = \cdots = (1.05)^nM_{t-n}$;

P-*series:* $P_t = P_{t-1} = P_{t-2} = \cdots = P_{t-n}$;

w-*series:* $(w/A)_t = (w/A)_{t-1}$
$$= \cdots (w/A)_{t-n}; (w_t/w_{t-1}) = (A_t/A_{t-1}).$$

The w-series follows on the presumption that, if P is to be stable, unit labor costs over time will also have to be (nearly) stable.

This last relationship is important: Friedman proposes to achieve, through monetary policy, a time pattern in which w is synchronized with A.[29] Whereas in Keynes this wage path would require trade union concession or legislative compliance, Friedman promises to order the result indirectly, through adherence to his monetary rule. Labor would be expected to make the adjustment "voluntarily," undoubtedly through the pain of unemployment. "Disorderly" wage demands would exact a penalty: prices would rise and unemployment would ensue.

Agreement and Dispute

On the relation of money to output and employment it appears that there is little to distinguish Friedman from Keynes; Keynesianism and Monetarism effectively coincide. It is on the price level or inflation that the camps divide, into Monetarist and wage sects. For Keynes the wage-productivity mesh was decisive. For Friedman it is the duel of money supply and output. In protesting some interpretations of his position, Friedman writes: [30] "The price level is then a joint outcome of the monetary forces determining nominal income and the real forces determining real income." Also: "I regard the description of our position as 'money is all that matters for changes in *nominal* income and for *short-run* changes in real income' as an exaggeration but one that gives the right flavor of our conclusions."

Thus the dispute must ultimately revolve about the respective theories of the price level and the policies advanced to combat inflation. The trend of wages under Friedman's projected rule 3 becomes particularly crucial; although under all of his rules there is an embodied wage policy, under rule 3 it has tended to be submerged. Presumably, unemployment is to be meted out if labor does not yield to the monetary clamp. Recent wage trends suggest that the theory may be incorporating an unduly sanguine estimate of future labor market behavior.

This optimistic wage trend assessment of Monetarism has not received the attention it deserves. For to stabilize P and w/A under rule 3 the instrument elected is that of a constant M-growth. Yet Friedman himself is the authority for the view that while ΔM bears a good relationship to ΔY, the split between $Q\Delta P$ and $P\Delta Q$ is vague. It is thus doubtful that the M-policy will hold P and w/A firm with (nearly) full employment unless the monetary rule succeeds in foisting a new docility on labor, or an imposed discipline through new laws, signifying either a voluntary or a legislated incomes policy.

For its policy success, unless it is to lead to unacceptable levels of both unemployment and inflation, Friedman's rule must therefore also secure labor's compliance; again we see the convergence in the theories: *both entail an appropriate wage trend.* Friedman assumes it can be achieved indirectly and harmoniously; others equally dedicated to P-stability contend that new institutions are needed to induce labor, through cajolery or coercion, to adopt a more reasonable wage stance.

Skepticism thus persists on the viability of Rule 3 unless its policies, when confronted by excessive annual wage demands and the persistence of unemployment, are enunciated. To keep paying the price of unemployment and unrealized output, with its damage to human lives, is undoubtedly harsh: a rule should not compound human misery. Can the rule curb union adamancy for 10, 12, or even 30 per cent annual increases in money wages?

In short: what is the Monetarist program for coping with unruly wage demands? For action in the face of persistent unemployment? If these events occur, what is the contingency plan? It would help to have the Monetarist view on these matters; it is evasive to contend that it cannot happen. It may happen, just as it has happened under the less mechanistic monetary policies of the past.

Final Note: Keynes as the Monetarist

The Monetarists are the modern descendants of the Currency School: set the monetary course and the economy can be charted while further thought with respect to Q, N, P, and w is superfluous. Inherently, the Monetarists believe, along with Mill, that money *doesn't* matter—except under the wrong rule. Delicate monetary parries in combating unexpected major convulsions or minor disruptions in the evolving economy are rejected.

Keynes regarded money as a lubricating prerequisite to sustain the transactions purposes and to sate the liquidity demands which might take unpredictable turns. In his view, monetary policy could have decisive influence on the outcome when unusual events erupted. Conceivably, Keynes may be better suited for the honorific Monetarist title than those who insist that by implementing a single rule, money, thereafter, does not matter.

NOTES

1. The 1969 adoption of SDRS by the IMF is a belated vindication of Keynes's plan to enlarge international monetary reserves. For a bibliography of Keynes's writings on money, see S. E. Harris, ed., *The New Economics* (New York: Alfred A. Knopf, 1947).

2. In some passages the old Quantity Theory survives among the Monetarists. Karl Brunner writes: "An assemblage of all the inflationary experiences, new and old, demonstrates that the Monetarist thesis explains the whole range of experience with respect to both occurrences and orders of magnitude." See Karl Brunner, "The Drift into Persistent Inflation," *The Wharton Quarterly*, IV, no. 1 (Fall 1969), 26. Friedman: "Inflation is always and everywhere a monetary phenomenon. . . ." See M. Friedman, "What Price Guideposts," in George Shultz and Robert Aliber, eds., *Guidelines, Informal Controls, and the Market Place* (Chicago: University of Chicago Press, 1966), 18. Darryl R. Francis, President of the FRB of St. Louis: "The growth of money is thus the key to inflation . . . ," in "Controlling Inflation," Federal Reserve Bank of St. Louis, *Monthly Review*, 51, no. 9 (1969), 11.

3. Milton Friedman, *The Optimum Quantity of Money and Other Essays* (Chicago: Aldine Publishing Co., 1969), 226; Milton Friedman and David Meiselman, "The Relative Stability of Monetary Velocity and the Investment Multiplier in the United States," in Commission on Money and Credit, *Stabilization Policies* (Englewood Cliffs: Prentice-Hall, 1963), 171.

4. On the Keynesian ingredients, see Don Patinkin, "The Chicago Tradition, the Quantity Theory, and Friedman," *Journal of Money, Credit and Banking*, 1, no. 1 (1969).

5. Friedman, *The Optimum Quantity of Money*, 215; also Friedman, *A Program for Monetary Stability* (New York: Fordham University Press, 1959), 87–88.

6. Friedman, *The Optimum Quantity of Money*, 279; also, with David Meiselman, "The Relative Stability of Monetary Velocity," 172. Anna Schwartz remarks: "Indeed, this issue of the forces determining the division of a change in income between prices and output is per-

haps the major gap in our present knowledge of monetary relations and effects." See A. Schwartz, "Why Money Matters," *Lloyds Bank Review,* 94 (1969), 11.

7. Friedman, *The Optimum Quantity of Money,* 170, 179.

8. *Ibid.,* Chap. 1.

9. David Hume, "Of Interest," *Political Discourses* (1752).

10. Friedman, *The Optimum Quantity of Money,* 278.

11. John Stuart Mill, who is quoted with favor by Friedman, wrote long ago: "There cannot, in short, be intrinsically a more insignificant thing, in the economy of society, than money; except in the character of a contrivance for sparing time and labour." And "it only exerts a distinct and independent influence of its own when it gets out of order." *Principles of Political Economy* (1848) (London: Longmans, Green and Co., Ashley edition, 1915), 488.

12. The word "wages" does not appear in the index of *The Optimum Quantity of Money* though a few inconclusive passages are devoted to the subject. Anna Schwartz likewise fails to refer to wages in the article cited in n. 6.

13. In an earlier article Friedman has written: "The crucial fallacy is the so-called 'wage-price spiral.'" See M. Friedman, "The Case for Flexible Exchange Rates," *Essays in Positive Economics* (Chicago: University of Chicago Press, 1953), 181.

14. Apparently, Keynes's castigation of this theory has never been pondered. J. M. Keynes, *The General Theory of Employment, Interest and Money* (London: Harcourt, Brace & Co., 1936), 257–260. Cf. my criticism based on J. M. Keynes, *An Approach to the Theory of Income Distribution* (Philadelphia: Chilton Book Co., 1958), 14–18.

15. Gottfried Haberler, *Prosperity and Depression* (Cambridge: Harvard University Press, 1960); Don Patinkin, *Money, Interest and Prices* (New York: Row, Peterson and Co., 1956).

16. Axel Leijonhufvud, *On Keynesian Economics and the Economics of Keynes* (New York: Oxford University Press, 1968), 132n.

17. On the importance attached to the 45° diagram, likening it to Marshallian demand and supply curves in micro-theory, see P. A. Samuelson, "The Simple Mathematics of Income Determination," in *Income, Employment and Public Policy: Essays in Honor of Alvin H. Hansen* (New York: W. W. Norton & Co., Inc., 1948), 135.

18. Cf. my earlier critique in *Classical Keynesianism,* Chap. 11.

19. On this issue of the choice of units (which I regard as vital for the *P*-theory), Alvin Hansen wrote: "Fundamentally the matter

is of no great consequence." See *A Guide to Keynes* (New York: McGraw-Hill Book Co., 1953), 44.

20. For an early statement of the "symmetrical" theory, see Robert L. Bishop, "Alternative Expansionist Fiscal Policies: A Diagrammatic Analysis," in *Essays in Honor of Alvin H. Hansen, op. cit.* Cf. the remarks on "an overly simple model which my generation of economists learned and taught," by James Tobin, "Unemployment and Inflation: The Cruel Dilemma," in Almarin Phillips and O. E. Williamson, eds., *Prices: Issues in Theory, Practice and Public Policy* (Philadelphia: University of Pennsylvania Press, 1967), 101. Keynes had cautioned earlier that deflation in employment and inflation in prices were not symmetrical concepts, *General Theory*, 291–303.

21. I have suggested, in all seriousness, that those who advocate unemployment through public policy as an inflation remedy should be the first to join the ranks of the unemployed to ensure the success of the policy. Cf. R. F. Harrod: "I would suggest that any policy measures deliberately designed to increase the level of unemployment are morally wrong." *Towards a New Economic Policy* (Manchester: University of Manchester Press, 1967), 16.

22. Keynes wrote: ". . . by acting on the pessimistic hypothesis we can keep ourselves forever in the pit of want." J. M. Keynes, *Essays in Persuasion* (London: Harcourt, Brace & Co., 1931), vii-viii.

23. Keynes, *General Theory*, 12, 295, 302.

24. For Keynesian corroboration of this interpretation of the especial importance of money wages for inflation, cf. R. F. Harrod, *Reforming the World's Money* (London: Macmillan and Co., 1965), 26–27; R. F. Kahn, Radcliffe Commission, *Memorandum of Evidence,* 3 (1958), 140; Nicholas Kaldor, "Economic Growth and Inflation," *Economica*, XXVI (1959), 292; A. P. Lerner, "Employment Theory and Employment Policy," *American Economic Review*, Proceedings, LVII (May 1967); Joan Robinson, review, *Economic Journal* (1938), 510.

25. See Lloyd W. Mints, *A History of Banking Theory* (Chicago: University of Chicago Press, 1945).

26. Friedman, *Optimum Quantity of Money*, 48. Page references in this section are to this work. Cf. some parallel remarks in my "Incomes Policy in the Monetarist Programme," *The Bankers' Magazine*, CCX (1970), 75.

27. While Professor Friedman's lags are thus not correctly reproduced, the results will apply along the ultimate path traversed.

28. Cf. Keynes: "The maintenance of a stable general level of money wages is . . . the most advisable policy for a closed system; whilst the same conclusion would hold good for an open system, provided that equilibrium with the rest of the world can be secured by means of fluctuating exchanges." *General Theory*, 270.

29. On the option "of allowing wages to rise slowly whilst keeping prices stable," Keynes wrote that "on the whole my preference is for the latter alternative. . . ." *Ibid.*, 271.

30. Milton Friedman, "A Theoretical Framework for Monetary Analysis," *Journal of Political Economy*, 78, no. 2 (March–April 1970), 217.

2 The Keynesian Light That Failed*

Kipling told of the military artist ultimately blinded by a head blow. The Keynesian vision has been clouded by a body punch. Monetarists suspect a congenital defect. Others in Keynes's camp had worried about a Keynesian habit of blinking at disconcerting facts in poring over disfigured models of the original subject.[1]

Keynesianism bumbled the inflation issue and now stands in disarray. Divining the Keynesian eclipse, Monetarists have injected the rhetoric of a New Quantity Theory in lieu of a determinate price-level formulation, nonetheless persuading an influential audience (anxious to believe) that monetary discipline will, after an unfathomable lag, win the day—despite a dismal unemployment slide and a persistent price climb. Some frustrated Keynesians have, in some gambol, flirted with Monetarist rules with restrained ardor for the belief that money is the root of all inflation. Establishment Keynesians, mindful of their Democrat sponsors, treat inflation as a frivolous distraction worth a mild rebuke. Professor Minsky, in discussing President Ford's Potomac inflation "summit," chided their performance as futile.[2]

Currently (1975), with 9 per cent unemployment, assorted Keynesians breathe new life: the sect is always intellectually comfortable with unemployment. Some even assert the price battle is over; the price of sugar is lower. And those car rebates . . . and other flimsy straws.

* I thank Professor Davidson for helpful comments on a previous draft. While I have not cited those writings responsible for what I regard as "Wayward Keynesianism," references are readily available. Documentation could be massive and still incomplete. (This was prepared as a presentation to the Mid-West Economic Association).

Keynes and Keynesians

Keynesians are widely identified by their technical baggage and their full employment advocacy secured mainly by fiscal means. On "money matters" some do short-term borrowing from Monetarists despite intermittent violence to Keynes's money principles.

Leijonhufvud has shown that Keynes and Keynesianism can be differentiated goods.[3] Loose handling of Keynes's legacy led Mrs. Robinson to castigate *Bastard*-Keynesianism, and to warn of an impending crisis.[4] Long ago I protested the hampers of Classical Keynesianism.[5] Transcending doctrinal deviation, at stake is the state of western economies.

Fiscal remedies for unemployment, with a modicum of intervention, united most Keynesians; the mantle of respectability encouraged even Republican presidents to confess a symbolic conversion when publicly embarrassed by huge deficits. Keynes's inflation theory, and remedy, has been generally shrugged off by the widest Keynesian community as politically inexpedient and so, superfluous—at least by those who have heard about it, for there is much evidence that few have read appropriate pages in *The General Theory*, fewer have absorbed the content, with only a smaller number (in the United States) being willing to act on its principles. The neglect marks the plight of modern Keynesianism, and is at the bottom of our economic morass.

Except in tax and transfer contexts, income distribution attitudes in Keynes have been just skimmed.[6] Inadvertence to the monetary framework behind *The General Theory* opened a vacuum for the short-lived Monetarist coup that battered Keynesianism. Keynes survived the ordeal.[7]

Episodic Keynesianism and Keynes

Keynes, it is alleged, has thus been victimized (traduced?) by Keynesians on vital matters. He deserves better than to be identified as ushering in an inflationary age. Once, he uttered the hope that economists might "manage to get themselves thought of as humble, competent people on a level with dentists."[8] The modest aspiration has been dashed as prominent Keynesians mutter that simultaneous inflation *and* unemployment defy eradication. Keynes, however, would tackle, and unravel, the dual malaise for sterile economics led him to decry "our miserable subject"—meaning the anomalous policy recipes concocted by its practitioners.[9]

The Keynesian indictment can be highlighted in almost chronological sequence tracing the metamorphosis of policy-oriented Keynesian theory. Some prominent Keynesians participated in each phase of the convolution; laggards, dropouts, and escapists seeking happiness with Monetarists, could also be cited. Textbooks abound in some confused eclecticism. Ways to put more Keynes in Keynesianism will follow later.

THE METAMORPHOSIS OF KEYNESIAN THEORY IN POLICY

Keynes, in declaring that we were not prisoners fenced in by either the Treasury View or by Dr. Pangloss, carried a cogent message of release. A dose of budget policy might suffice. Investment management might be required later, while the euthanasia of the rentier need not be mourned. (Double-digit long-term interest rates have postponed the demise indefinitely.) The latter were less urgent themes than salvaging capitalism through providing jobs and allowing the decentralized market economy to operate efficiently. Restoration could fend off destructive totalitarian adherents.

Acting on the Keynesian wisdom, countries have succeeded in minimizing unemployment: the record has been incomparably better than in the pre-war world. For a time the United Kingdom and Australia reported practically no unemployment; Germany imported labor. Our own reports prior to the Nixon years were also good.

In offering a way out Keynes conveyed an optimistic spirit, though some saw a pessimistic Marxian streak in his distrust of the automaticity of the full-employment market mechanism.[10] Remarkable debates have raged, especially under the protection of high employment and growing government expenditures, on the *logic* of underemployment equilibrium. Walrasian models often "prove" its absurdity, most often by *assuming* the market equilibrium of labor demand and supply. The models score high in convincing economists who regard barter states as replicas of the real world.

Keynes might be allowed to use words in his own meaningful sense; annual rates of unemployment of 10 to 22 per cent in the United Kingdom from 1921 to 1935 (just prior to *The General Theory*) could be described as an underemployment balance requiring a stiff nudge to dislodge the settled state.[11] (Maybe "neutral" equilibrium would have been a better word, as he remarked in a letter to Kaldor.)[12]

The GT as Depression Economics

Keynes might be exonerated for underplaying inflation. He was keenly aware of the hyperinflations in central Europe.[13] In the 1930s, after the price roof caved in and unemployment abounded, useful jobs were the objective. Further, the 1925–1929 U.S. price trend before the debacle was quite flat. Inflation was hardly imminent. (Many feared inflation even in 1933. Proponents of "expectations of inflation" should ponder the "inflationary" effect of the run on gold.)

Nonetheless, for those willing to read *The General Theory* to the end, and reflect on the wage unit from the beginning, all the necessary ingredients of an inflation theory are liberally sprinkled about, briefly in Chapter 2 and extensively in Chapters 19–21.

Early 45-Degree and IS-LM Classical Keynesianism

Despite the passage of the Great Depression into history, inflation has always mystified Keynesians who detached themselves from his wage-unit device. Almost 20 years of teaching 45-degree lines and IS-LM curves (consumers and purveyors should read Hicks's admission of his own misunderstanding) had "explained" that inflation and unemployment were mutually exclusive, having a neat symmetry whereby unemployment would commend a relaxation of the money and fiscal screws while inflation would countenance tightening.[14] Judicious policy would walk the tightrope just short of full employment.

God was good. He would not sabotage Keynesians doing His work to maintain jobs. Inflation, if it did erupt, could be summarily extinguished.

Unfortunately, mainstream Keynesians never bothered to glance at underdeveloped economies where simultaneous inflation and unemployment were rife. Still, our textbooks conquered the world, with their irrelevance hailed as a sort of virtue.

To compound the confusion, the analysis ran in *real* terms, accomplishing the feat of explaining inflation in models where price changes were precluded. Constant-dollar models of "inflationary-gaps" earned Ph.D.s.

Phillips-Curve Keynesianism

The money wage enjoyed only desultory mention by Classical Keynesians, despite Keynes's exposition, until Phillips's publication compelled recognition of the association of money wages, prices, and unemployment. Credibly, the Phillips-curve phenomena imparted at least a logic to the theory of inflation, with money wages (w) and the price level (P) moving inversely to the unemployment rate. Empiricism now sustained theory; Phillips-curve data generated Phillips-curve Keynesianism.

Less credibly, it fostered a trade-off complacency, abnegating Keynes's ideology, on the conviction that the inflation ill could be mitigated only by the unemployment ailment.[15] With Phillips curves being hailed as reflecting "natural laws," a new prison fence was erected to deter public policy. Full employment wore a high price tag. A flat price trend might cost intolerable unemployment.

All was endogenous, a wayward economy defied salvation. This was the inertia wrought by professed Keynes disciples. Even counting the cosmetics of the Kennedy Guideposts, requiring the president to deploy his prestige in what should be routine economic events, the Phillips-curve era was notable for a studied intellectual disdain of institutional reforms to abort "natural" Phillips-curve outcomes, as extracted from a data universe in which unrestrained labor bargaining prevailed. Pressed for solutions, Keynesians would aver that inflation was a "hard" problem, a coded euphemism for a wish that it would go away.

The 1968 Surtax

One reference point for marking the bankruptcy of Phillips-curve Keynesianism would be the Lyndon Johnson 1968 surtax. The economy, at the time, was making its strongest assault on the full-employment salient. Suddenly Keynesians feared "overheating"—this antedated the energy crisis. Phillips-curve mentalities advised a real-demand deflation to outwit inflation.

Uneasy at the outposts of the Promised Land, Keynesians thus sought refuge in a retreat toward unemployment where they could, at leisure, devise full-employment strategies.[16] Confidence abounded that the Phillips curve would banish inflation. Echoing Herbert Hoover, the Keynesian chairman of the Council of Economic Advisers uttered the immortal words: "We have turned the corner on inflation." Churchill might add: "Some corner. Some turn." The inflationary sequel is now history, with the end still not in sight.

The 1968 surtax is a classic illustration of the *static* myopia of "constant-dollar," Phillips-curve, Fiscal-Keynesianism. The personal income tax was the vehicle chosen to undo "excess" real demand. Wage earners, not being avid textbook readers, saw nothing sacred in constant money wages to match constant-dollar Keynesian calculations. With their after-tax pay thinned, pressures for unprecedented outsized pay increases were touched off, lifting the price level to the worst inflation in our industrial age.

Faith in the efficacy of the ideological monetary game plan of the new Nixon Monetarist team precluded any early confrontation of the wage surge. By August 1971, the re-election misgivings of the "stagflation" albatross outweighed the reiterated optimistic Monetarist assurances, culminating in the Nixon Phase improvisations. The "never" to price and wage controls was an impeachable principle.

Shifting Phillips-Curve Keynesianism

Keynes foresaw that when money-wage gains outran productivity, price stability would crumble.[17] Invoking the hypothesis of a given wage unit right from the start, he could hardly have been more explicit on wages and prices, except to the most unwary Keynesians. Joan Robinson, as early as 1939, delineated the wage-price spiral in a few pages.[18] Yet few Keynesians before, or after, 1968 had anything constructive to offer on wage policy. The subject seems to be taboo; tastes have run to the inertia of "natural-law" Phillips curves.

Especially after 1968 (in the United States) growing unemployment under tight-money antidotes for inflation incited some strange Phillips-curve doings; a N.E. flight pattern of deviant points was observed running amok in several market economies. Instant post hoc theory was born: *Shifting* Phillips curves became the in-thing. In a twinkling, what was previously hailed as a predictive law became transformed into an ex post explanation.

Shifting Phillips curves might have evoked a flurry of strategies to rein in the skyward money-wage drift. Instead, we have been titillated with sporadic tidbits on "expectations of inflation." Control blueprints to dam the wage-price tide frequently revert to Monetarist rules, despite a predictable unemployment outcome and a dubious price-level deterrent in the absence of money-wage discipline. Incomes Policy, which would appear to be a logical response to Shifting Phillips-curve phenomena, has had a limited appeal to the Shifting school; yet if money wages can mount sharply even as unemployment grows, with the unemployment ensuing from tighter monetary and fiscal policy, there would seem to be no alternative to direct money-income measures.

Correction-Keynesians

Prestigious Keynesians, engaged in collecting Shifting Phillips-curve data, frequently banded together in an informal Ignore-Inflation sect. The tribe flourished between about 1970–1972.

The guiding principle was that inflation would vanish if economists shut their eyes.

Ignore-Inflation-Keynesians tend to overlap with Indexation- or Correction-Keynesians. If inflation did not vanish, its inequiites—a concession?—could be "corrected." Learned papers were long on allusions to the correction parlor-game but very short on details on how to play it.

Recently, some Correction-Keynesians have become a trifle alarmed at double-digit inflation, and have urged a vague Social Compact whereby labor would renounce high-wage demands for a cut in Social Security taxes.

This might work as a temporary expedient. But it is a sad reflection on economic policy that "corrections" should be advanced in lieu of stable price-level proposals. If our economic institutions, and our political order, were really dedicated to "corrections," some obscene imbalances in income distribution would have been eliminated long ago.

Correction-Keynesians also find themselves holding hands with Indexing-Monetarists. Unless, by happenstance, indexing selects the right money-wage number, inflation or price-level gyrations will be a way of life until a new generation of economists, or political leaders wiser than economists, stop the charade of proposals for emulating the repressive Brazil or the chaotic Iceland experience.

The Money-Wage and Incomes Policy Omission

Standing in the wings in all the twists of policy-oriented Keynesianism is the ubiquitous theme of unemployment as an inflation spoiler. An endogenous, indirect, labor-market determination has been premised for money wages, contingent on unemployment. Not unexpectedly, the endogenous Keynesian money-wage theory makes an alliance with Monetarism irresistible: both avenues end in an unemployment bath to thwart inflation (in their theory, not in fact). The Shifting Phillips curve, a precious circumlocution for *some* money-wage exogeneity, has blasted the endogeneity pitch, though Keynesians are reluctant to admit it.

Keynes's message revolved about useful jobs and income. Wage exogeneity, meaning trade-union power, could upset price stability even prior to full employment.[19] A money-wage policy could prevent it, for full employment without inflation was the rational goal.[20] Employment, obviously, was the overriding objective in the depressed 1930s.

Lack of an appreciation for the money wage in inflation and the absence of a serious long-range Incomes Policy thus separates Keynes from Keynesians: employment advocacy buys only half a stability loaf.[21] Restraining inflation by inducing unemployment is misanthropic Keynesianism. Abiding inflation is mischievous Keynesianism.

Money-Wage Exogeneity and Quantity-Theory Conclusions

Money-wage exogeneity can be construed, perhaps least controversially, as the a priori indeterminateness of the ultimate agreements emerging from the bargaining table in key contracts, which have a way of spilling over in smaller union agreements and being emulated in the pay treatment of nonunion employees. Some may prefer to interpret the money-wage results as a bilateral-monopoly phenomenon, while others, in denouncing union power, may term it "monopoly," though without specifying the maximization objective this may dissolve into a generic name, conceivably embracing even competitive outcomes. Charitably, union-management negotiation might even be idealized as a modernized Walrasian auctioneer seeking a settlement balance.

Keynes titled his Chapter 19 as *Changes in Money Wages,* not *The Theory of Money Wages* as convention, and his own book title, would dictate. There is a difference. On his methods he set about to develop the *effects* of money-wage changes injected into an otherwise "equilibrium" setting; he refrained, however, from any venture designed to classify the determinants of the money wage. Other prices positioned themselves about any new money-wage site that was established, with the precise money-wage figure left open and dangling, as a money sum emerging from custom, history, concepts of "fairness," or trade-union bargaining. It is on this interpretation that the "exogenous" characterization is defensible.

On his main argument, including expectations, income shifts, bankruptcies, interest rates and monetary policy, open-economy repercussions, and the like, labor demand would be largely invariant to money-wage cuts. Conceptually, a vertical labor-demand curve would constitute a graphic image, so that the money wage would be in "neutral" equilibrium, to be settled by other forces: trade-union supply fixation could thus govern the outcome. This was, of course, before the theory of Pigou effects was exploited. More on this later.

The price level bounced whenever the money wage lodged at a new point, for whatever reason, while the economy moved out in time.[22] It thus hardly comports with Keynes's image to *assume* full employment, and an attendant "fixed" full-employment output, and then to dump more money on the scene. In this version, on the proviso that households directly acquire the "loose" money, and disburse some or all of it, prices respond in a new equilibrium balance. The ensuing price-cost imbalance —disequilibrium state—is supposed to lead to a subsequent money-wage uplift while prices hold at their same equilibrium level. While this is good Quantity Theory doctrine, it is nonetheless at odds with Keynes's image of money-wage—and money —mechanics.

MORE KEYNES IN KEYNESIANISM?

A set of numbered impressions are offered to render Keynesianism more consistent with Keynes, and to cope with our formidable unemployment and inflation anomalies. Other readers of the Good *General Theory* Book will interpret it differently. Religious quarrels over textual exegeses are usually more contentious than conclusive. There is an uncanny methodological wisdom in the Biblical injunction that "by their fruits ye shall know them" (Matthew, 7:20).

1. Any model purporting to capture the flavor of Keynes which omits a money-wage parameter is suspect. It has little to do with the *General Theory*. In the *Treatise*, dropping Keynes's special definition of profits as containing "windfall" income re-

sponsible for the saving-investment discrepancy, his "fundamental" equation would read: $P = Y/Q$, where Y = money income, and Q = aggregate output.[23] Movements in money income (with money wages and salaries comprising the income bulk) relative to output are truistically linked to the price level so that we have either conscious or unconscious Incomes Policy. Abandoning money incomes to the whimsy of labor negotiators is bound to have P-effects.

Curiously, most Keynesian models simply eschewed a P-equation. Two of the best expositions of early Keynesianism tacked on, implicitly, a Fisher version. To their credit, though the form was anomalous for a "Keynesian" model—for Keynes attacked the Quantity Theory formulae—the two statements discerned the need for a P-equation to complete the system.

Recently, Monetarists have discovered that they, too, require an explicit P-equation after a long, and now embarrassing, confusion of a money-demand equation with a P-formula; their choice falls between Fisher and Cambridge cash-balance varieties to fit their system.[24] Their current struggle revolves about imparting P-determinateness in a world of varying Q. Ultimately, when the issue is squarely faced, exogenous, that is, negotiated, money-wage fluctuations will qualify the Monetarist theory and affect its policy views.

Keynesian P-equations will have to stress money wages and salaries. My own preference has been for a unit wage-cost mark-up relation.[25] Of the few competing mark-up equations, those that embody K—the stock of capital—become fuzzy as measured capital reveals its elusive features explored by Mrs. Robinson.[26]

Some econometric models embody wage/mark-up equations with lingering Phillips-curve remnants. With the erratic S.E. and N.E. path, and flights in-between on the money-wage/unemployment grid, mechanical calculations will have to yield to judgment in "exogenous" money-wage guesses.

2. Walrasian-descendent money-wage and price models seem to have a compulsion to "explain" all prices endogenously. Yet for about 130 years (with a few interruptions) the price of gold

was "exogenously" (legally) fixed, a "given" number. Under bimetallism, we had two fixed prices.

Similarly, in the current environment labor contracts often extend for 2 to 3 years into the future. These "prices" are "given." We *know* them. The more universal the bargaining practice (and its spillovers to professors and other non-union employees) the less plausible are models which "lag" money wages, and "determine" them from evolving P or U (= unemployment rate) phenomena. Whatever the influence of recent or remote *past* P and U facts, once money wages are set at t_0 to run out to t_1, t_2, t_3 . . . it must be that product prices adapt to money wages, rather than as the nebulous derived-demand theory would have it, of product prices scaling money wages. "Predicting" money wages often means guessing what we already know. There is a tenacious reverse logic in much of the $P \dashrightarrow w$ (= money wages) doctrine, and some unfathomable opposition to the $w \dashrightarrow P$ causality which conforms to Keynes's version of events.

Escalator clauses do not really upset this conclusion. Though they cover only marginal amounts of the annual wage increment in the usual case, using time subscripts there is a $P_1 \dashrightarrow w_2$ relation. But there is also embedded Keynes's simultaneous $w_2 \dashrightarrow P_2$ interaction. Universal indexing of wages would make the $w_2 \dashrightarrow P_2$ interaction contingent on the size of the previous $\triangle P_1$ advance, and the duration of the t_2 time interval for which the new w_2 prevails, whether this covers a day, month, year, or other time span. Indexing itself becomes merely one way of extracting a number to control w_2. It may, or may not, impart better stability to the price level than prevailing collective bargaining practices.

"Expectations of inflation," as a stylish transplant elevated to determining status in recent money-wage theory, constitute a back-door espousal of money-wage exogeneity: what people *think* is fair and right on money wages in the evolving price climate affects the money-wage level. Philosophers undoubtedly can detect a hair-line fracture of the "exogeneity" theme of that which negotiators "think" is fair determines the money-wage bargain. Fancy splashing has been designed to conceal the embrace of an older idea.

3. Attributing Keynes's underemployment equilibrium to "rigid" money wages is bad theory and worse semantics.

Confronted with almost daily reports of rising money wages, inflation, and unemployment, students must find it hard to digest the view that unemployment is due to "rigid" money wages. Surely our problems are linked to excessive upward flexibility, not wage "rigidity."

Instead of the full-employment attributes of the Pigou effect under sharply falling money wages, a theorem predicting riots and revolution might be as apt as the full-employment deduction. Recognizing fixed contractual payments may also mean that the Pigou effect creates full employment through limitless jobs for referees in bankruptcy and for court attendants.

Contracts and *flexible* money wages reflecting changes in the wage unit inhabit Keynes's world. Models possessing a different personality are bound to have a separate life-style.

4. After protracted revelations in praise of the "Keynesian" system, an astonishing number of successful textbooks are not above drawing a "classical" labor-demand curve. If this is valid, why waste time on the "Keynesian" part? Keynes assailed the view that money-wage cuts would end joblessness. Futility of money-wage cutting inspired the *General Theory* and spurred the Keynesian Revolution. Keynes insisted that movements in money wages, the fundamental unit in which he couched his analysis, vastly overshadowed the price-level effects of price changes in bananas—or peanuts. Widespread money-wage changes might not be more successful than monetary policy in providing jobs; the price level would alone be dislodged through wage changes.

Journals, textbooks, and monographs abound with diagrams and functions linking labor demand (N) with real wages (w/P). The result is a monumental confusion whereby a *ceteris paribus* clause is invoked to cover a *mutatis mutandis* situation. In tracking the function, eminent authors "assume" P-constant regardless of the w-variation, from zero depths to infinite heights. The dismal "theorizing" prevails in Keynesian "exposés" and among supposedly Keynesian "supporters." One may be forgiven for thinking that "with friends like that. . . ."

Acknowledging his own failure to apprehend Keynes's wage-unit technique—an admission which should be relayed to dedicated IS-LM expositors—Hicks has recently propounded what he terms Keynes's wage-theorem:

> When there is a general (proportional) rise in money wages . . . the *normal* effect is that all prices rise in the same proportion . . . provided that the money supply is increased in the same proportion (whence the rate of interest will be unchanged.)[27]

Deferring the M-aspects which involve Q and N, a correct theorem is both broader, and narrower, than Hicks professes. Broader, for with a constant wage-salary *share* a proportionate *average* pay advance would have the same P result. Also, with the constant share and constant average labor productivity, the monetary reservation is redundant. Theoretically, the theorem is too narrow in ignoring *user* costs (involving anticipations) and excise (or sales) taxes. While welcome, the archaeological find duplicates earlier excavations.

Some immediate revision in the IS-LM apparatus is urgent before too many more innocent Keynesian students become hopelessly indoctrinated.

5. Acknowledging $w \mathrel{-\mathord{-}\mathord{-}} \to P$ as the modern causal force in inflation, the uneasy alliance of some Keynesians with Monetarists would wither. Money wages *and* money supplies cannot both be cited as the current inflation culprits—despite the superficial wisdom that anything can happen.

Money could bear the causal onus in a Profit Inflation, to revert to the *Treatise*, or in a printing-press hyperinflation, though the latter would still have to incorporate the vertical take-off in money income (as Joan Robinson noted in her review of Bresciani-Turroni). In an Income Inflation, entailing a mounting Y/Q ratio, money wages and salaries dominate. Considering the typical macro-markup stability of prices over unit labor costs, Profit Inflation has not been our big trouble.[28]

6. It follows from (5) that once money wages are assigned causal power over the price level, money supplies must be envisaged in a non-Monetarist fashion. Under $w \text{-} \text{-} \text{-} \rightarrow P$ causation, money is required to *accommodate* transactions, to finance output volume at a stipulated price level.[29] A Banking Principle stamp covers at least part of monetary theory. $M \text{-} \text{-} \text{-} \rightarrow P$ causality, the Quantity Theory view of Currency Principle doctrine, was at odds with Keynes's thinking.

7. The portfolio approach, listing money as one among many in the stock of assets, has the virtue of generality at a risk of undermining the top perch occupied by money in the flow of daily transactions. Stock-flow distinctions tend to be submerged. Attaching special properties to money only in particular circumstances also weakens the whole classification scheme: liquidity bouts have special characteristics beyond the usual uncertainty. When lender's risk mounts, and liquidity is menaced by the sword of either insolvency or bankruptcy, money acquires a status akin to food and drink for the starving man in the desert, in the older demand parables. How much will he pay? How much of stockholders' resources will management commit for survival?

Financial linkages in an era of undercapitalization and queasy ventures have attracted too little attention: however we react to particular Monetarist theories, money as finance should be released from the exile imposed by too many Keynesian models. In the *Treatise* Keynes elaborated his understanding of the older institutional relationships. Kaldor, Davidson, Minsky, and others have provided insights for Keynesian development. Minsky has performed a service in conjecturing prospects of a 1929 recurrence, of events which "can't happen again." Some tenuous fast-buck relations may bode danger ahead.

8. It is a stale joke to transcribe Keynes in models without contracts and without flexible exogenous money-wage payments. It is something of a hoax to put him in nonproduction pure exchange economies. Or to associate him with the assumption of

$M = \bar{M}$, regardless of the money wage or the employment level
(where the latter is visualized as a determinant of Fed behavior).[30] Or to transcribe him in economics of "fixed" output
where the natives are bombarded by a helicopter dropping fresh
currency instead of "smart" bombs. Keynes surely was preoccupied with *variable* output and employment. Small wonder,
then, if we reject Keynes's world, we can emit Walrasian and
Monetarist conclusions.

9. Decisions on labor hire in advance of sales at accepted
money wages—Keynes's "daily" short-term expectations—not only
set up the cost side of price calculations but also thrust forward
the fact that the same money-income sums entered as costs
comprise the mainstay of consumption outlays. "Cost-push" and
"demand-pull" are more nearly two sides of the same coin in
consumer markets, rather than independent inflation forces.[31]

10. Keynesians have rightly focused on the consumption function. However, the subject has come to border on the esoteric
and has lost in concreteness. Hidden behind "households" there
has been some dimming of the fact that the C-function is primarily a wage-salary earner intake function, and that consumption outlays are strongly geared to employee payments.

The Kalecki-Kaldor-Robinson generalizations admit some remarkable illumination and insights. Graduate students probing
the complexities of the permanent income stream have become
burdened with formulae to assess lower-income wage-earner behavior—or their personal expenditure habits. At the highest incomes where long-range rational computations might fit better,
it is doubtful whether Rockefeller, Hunt, or Getty, require the
niceties of the stream view. Over most of the world, and India
weighs in with heavy numbers, a simpler statement would suffice.

11. By itself the investment function has erected a mini-
Keynesian specialized literature. A variety of functions for sub-
sectors has evolved, with lags, accelerators, internal finance, and
anticipations accorded modest or dominant roles. In those "rude"
days of Classical Keynesianism, writing $I = I(r)$ stored all the intriguing phenomena implicitly in the shape of I.

"Animal spirits" motivated investment for Keynes. His model was instantly "dynamic" through its psychological setting; it was inherently vague, indeterminate, instable, volatile (depending on tastes in language) in a time context. Static Walrasian worlds lacked appeal for him, as he understood events. With Marshall as his mentor, the statical *method*, not the stationary model, was embossed on Keynes's methodological passport.[32]

Covering the cycle, Keynes wrote: "A boom is a situation in which overoptimism triumphs over a rate of interest which, in a cooler light would be seen to be excessive" (*The General Theory*, p. 322). One may thus wonder how a stable, mechanical *I*-function would appeal to Keynes. It would lose some of the irrational "will to act" to which he attached importance, and which businessmen describe as "confidence." Considering the dynamic behavioral factors that animate investment in Keynes's model dispels any easy transform to Walrasian statics or even econometric mechanics.

12. Considering its origins in his "widow's cruse," and the multiplier, Keynes could be at home with the Kalecki-Kaldor-Robinson propositions linking investment and profits; the tie would assign even greater importance to investment and animal spirits for moving a capitalist economy.

On Keynes's latter-day fascination with Kalecki's constant wage-share data, the Sraffa critique of marginal productivity doctrine would cause him no grief; some revision of the limited *General Theory* space devoted to monopoly and administered prices was imperative anyway.

13. Early on, in the most methodical statement of his theory, Keynes assigned commensurate prominence to Aggregate Supply with Aggregate Demand as the employment determinants. Classical Keynesians, and their several offspring, sloughed off the Supply skin and latched on solely to Demand.

Aggregate Supply was used extensively in my own interpretations of Keynes's theory.[33] Recently the concept has surfaced implicitly in the "capacity" constraints of econometric models. Capacity is a vague word, dependent on time intervals and "normal" operating conditions, aside from measurement compli-

cations. Cobb-Douglas and CES functions show some bruises
from past skirmishes. Something can thus be said for an Aggregate Supply concept designed in the Marshallian spirit of industry supply, modified for aggregate phenomena. Money wages,
taxes, user costs, productivity, and monopoly would have to
mesh into the pattern.

The elements would display Q, N, and P effects independently
of Aggregate Demand influences. Using Aggregate Supply as a
mutual determinant of Macro-equilibrium would have averted
several of the errors of Keynesianism. Money wages, productivity,
taxes, user cost, expectations, and monopoly would have figured
in the inflation discourse, and their impacts would have been
unraveled at an earlier date. The foolish business of discussing
inflation in a constant-price model would have been instantly
suppressed.

Hicks's admission of wage-unit omissions compels a reconsideration of the whole IS-LM apparatus. The Aggregate Supply/
Aggregate Demand concepts may emerge as a suitable replace-
ment, possessing some natural extensions for growth theory
which generally lacks a demand component.

As an important addendum, Fiscal Keynesianism has tended
to regard taxes which lower real income (and employment) as
being deflationary with respect to prices. But this theory cannot
always be right. Aggregate Supply concepts could put a cleaner
edge on the subject, with some relevance in our high inflation
and high tax environment.

14. Heavy weather has been made lately of search costs as
an unemployment factor and a job obstacle. Successful search
rests, in part, on smoother geographical mobility.

Nine per cent unemployment should dampen the ardor for
costly locational shifts. A healthy recovery in housing and in
auto demand—or in building mass transit facilities—could be a
lot less expensive, in pecuniary and psychic costs (including
costly duplications in municipal infrastructure). Statistics of unemployment since 1969 resemble more of a depression predicament than a sloppy failure in job search.

15. To reiterate, Keynes leaned on the static method, rooted

in Marshallian precedents, rather than the static model. In embodying animal spirits as a behavioral characteristic, contracts as a device to circumvent uncertainty, stock exchanges to provide some scope to speculation, and an institutional mode of settling a basic "bundle" of money-wage prices, and under government economic participation, Keynes was preoccupied with strings still to be played on Walrasian fiddles.

Walrasian static theorems may often be able to leap the institutional chasm. At other times, the space is too vast. Until Walrasian models include Keynes's elements, some modern criticisms of the *General Theory* should be muted.

A CLOSING NOTE

Economists will have to resolve the inflation problem to enhance the prospect for minimal unemployment. Otherwise we shall merely wait for happenstance to establish a better, or worse, price trend. The situation is not unlike the pre–General Theory time when the inter-war generation was wasted in waiting for unemployment to vanish.

It should give us pause that despite our vaunted analytic methods, our high-level mathematics and the computer, and piles of data, we have succeeded in creating an uncommon failure in simultaneous high inflation and high unemployment. New names have had to be invented: stagflation, slumpflation, and the latest monster, "inflump."

With a flat price trend and full employment it would be in the spirit of Keynes to deal constructively with the new problems of a new age. With a remarkable prescience and a fresh timeliness, writing in 1925 Keynes listed the five problems ahead: (1) Peace Questions, (2) Questions of Government, (3) Sex Questions, (4) Drug Questions, and (5) Economic Questions.[34]

Environment, urban chaos, the auto mess, energy, and the new Middle East money power, above all the quality of life, would undoubtedly concern him in his contemplation of what he envisaged as "the prospect of civilization," to which economists would contribute.

Despite the Nobel prize for eminent practitioners of our subject, public esteem today probably ranks our craft below . . .

dentists. The depreciation is undoubtedly attributable to our inflation and unemployment derelictions.

If Keynesianism has failed, might we not try Keynes? With apologies to Eugene McCarthy in nominating Adlai Stevenson: Implementing Keynes's inflation theory may again make us proud to call ourselves economists.

NOTES

1. Paul Davidson has classified varieties of Keynesianism in his *Money and the Real World* (London: Macmillan, 1973), Chapter 1. My own classification runs more in terms of the evolution of the "neo"-Classical Keynesian grouping. Adjectives, I think, will be generally descriptive of the point of view being distinguished.

2. Hyman Minsky, "The Futility of President Ford's Economic Summit," September 25, 1974 (mimeo).

3. Axel Leijonhufvud, *On Keynesian Economics and the Economics of Keynes* (New York: Oxford, 1968).

4. Joan Robinson, *Economic Heresies* (New York: Basic Books, 1971), p. 90, and "The Second Crisis of Economic Theory," *American Economic Review*, May 1972.

5. Cf. *Classical Keynesianism, Monetary Theory and the Price Level* (Philadelphia: Chilton, 1961).

6. Among 17 economists responding to an invitation to select their own topics for a symposium on *Income Inequality*, Professors Davidson and Minsky both focused on Keynes's rentier as a largely neglected theme of the GT. See Davidson, "Inequality and the Double Bluff," and Minsky, "The Strategy of Economic Policy and Income Distribution," *Annals of the American Academy of Political and Social Science,* ed. S. Weintraub (September, 1973).

7. Interestingly, considering his criticisms of Keynesians on "money matters," Friedman writes: "Re-reading the *General Theory* . . . has also reminded me of what a great economist Keynes was and how much more I sympathize with his approach and aims than with those of many of his followers." Later, however, and erroneously in my view, he remarks that "Keynes . . . has no theory of the absolute level of prices." See his "Comments on the Critics," *Journal of Political Economy,* September-October 1972, pp. 908, 931 n.

8. J. M. Keynes, *Essays in Persuasion* (London: Harcourt Brace, 1930), p. 373.

9. *The Collected Writings of John Maynard Keynes* (London: Macmillan, 1973), Vol. 14, p. 190.

10. For William Fellner the "stagnation" theme ascribed to Keynes was a pessimistic slant. See his *Trends and Cycles in Economic Activity* (New York: Holt, 1956), p. 390.

11. See William Beveridge, *Full Employment in a Free Society* (New York: Norton, 1945), p. 27.

12. *Collected Writings,* Vol. 14, p. 242.

13. See J. M. Keynes, *A Tract on Monetary Reform* (London: Macmillan, 1923).

14. James Tobin, for example, wrote that "much discussion of current policy is based on an overly simple model which my generation of economists learned and taught . . ." in "Unemployment and Inflation: The Cruel Dilemma," *Prices: Issues in Theory, Practice and Public Policy,* ed. A. Phillips and O. Williamson (Philadelphia: University of Pennsylvania Press, 1967), p. 101.

15. Cf. "Keynes and the Monetarists," Chapter 1 above.

16. For some criticism at an earlier date, see my "In Defense of Wage-Price Guideposts. . . . Plus," (1967), Appendix.

17. J. M. Keynes, *The General Theory of Employment, Interest and Money* (New York: Harcourt Brace, 1936), p. 270, also, for example, pp. 209 and 301. Keynes had, in the *Treatise,* been working toward what is here termed money-wage exogeneity with the concept of "Spontaneous" money-wage changes, with "Induced" changes being a Phillips-curve idea. See Vol. 1, pp. 166-170, 271-272, and Vol. 2, p. 351. Remarks on monetary policy in the circumstances are included.

18. Joan Robinson, review of Bresciani-Turroni, *Economic Journal,* September 1938, p. 510.

19. Cf. the *General Theory* remarks on "semi-critical" points, pp. 301, 307.

20. On Keynes being "often ahead even of himself," see A. P. Lerner, "From the Treatise on Money to the General Theory," *Journal of Economic Literature,* March 1974, p. 42.

21. See the lament for economists' evasion of wage costs in inflation by Peter Wiles, "Cost Inflation and the State of Economic Theory," *Economic Journal,* June 1973.

22. Cf. D. W. Katzner and S. Weintraub, "An Approach to a Unified Micro-Macro Model," *Kyklos,* 1974.

23. J. M. Keynes, *A Treatise on Money* (London: Harcourt Brace, 1930), Vol. 1, p. 135. Keynes's Fundamental Equation, dropping the savings/investment definitional distortion and redefining money income, can be turned to read $P = Y/Q$. Keynes, however, uses his relation only for the consumer price level in view of his definitions.

24. Milton Friedman, "A Theoretical Framework for Monetary Analysis," *Journal of Political Economy,* March-April 1970.

25. Cf. Lawrence Klein, *The Keynesian Revolution,* 2d ed. (New York: Macmillan, 1966), pp. 218–219.

26. Joan Robinson, "The Measure of Capital: The End of the Controversy," *Economic Journal,* September 1971.

27. Sir John Hicks, *The Crisis in Keynesian Economics* (New York: Basic Books, 1974), pp. 59–60.

28. *Treatise,* Vol. 1, p. 155.

29. Cf. "Money as Cause and Effect," Chapter 8 below.

30. Commenting on Oskar Lange's work, Keynes remarked that "my analysis is not based . . . on the assumption that the quantity of money is constant." *Collected Writings,* Vol. 14, p. 232 n.

31. Cf. "Cost Inflation: A Comment," Chapter 14 below.

32. Cf. Alfred Marshall, *Principles of Economics,* 8th ed. (London: Macmillan, 1920), p. 369.

33. See my *Approach to the Theory of Income Distribution* (Philadelphia: Chilton, 1958), Chapter 2. It was this version of Keynesianism, incorporating Aggregate Demand and Aggregate Supply, that was branded as a "maverick" formulation by Paul Samuelson in "A Brief Survey of Post Keynesian Developments," *Keynes' General Theory, Reports of Three Decades,* ed. R. Lekachman (New York: St. Martin's, 1964). Nonetheless, for a later stress on the need for the inclusion of a supply function in a "new" approach to macrotheory, see Robert Solow and Joseph Stiglitz, "Output, Employment, and Wages," *Quarterly Journal of Economics* 1968, and my "Solow and Stiglitz on Employment and Distribution: A New Romance with an Old Model?" Appendix 3. The interchange reveals some Keynesian misgivings at the lack of a supply component. Solow-Stiglitz, however, lean on Phillips-Curve, money-wage, and price-level relations.

34. *Essays in Persuasion,* p. 330.

3 Keynes and the Quantity Theory Elasticities

with Hamid Habibagahi

Considering its enormous influence, and the fact that *The General Theory* has been finecombed for theoretical and practical insights, it is somewhat mystifying that practically no attention has been devoted to Keynes's conjectures on the Quantity Theory of Money and how it could be salvaged for analytic implementation. Astonishment deepens in this decade of Monetarist revival for Keynes's remarks have an undiluted bearing on the Monetarist point of view. The neglect is compounded when it is apprehended that Keynes's quantity theory concepts are amenable to the econometric method that has flourished since Keynes wrote.

In fragmented and separated passages Keynes sought a "Generalised Quantity Theory of Money." Not only do the passages convey his attitude on monetary phenomena, but they are decidedly relevant to some very recent and perplexing issues raised by Professor Friedman. On several occasions Friedman has made the point that: "the general subject of the division of changes in money income between prices and quantities badly needs more investigation," and that "none of our leading theories has much to say about it." [1]

Interestingly, Keynes wrestled with this very issue.[2] In what follows we shall consider Keynes's analysis in terms of the elasticities he designed to cope with the question, modified in part to make price-level determining aspects stand out more sharply.

Finally, some estimates of the magnitudes involved in the concepts, which are directly subject to quantification, will be offered.[3]

First, we proceed to sketch some background for comprehending Keynes's elasticity approach.

KEYNES'S CRITICISM OF THE QUANTITY THEORY

The Friedman problem may be put fairly succinctly. Write:

$$dY = PdQ + QdP \tag{1}$$

$$Y = \text{money income}$$
$$Q = \text{real output}$$
$$P = \text{price level}$$
$$dY, dP, dQ = \text{variations in } Y, P, Q$$

The Friedman puzzle is concerned with the separate magnitudes in (1) which, in incremental form, may be written as $P\Delta Q$ (= the output variation) and $Q\Delta P$ (= the price variation). For a discrete movement the $\Delta P\Delta Q$ term must also be included. Friedman's own analysis stresses the importance of monetary factors in determining ΔY with the theoretical obscurity extending to the explanation of the historical aberration in the ΔQ and ΔP components.

Keynes's Critique of the Quantity Theory

Elsewhere the authors have endeavored to resolve the Friedman puzzle in a way compatible with Keynes's theorizing on the subject.[4] With respect to the ΔQ variations, Keynes wrote: "The primary effect of a change in the quantity of money on the quantity of effective demand is through its influence on the rate of interest."[5]

For effective demand we can read money income (Y). Output variations stemming from monetary policy thus hinged on movements in the interest rate level (r). Thereupon, for Keynes, investment (I) would be influenced through the schedule of the marginal efficiency of capital. From investment the income path would assume its full dimension through the operation of the "multiplier."

As to ΔP, the price level movement, Keynes wrote:

> For the purpose of the real world it is a great fault in the Quantity Theory that it does not distinguish between changes in prices which are a function of changes in output, and those which are a function of changes in the wage unit.[6]

This is a penetrating insight. Moving upward (to the right) along industry supply curves under diminishing returns (the competitive hypothesis), equilibrium prices would have to be higher, as Keynes saw it, even if money wages remained constant. This is the sense of his remarks on "changes in prices which are a function of changes in output."

But this was the far lesser cause of price level changes; it was not *the* inflation factor.[7] Keynes reserved this part for *movements in money wages*. Price level surges were primarily the result of wage level upheavals. This emphasis on wages, which we shall document, contrasts sharply with some later Keynesian practice that became preoccupied with "excess demand," to an almost cynical disregard of wage movements, as the main ingredient of an inflationary flare-up, whether under an explosive hyperinflation or in the more typical persistent erosion of the value of money in western economies.[8]

For Keynes, not only would the inflation battle rage mainly on the wage frontier but changes in the money supply (M) would exert little influence, for the chief impact of ΔM was on ΔQ, via Δr. Movements in *money* wages were regarded by Keynes as exogenous, as inexplicable under the ordinary techniques of economics.[9] Since Keynes there has been the Phillips curve fascination entailing an association of wage movements with unemployment; in Keynes's terms this would fail as a *predictive* instrument for determining the precise *degree* of wage change: past, present, and future institutional factors would combine to govern wage movements. The "institutional" aspect embraces political, psychological, and personality elements which combine with eco-

nomic ingredients in collective bargaining to condition the ultimate wage outcomes in the continuous and successive rounds of
wage negotiations.

A Price Level Formula

Taking only mild liberties with Keynes, his theory of the price
level can be specified in a simple formula involving a wage-cost
markup (WCM) relation:

$$P = kw/A \qquad (2)$$

w = average annual wage
$A = Q/N$, the average product of employed
    labor (N)
k = the average markup of prices over unit costs
    (the reciprocal of the wage share)

Empirical evidence supports writing $k = \bar{k}$, a constant (or near
constant).[10] Manifestly, unit labor costs (w/A) then exercise determining significance. In the temporal sequences of advancing
economies, the average productivity of labor (A) tends to rise
rather than to fall (as it would under the static laws of return
which Keynes had in mind in referring to price changes "which
are a function of changes in output"). Where annual increases
in A approximate 3 per cent, average annual money wage movements in excess of this figure tend to lift the price level.[11]

THE QUANTITY THEORY ELASTICITIES

The foregoing should provide ample background for Keynes's
analysis of the Quantity Theory of Money and for the elasticity
form recommended by him for its reconstruction.

The Price and Output Elasticities

Keynes's Quantity Theory conjectures turn on the very $P\Delta Q$ and
$Q\Delta P$ magnitudes whose omission and vagueness have perplexed

Professor Friedman. That Keynes should have focused on these matters is not surprising; his whole mission was oriented toward lifting a depressed economy; his inquiry was bound to fasten on the ΔP and the ΔQ aspects of economic recovery. Thus he wrote:

> . . . the sum of the elasticities of price and of output in response to changes in effective demand . . . is equal to unity. Effective demand spends itself, partly in affecting output and partly in affecting price, according to this law.[12]

Algebraically, from $Y = PQ$ and $dY = PdQ + QdP$ this involves:

$$\frac{dY}{Y} = \frac{dP}{P} + \frac{dQ}{Q} \tag{3a}$$

$$E_q + E_p = 1. \tag{3b}$$

Equation (3b) comprises Keynes's elasticity relation; it involves a concern with the same income split noted by Friedman.[13]

Keynes and the Quantity Theory: A First Step

With respect to the Quantity Theory and its shortcomings, and on its reconstruction and admissability, Keynes proceeds in two stages. Advancing "as a first step to a generalized Quantity theory of money," [14] he writes:

$$E_p = 1 - E_{qw}(1 - E_w) \tag{4}$$

$$E_p = YdP/PdY$$
$$E_w = Ydw/wdY$$
$$E_{qw} = Y_w dQ/QdY_w$$

Y_w, and $\Delta Y_w = Y$ and ΔY, measured in wage units

In (4) Keynes is clearly analyzing Friedman's income split. According to (4), the ratio of the relative price movement to the relative money income increment depends on output and money wage phenomena. Keynes notes that with $E_w = 1$, or $E_{qw} = 0$, then $E_p = 1$ as the strict Quantity Theory (of rigid output levels) would have it. High values for E_w and low E_{qw} responses would lift E_p.

This schematic statement by Keynes contrasts sharply with some later Keynesian neglect of money wages in the context of inflation and price level theory.

A Money Income Formulation

To purge the wage unit remnants from (4), Keynes's formula can be rewritten as follows:

$$E_q + E_p \equiv E_q + E_w + E_k - E_a = 1 \qquad (5a)$$

$$E_p = E_w + E_k - E_a \qquad (5b)$$

$$E_a = YdA/AdY$$
$$E_k = Ydk/kdY$$

In (5) the elements of the WCM equation are incorporated. If $\Delta A = \Delta k = 0$, then the change in real output and the movement in money wages absorb (in a non-causal sense) the entire variation in money income. Or in (5b) the price movement is fully proportional to the wage trend. An improvement in A will act to neutralize the effect of wage changes; a fall in k will also subdue the price level impact of wages. Variations in A and k can reenforce or neutralize the effect of money wages as the critical price level influence.

Keynes's Generalized Quantity Theory

In the second step Keynes links the price level to money supplies, or P to M:

$$E'_p = E'_y(1 - E_n E_{qw} + E_n E_{qw} E_w) \qquad (6)$$

$$E'_p = MdP/PdM$$
$$E'_y = MdY/YdM$$
$$E_n = YdN/NdY$$

Referring to (6), Keynes remarks: "Since this last expression gives us the proportionate change in prices in response to a change in the quantity of money, it can be regarded as a generalized statement of the Quantity Theory of Money." [15]

At this point, while Keynes expresses skepticism over mathematics and "manipulations of this kind," he remarks that they do "exhibit the extreme complexity of the relationship between prices and the quantity of money, when we attempt to express it in a formal manner." [16]

As a Marshallian descendant Keynes observes that if a constant proportion of income is held in money—as in the Cambridge cash-balance equation marked by a constant income velocity of money—then $E'_p = 1$. The outcome will also follow if $E_w = 1$, or if $E'_y = 1$ and $E_q = 0$. These results would confirm the Old Quantity Theory. With a "flight from the currency," E'_y and E_w would become very "large." Otherwise $E'_p < 1$. Only for extremely large E_w values and simultaneous Q-declines would $E'_p > E'_y$.[17]

Reflecting on Keynes's "generalized statement" in (6), the prominence attached to money wages is crucial in both E_{qw} and E_w. A "diminishing returns" aspect is also present, along with the response of money *income* to money supplies, as in Friedman's revision of the Quantity Theory as entailing $MV = Y$, rather than $MV = PQ$ with the $M \to P$ causation of the Old Quantity Theory being partially suppressed.

An Alternate Price Level–Money Supply Elasticity

An alternate expression to (6), eliminating the wage unit measurement, might be written thus:

$$E'_p = E'_y(E_w + E_n + E_k - E_q). \tag{7}$$

The importance of the wage drift for the price level regardless of money supply variations emerges indelibly in (7).

An Output–Money Income Elasticity

Arguing from the stimulative effect of M on Q suggests writing:

$$E'_q = E'_y - (E'_w + E'_k - E'_a). \tag{8a}$$

The E'-notation, as defined earlier, denotes elasticities with respect to money supplies.[18]

On the proviso of constancy in $A = \bar{A}$ and $k = \bar{k}$, the formula reduces to:

$$E'_q = (E'_y - E'_w). \tag{8b}$$

Equation (8b) reveals again that the Q-response to a given relative money increment is reduced by the wage movements accompanying the $\Delta M/M$ augmentation.

The Income Elasticity of Money

Rearranging (8), Professor Friedman's "income elasticity of money" appears:

$$E'_y = E'_q + (E_w + E'_k - E'_a) \tag{9a}$$

or, with $A = \bar{A}$ and $k = \bar{k}$:

$$E'_y = E'_w + E'_q. \tag{9b}$$

In (9b) the impact of money wages is striking; the output influence in money income is tempered by ascending wage scales. Professor Friedman has written E'_y as follows:

$$E'_y = \frac{d(\log Y)}{d(\log M)} = f(\omega, \delta, \eta) \approx 1.83. \tag{10}$$

In (10) the logarithmic derivation is the standard elasticity relation. The Y-term refers to national income, $\omega =$ "permanent" income which, in Friedman's definition, involves some statistical normalization of current income, $\eta = E_p$ or the price level money income elasticity, while $\delta =$ other variables in the specified demand function for money (such as interest rates, income distribution, and price expectations).

While Friedman has estimated E'_y, it is in the split of E'_q and E'_p that he finds prevailing theory deplorably vague. In contrast to Keynes, Friedman's work is laconic, even mute, with respect to money wages; terms for E_w or E'_w are noticeable by their omission.[19] Keynes, in contrast, is invariably explicit on money wages despite a tendency on the part of some Keynesian disciples to ignore this indispensable ingredient in his analysis.[20]

TABLE 3.1

Elasticities of Gross Business Product and Money Supplies,
United States, 1949–1968

Elasticity	Estimated Elasticity	Mult. Correlation Coeff.	Standard Error of Est.	Student's T	Beta Coefficient
$\dfrac{YdN}{NdY}$	0.2536	0.963	0.024	15.26	0.9635
$\dfrac{YdQ}{QdY}$	0.7761	0.987	0.037	25.58	0.9865
$\dfrac{YdP}{PdY}$	0.3231	0.986	0.019	24.79	0.9857
$\dfrac{Ydw}{wdY}$	0.8043	0.995	0.028	41.33	0.9948
$\dfrac{Ydk}{kdY}$	−0.0585	0.806	0.014	5.779	0.8061
$\dfrac{YdA}{AdY}$	0.4822	0.975	0.032	18.75	0.9754
$\dfrac{YdM^{\circ}}{M^{\circ}dY}$	1.1420	0.982	0.064	21.98	0.9819
$\dfrac{M^{\circ}dw}{wdM^{\circ}}$	0.9099	0.968	0.068	16.29	0.9677
$\dfrac{M^{\circ}dk}{kdM^{\circ}}$	0.0627	0.743	0.016	4.703	0.7428
$\dfrac{M^{\circ}dA}{AdM^{\circ}}$	0.4211	0.991	0.020	30.69	0.9906
$\dfrac{M^{\circ}dQ}{QdM^{\circ}}$	0.6747	0.997	0.017	55.96	0.9971
$\dfrac{MdQ}{QdM}$	1.4799	0.943	0.027	11.28	0.9426
$\dfrac{Mdw}{wdM}$	1.8546	0.979	0.055	20.40	0.9791
$\dfrac{Mdk}{kdM}$	−0.1384	0.814	0.014	5.946	0.814
$\dfrac{MdA}{AdM}$	0.9676	0.971	0.0557	17.36	0.9714
$\dfrac{MdY}{YdM}$	2.3204	0.990	0.047	30.28	0.9903

Source: See Table 3.2.

Y = Gross Business Product, in current dollars.

Q = Gross Business Product, in constant dollars.

$A = Q/N.$

$k = Y/W.$

$w = W/N.$

TABLE 2.2

United States Gross Business Product and Related Data, 1929–1968

Year	Gross Business Product, Current Dollars (Y)	Compensation of Employees (W)	Gross Business Product, Constant Dollars (Q)	Price Index (1958 = 100) (P)	Business Employment (N)
1929	095.1	044.4	182.1	052.2	30.4
1930	082.4	040.2	161.4	051.1	28.3
1931	068.3	033.4	147.7	046.2	25.4
1932	051.3	025.3	123.8	041.5	22.2
1933	048.9	023.6	120.6	040.6	22.3
1934	057.4	027.4	131.1	043.8	24.5
1935	064.1	030.0	144.9	044.2	25.5
1936	072.9	034.1	165.4	044.1	27.4
1937	081.0	039.3	176.4	045.9	29.2
1938	074.5	035.8	164.6	045.3	27.0
1939	080.3	038.6	180.7	044.4	28.3
1940	089.1	042.6	197.1	045.2	29.3
1941	112.2	053.5	228.1	049.2	33.8
1942	139.5	068.0	248.7	056.1	36.3
1943	162.4	081.6	264.9	061.3	37.8
1944	173.8	086.2	278.9	062.3	36.7
1945	172.3	084.8	274.6	062.7	35.1
1946	182.7	093.7	267.0	068.4	37.3
1947	208.6	108.5	272.8	076.5	39.2
1948	233.5	120.0	286.0	081.7	41.2
1949	230.1	117.6	284.7	080.8	38.6
1950	256.3	129.3	314.2	081.6	40.0
1951	292.8	148.7	334.5	087.5	42.3
1952	305.8	159.5	343.2	089.1	42.9
1953	323.6	172.2	360.7	089.7	42.9
1954	322.7	170.5	355.4	090.8	42.4
1955	353.9	184.6	385.4	091.6	43.7
1956	370.8	200.3	392.2	094.5	44.8
1957	389.3	210.5	397.5	097.9	44.7
1958	391.7	208.8	391.7	100.0	43.2
1959	425.0	227.6	419.4	101.3	44.4
1960	440.7	239.1	429.5	102.6	45.0
1961	452.3	244.0	436.9	103.5	44.6
1962	489.4	260.9	466.7	104.4	45.6
1963	513.0	274.5	486.6	105.4	46.3
1964	548.2	293.9	513.3	106.6	47.3
1965	594.4	316.9	548.9	108.3	49.2
1966	646.7	349.2	584.9	110.9	51.6
1967	681.0	371.4	597.3	114.1	52.6
1968	740.6	406.9	627.5	118.6	54.1

Source: Department of Commerce, *National Income and Product Accounts of the United States, 1929–1965; Survey of Current Business,* July issues, 1967, 1968, and 1969.

ELASTICITY MAGNITUDES

Some indication of the magnitudes involved are enumerated in Table 3.1; the usual computational aspects are also included.[21] The income concept utilized is that of Gross Business Product (GBP) for the United States for the 1949–1968 period, in the thought that this corresponds most closely to the $Y = PQ$ concepts of economic analysis: economic theory revolves about the market sector of the economy, and this is captured in the GBP data.

For the money supply elasticities, separate computations are made on the basis of the inclusive Friedman-Schwartz definition of money involving currency, demand deposits, and commercial bank savings deposits (M^*) against the more usual definition excluding savings deposits (M).

What stands out most markedly is the magnitude of the wage elasticities; compared to average productivity they spell the price inflation of our times. The markup (k) has tended to play a minor deflationary part; insofar as the k-values are associated with "monopoly," or embody "expectations of inflation," the elasticity values indicate a dwindling importance of these factors as inflationary elements.

SOME ELABORATION AND INTERPRETATION

It will be useful to assess the elasticity estimates in terms of the several formulae. The general order of elasticity magnitudes is written in descending sequence and carried to two decimal places in each parenthesis.

Money Income Elasticities

The money income elasticities involve relative movements with respect to Gross Business Product:

$$E_w(.80) > E_q(.78) > E_a(.48) > E_p(.32)$$
$$> E_n(.25) > E_k(-.06). \quad (11)$$

Recalling equation (5b) the price level seems to be governed mainly by the upward pull of wages as against the ameliorating facts of productivity advance.

Money Supply Elasticities

Considering the elasticities with respect to money supplies, beginning with the more conventional currency-demand deposit definition of money, we have:

$$E'_y(2.32) > E'_w(1.85) > E'_q(1.48)$$
$$> E'_a(.97) > E'_k(-0.14). \quad (12)$$

Recalling (9), the money income elasticity is a resultant of output and money wage movements reduced by productivity improvements.

On the Friedman-Schwartz measure of the money supply (noted by E^*) the array follows the same pattern:

$$E^*_y(1.14) > E^*_w(.91) > E^*_q(.67)$$
$$> E^*_a(.42) > E^*_k(-.06). \quad (13)$$

SOME CONCLUSIONS

This essay has been concerned chiefly with a bit of doctrinal history which should correct at least some part of the record with respect to Keynes's views on the importance of wages in inflation and his chronic reservations on the Older Quantity Theory ideas as an explanatory framework. For modern work it is apparent that he did try to stake out the important elements in the problem discussed by Professor Friedman, involving the price-quantity dimensions of a money income variation.[22] Since this paper has been preoccupied mainly in relating some important price level–real output–money income truisms, explicit and implicit in Keynes, and estimating the size of the major components, aspects of causation and functional interdependence have been skirted. Nevertheless the following conclusions do not appear to be unwarranted even within the bounds placed upon the study:

1. Interpreting Keynes as regarding the money wage level—the "wage unit"—as essentially an exogenous phenomenon not amenable to explication by the usual methods of economic analysis, the price level thereupon becomes a resultant of the tug-of-war between wage movements and the progress of productivity. (See equations 2 and 5b.)

2. Keynes was dubious of the Old Quantity Theory linkage between money supplies and prices, not only for the obvious reservations for output variations but also in its neglect of wage levels and productivity (or output-employment elements) phenomena as price-making forces. (See equations 6 and 7.)

3. While the elasticities have been estimated to apprehend their magnitude, and causal aspects have been eschewed, the special characteristics of the period to which they pertain should be noted. The era was one of technological improvement (so that $E_a \approx .5$), one of some unemployment with a growing labor force (so that $E_n \approx .25$), and one in which the business spirit of growth and expansion, with its special implications for monetary demand, was generally pervasive.

Thus, while in the narrower definition of money it appears that a 1 per cent increase in money supply carries a 2.3 per cent increase in money income (business gross product), and on the broader definition of money, a 1.1 per cent increase in money income, any predictive significance must be tempered; the conclusion only applies on an ex post view of the period covered. Everything would depend on: (1) entrepreneurial behavior with respect to investment and output; (2) the availability of extra productive resources; (3) the demand for money, especially "speculative-balances," on a Keynesian view; (4) the supply response of the banking system and its network of intermediaries. The elasticities could be applied for predictive purposes only on the proviso that the future would replicate the past. Nonetheless, even underscoring this disclaimer, the results have some interest as a part of quantitative history and carry a presumption of some stability if past behavorial and technological patterns are substantially reproduced.

NOTES

1. Milton Friedman, *Optimum Quantity of Money*, p. 279; "Theoretical Framework for Monetary Analysis," pp. 222–223, 234.

2. Axel Leijonhufvud makes the same point in a passing remark: Keynes's "analysis focuses upon the *changes* in the price and quantity vectors refining system states . . ." (italics in original). *On Keynesian Economics*, p. 132n.

3. Alvin Hansen devotes a few passages to this in his *Guide to Keynes* (New York: McGraw-Hill Book Co., 1953), pp. 197–199. See also a two-page comment dealing with a slip by Keynes in T. H. Naylor, "A Note on Keynesian Mathematics," *Economic Journal*, Vol. 78 (March 1968). Naylor seems to be correct with respect to equation 6 (below) in Keynes.

4. See below, Chapter 7.

5. J. M. Keynes, *General Theory*, p. 298.

6. *Ibid.*, p. 209.

7. That Keynes was prone to admit the relative unimportance of this factor is a by-product of the controversy on movements of real wages as employment advanced, following studies by Dunlop and Tarshis. For a modern appraisal, see Ronald Bodkin, "Real Wages and Cyclical Variations in Employment," *Canadian Journal of Economics*, August 1969.

8. Cf. the essay on "Classical Keynesianism: A Plea for Its Abandonment" in S. Weintraub, *Classical Keynesianism*.

9. Cf. Keynes, *General Theory*, Chap. 19, titled "Changes in Money Wages," concerned with the *effects* of money wage changes instead of a preoccupation with a theory of the *determination* of money wages.

10. Keynes recognized this in pondering Kalecki's work. See J. M. Keynes, "Relative Movements of Real Wages and Output," *Economic Journal*, 1939.

11. It is mischievous to regard this as a mere "cost-push" theory of inflation for, in a fuller account, it can be demonstrated that money wages (and salaries) not only comprise the major cost category but that they also dominate demand in consumer markets. Wage (and salary) earners buy almost 90 per cent of the output even in the United States: the consumption-function is a misnomer for what is better described as substantially a wage-earner intake function.

12. Keynes, *General Theory*, p. 284.

13. It is thus not correct to allege that for Keynes "all adjustments are in Q," with none in P. Cf. Friedman, "Theoretical Framework for Monetary Analysis," p. 209.

14. Keynes, *General Theory*, p. 285. Keynes omits a prime over his elasticity for output (in his notation) to denote that money income is measured in terms of wage units for his formula. In our notation the wage unit elasticity is written E_{qw}.

15. Keynes, *General Theory*, p. 305. The inclusion of E_n seems to be an error in Keynes unless it is assumed that $E_n = 1$. But this restricts the formula unduly.

16. From this and so many other statements, it is inaccurate to suggest that for Keynes, money does not matter. Cf. Friedman, "Theoretical Framework for Monetary Analysis," p. 210. To the man who gave currency to the concept of monetary management, and who left as a legacy the World Bank and the International Monetary Fund, besides being the author of *The Treatise on Money* and a prominent figure in *The Macmillan Report*, money mattered indeed.

17. The last relation may characterize the United States in 1969–70.

18. From $Y = PQ$, $dY = PdQ + QdP$, $P = kw/A$ and $dP = kdw/A + wdk/A + \cdot \cdot \cdot$, it is possible to derive (8a).

19. Friedman's infrequent discussions sometimes refer to the "prices of factor services," as if wages were not the dominant phenomenon or as if they would disappear if they were ignored.

20. It is possible to distinguish between "two-theories" in Keynes, a theory of output or employment—a Q or N theory—and a theory of the price level (a P-theory). In the Q-theory the wage level is held constant; in the P-theory, with inflation or price level significance, the wage level rises. See Chapter 1, above.

21. Basic data appear in Table 3.2.

22. For a more complete analysis of this problem, see Chapter 7 below.

4 Keynes and the Theory of Derived Demand *

The Theory of Derived Demand permeates the analytic frame of economics so deeply that propositions are often advanced without a full appreciation of the linkage. For example, it is commonly argued that control of the money supply will contain inflation and control the price level. Keynes held a different view, of money wages determining prices. Those who advance the former theory imply that, in the process of stopping the price rise, wage levels will also be repressed. This is really the macroeconomic version of the microeconomic derived-demand doctrine.

Some of the key hypotheses of the underlying theory, when directly applied to substantive issues, are probably in error while the situations for which the doctrine can be preserved are generally fairly trivial. If this assessment is even partially correct much of our thinking may have to be revised and textbook pages rewritten.

For perspective we trace the early stages of the theory, tied as it was to the Demand Revolution of the 1870s. Finally, we consider Keynes's extensive statement in condemnation of the Derived-Demand ideas before appraising the contemporary macroeconomic version of the doctrine.

MODERN ORIGINS

Classical value theory generally assumed that goods had utility, and thereupon proceeded to demonstrate that value depended

* I am grateful to Professor Arthur Bloomfield for several helpful comments.

on either the labor embodied, as in Ricardo, or on the psychic "real costs" of production, as in Senior. The cost aspect was paramount despite the qualifications that latter day exegesis has detected.

John Stuart Mill

The "wage-fund" doctrine was generally central to the analysis. As John Stuart Mill explained: [1]

> Demand for commodities is not demand for labour. The demand for commodities determines in what particular branch of production the labour and capital shall be employed; it determines the direction of the labour; but not the more or less of the labour itself, or of the maintenance or payment of the labour. These depend on the amount of the capital, or other funds directly devoted to the sustenance and remuneration of labour.

Mill goes on:

> This theorem, that to purchase produce is not to employ labour; that the demand for labour as constituted by the wages which precede the production, and not by the demand which may exist for the commodities resulting from the production; is a proposition which greatly needs all the illustration it can receive (p. 80).

In a sense, Mill first promulgates a macrotheory; for overall employment the size of the "Wages Fund" governs.[2] Later, Mill was to recant (Ashley ed., pp. 991–993) though his concession is not an issue here. To reject the concept of a "wage goods" inventory demonstrates how far we have come from the agricultural economy envisaged by Mill, with its lagged production sequences which are germane to the discontinuous farm-based economies of his time. When Mill argues that the demand for commodities determines the *direction* of labor, or its distribution among different outputs, he is properly applying "derived demand" as a microtheory, and presuming some unemployment—with full employment as a limit where population was quickly responsive to real-wages gains. As market demand for commodities could not enlarge the available size of the wages fund, demand could not affect total employment under given wage conditions; the acquiescence of labor to higher or lower real-wages, however, could alter the number employed but it could not influence the total consumption of the labor force.

Jevons-Menger-Walras

The theory of "Derived Demand" originates consciously with the celebrated trio of Jevons-Menger-Walras. Architects of the Marginal Utility Revolution, their work set much of the foundation for neoclassical, and modern, theory.

Jevons, despite his clarity and freshness, offers only a fragment, but an important one, on the price level theme.[3] When he declares, "Final degree of utility determines value" (p. 165), the theory of derived demand is implicit, with product value determining factor value. (For Ricardo, while embodied labor determined value, rent was price-determined.) If confronted with the question Jevons would undoubtedly assent to the view that the path of causation runs from products to factors. Yet he seldom conceives the issue in precisely this form although a page prior to his memorable lines on the false lead given by Ricardo, "that able but wrong-headed man" (p. li), he observes: "Thus wages are clearly the effect not the cause of the value of product" (Preface, *Second Edition*, 1879, p. 1).

In Menger, the theory of derived demand is unalloyed and indisputable.[4] Immediately, he distinguishes between "goods of first order"—consumer goods "that serve our needs directly"—and goods of higher order, encompassing semifinished goods and intermediate goods, which stretch out until the ultimate productive factors are reached.

There is the topical sentence, "The goods character of goods of higher order is derived from that of the corresponding goods of lower order" (p. 63).

Also, ". . . the value of goods of the higher order is always and without exception determined by the prospective value of the goods of lower order in whose production they serve" (p. 150). By "goods character," Menger means their power to satisfy wants by being brought into a "causal connection" to human needs. He writes: "the law that the goods-character of goods of higher order is derived from the goods-character of the corresponding goods of lower order in whose production they serve . . ." (p. 66).

Reiterative statements abound in Menger; indeed, the book devolves from this theme, of marginal utility determining value, with productive agents possessing an economic significance only because of their contribution to final want-satisfying output. The theory of "derived demand" permeates the work: Menger insisted that goods were not valuable because labor was expended on them, as the classicists *appeared* to hold—they did take utility for granted, as indispensable to value—but labor was expended because the final goods were valuable. Labor (and other factors) would be expended in amounts, and acquire a value, depending on the value of final goods, i.e., on their marginal utility.

Walras, in his preface, warns us of the critical importance of the idea although he does not always pursue its ramifications for factor price determination. Walras remarks: [5]

> Jevons wrote ten remarkable pages at the close of the preface to this second edition (pp. xlviii–lvii), in which he clearly stated the formula . . . of Ricardo and Mill, must be reversed, for the prices of productive services are determined by the prices of their products and not the other way round (p. 45).

He also notes:

> The Austrian economists . . . also carried this idea to its logical conclusion . . . they established exactly the same relation . . . that I established between the value of products, on the one hand, and the value of raw materials and productive services, on the other (*ibid.*, p. 45).

In the same paragraph, Walras makes the point on causation rather clearly:

Jevons became aware of a point he had missed in the first edition, namely, that if the *Final Degree of Utility* determines the prices of products, it must also determine the prices of productive services . . .

Introducing his *Theory of Production* (Part IV, Lesson 17) Walras adverts to the matter once again:

in other words, we still have to inquire whether the prices of productive services determine the prices of products, as it is often claimed [by classical writers], or whether the prices of products, having already been determined . . . by the operation of the law of offer and demand, determine, in their turn, the prices of the productive services by the operation of the law of . . . cost price (p. 212).

By the "law" of offer and demand Walras means his well-known equation of price = average cost, without profit or losses to entrepreneurs.

Beyond observing later (pp. 424–425) that, when rent arises as a residual, unit costs cannot determine prices in the classical system, Walras abandons serious interest in the theory of derived demand; his conception of simultaneous equations mutually determining all price-quantity variables really dispenses with a sequence descending from product prices to factor prices (as Menger would describe it) or the other way round, as the classicists would have it. Still, accepting marginal utility as the basic determinant of resource use, derived demand remains a fundamental concept.

MARSHALL AND THE MODERN THEORY

While the derived-demand theory crystallized in the revolution of the 1870s, it remained for Marshall to give it the prominence it enjoys in the modern day.[6]

Marshall (Chapter VI, Book V) initially explains:

. . . the demand for raw materials and other means of production is *indirect* and is *derived* from the direct demand for those directly serviceable products which they help to produce (p. 381, italics in original).

In the sentence leading to the famous footnote on the demand for knives and the handles-blades components, Marshall writes:

> . . . To use technical terms, the demand schedule for any factor of production of a commodity can be *derived* from that for the commodity by subtracting from the demand price of each separate amount of the commodity the sum of the supply prices for corresponding amount of other factors (p. 383).

This contains the thrust of the theory. With characteristic caution, Marshall also remarks:

> . . . it must be remembered that this Derived schedule [for blades and handles] has no validity except on the supposition that we are isolating this one factor for separate study; that its own conditions of supply are disturbed; that there is at the time no independent disturbance affecting any other element in the problem; and that therefore in the case of each of the other factors of production the selling price may be taken to coincide always with the supply price (p. 383n).

Over time, and in full long-run equilibrium, Marshall also accepts falling supply curves (p. 384n).

Marshall examines the conditions "under which a check to the supply of a thing that is wanted not for direct use, but as a factor of production of some commodity, may cause a very great rise in its price" (p. 385). These rules have been pondered closely, particularly after publication of Hicks's *Theory of Wages* (1932), which imparted some new precision to Marshall's results by aid of the elasticity of substitution.[7]

Marshall recognized the meliorative influence of a substitute available at constant supply price in a footnote reference to Bohm-Bawerk; in his less ambiguous *Elements of Economics of Industry* (3rd ed., 1899), he wrote:

> The tyranny which one factor of production of a commodity might in some cases exercise over the other factors through the Law of

Derived Demand is tempered by the Law of Substitution (p. 221).

Hicks and the Theory of Wages

In the opening passages of his influential study on wage theory, Sir John Hicks remarks:

> . . . labour is a factor of production, and is thus demanded . . . because it is to be used in the production of some other thing which is directly desired. Personal services are indeed an exception to this rule; but apart from this exception, the demand for labour is a derived demand. . . .

Hicks formulated the concept of the *elasticity of substitution* (σ) to refine Marshall's rules on the effects of a change in the supply of factors of production on relative and absolute shares (Mathematical Appendix: the Elasticity of Derived Demand); the amendments are attached to Pigou's work because of Marshall's reliance on the special fixed coefficient case. The technical details now occupy considerable literature; withal, Marshall's notion of *demand elasticity for the final product* as the ultimate determinant of factor demand has been preserved.

The Marshallian Demand Premises

Crucial to the Marshallian theory of derived demand is the demand curve for final output. If the theory is to be questioned in the large, rather than modified in subtleties, it is with respect to its foundations.

In constructing his product demand curve and specifying the elements governing its elasticity, Marshall (Book III, Chapter IV) points up the complications "of getting exact lists of demand prices," amid the complications arising from the passage of time (p. 109). Time, of course, matters only if the "given conditions" alter; Marshall reminds us that "other things seldom are equal in fact over periods of time sufficiently long for the collection of full and trustworthy statistics" (p. 109). Marshall's product demand curves premise: (1) the price level, or the array of product prices; (2) the income total; (3) the income distribution; (4) the employment level; (5) the individual taste structure; and (6) some taste variability, including new fashions, over time. (This dynamic aspect has been little noted.)

SOME MODERN USAGE

The Marshallian theory still pervades modern textbooks exemplifying higher analytic standards.

Boulding, in a section on *Determinants of the Demand for a Factor*, offers the subtitle: "The Demand for a Factor as a Derived Demand." He outlines "three (3) propositions on the magnitude of derived demand" and another three "on the elasticity of demand for a factor." [8] With Marshall, he notes that "the more elastic the demand for a product . . . the more elastic is likely to be the demand for the factors which go to make the product" (p. 255). Novel to his argument is the stress on *expected* product demand (p. 254) although, for equilibrium, this must coincide with actual demand. The hypothesis of "given product demand" dominates the presentation.

Stigler purveys the main idea with typical succinctness. Deriving the firm's demand curve for a factor on the assumption of (1) a constant product price by the industry, he then performs the necessary modifications when (2) *all* firms face a factor price reduction: a crosscut demand curve for a factor is extracted from the simultaneous factor and product price change within the industry. The crucial assumption, namely, that *the product curve of the industry is "given"* is spelled out in a statement of "the Rules of Derived Demand," with appropriate references to Marshall, Hicks, and Bronfenbrenner. [9]

Friedman offers an analogous discussion. [10] Noting that "much of the preceding discussion applies equally in passing from each industry considered separately to the economy as a whole" (p. 183), for "The Economy as A Whole," he concludes:

> . . . the demand curve for [a factor] for the economy as a whole is a value of marginal product curve for the economy as a whole (p. 186).

Also,

> The marginal product curve for the economy will tend to be more elastic than the sum of the marginal product curves for the firms . . . (p. 186).

For Friedman, too, the price level holds firm within the economy regardless of factor prices.

Some Macroeconomic Usage

The macrotheory of employment and real wage determination occasionally reveals its microtheory roots; despite the luminous giant thirty-five year shadow of Keynes's *General Theory,* some parts of the present theory have scarcely been affected by his work.

Bailey, for example, elaborates a production function in the form: [11]

$$\frac{Y}{P} = f(N). \tag{1}$$

where N = total employment
Y = money income
P = an index of the price level

Then:

> *We further assume that hiring by firms is competitive, so that each firm will hire up to the point at which the real-wage is equal to the marginal product of labor* (p. 33, italics in original).

For the demand curve for labor:

$$\frac{w}{P} = f'(N), \tag{2}$$

where w is the money wage rate and $f'(N) =$ "labor's marginal product in generalized units of product" (p. 33). A labor supply function $[N = j(w/P)]$ is also included.[12] A geometric argument on (real) wage determination follows from the intersection of the demand and labor-supply function.

Essentially, this is a direct importation of micro-concepts into macroeconomics, with the real-wage and employment level resolved sans money, sans prices—and as if Keynes never wrote.

The influential book of Patinkin furnishes an identical account; the argument is conducted in real terms; a money wage–price economy operates on all squares with a barter world.[13]

From this (limited but not untypical) sample we can conclude that the prevailing macroeconomic demand-supply approach to *real* wage, and employment, determination has essentially been unaffected by Keynes and *The General Theory*, despite some general reference to his ideas. The theory of derived demand remains entrenched despite his weighty efforts to dislodge it.

KEYNES ON THE LABOR-DEMAND FUNCTION

Keynes's attitude was one of dismay at the state of the theory of labor demand. Finding it faulty at the core, Keynes abandoned any attempt at theoretical reconstruction; he disclaimed as spurious the efforts to treat money wages (for homogenous labor) as an endogenous phenomenon governed, in the manner of price theory, by supply and demand. Instead, his thrust was to consider the *effects* of changes in money wages; for Keynes, money wage movements comprised an *exogenous* phenomenon.[14]

Several of Keynes's key sentences deserve to be quoted: [15]

. . . the Classical Theory has been accustomed to rest the supposedly self-adjusting character of the economic system on an assumed fluidity of money-wages; and when there is rigidity, to lay . . . the blame of maladjustment (p. 257).

The generally accepted explanation is . . . quite a simple one. It does not depend on roundabout repercussions . . . the argument simply is that a reduction in money-wages will *cet. par.* stimulate demand by diminishing the price of the finished product, and will therefore increase output and employment up to the point where the reduction which labour has agreed to accept in its money-wages is just offset by the diminishing marginal efficiency of labour as output (from a given equipment) is increased. (p. 257)

Keynes's subsequent remarks have gone virtually unheeded, and almost unnoticed, in the post-Keynesian literature:

In its crudest form, this is tantamount to assuming that the reduction in money-wages will leave demand unaffected. There may be some economists who would maintain that there is no reason why demand should be affected, arguing that aggregate demand depends on the quantity of money multiplied by the income-velocity of money and that there is no obvious reason why a reduction in money-wages would reduce either . . . Or they may even argue that profits will necessarily go up because wages have gone down. But it would, I think be more usual to agree that the reduction in money-wages may have *some* effect on aggregate demand through its reducing the purchasing power of some of the workers, but that the real demand of other factors, whose money income have not been reduced, will be stimulated by the fall in prices, and that the aggregate demand of the workers themselves will be very likely increased as a result of the increased volume of employment, unless the elasticity of demand for labour in response to changes in money-wages is less than unity. Thus in the new equilibrium there will be more employment than there would have been otherwise, except, perhaps, in some unusual limiting case which has no reality in practice.

He concludes:

It is from this type of analysis that I fundamentally differ; or rather from the analysis which seems to lie behind such observations as the above. For whilst the above fairly represents, I think, the way in which many economists talk and write, the underlying analysis has seldom been written down in detail. (p. 258)

Keynes then examines the theory of labor demand by a particular *industry*, with aggregate demand constant—a modern exercise in microeconomics. He then remarks:

> But if the classical theory is now allowed to extend by analogy its conclusions in respect of a particular industry to industry as a whole, it is wholly unable to answer the question what effect on employment a reduction in money-wages will have. For it has no method of analysis wherewith to tackle the problem. Professor Pigou's *Theory of Unemployment* seems to me to get out of the Classical Theory all that can be got out of it; with the result that the book becomes a striking demonstration that this theory has nothing to offer, when it is applied to the problem of what determines the volume of actual employment as a whole.

Keynes's Reconstruction

Breaking with tradition Keynes foregoes any effort to revive the labor demand and supply functions; instead, he focuses on the frequently advocated policy of his time, namely, the cutting of money wages to erase unemployment. Changes in money wages are injected as an *exogenous* phenomenon rather than resulting from market pressures. Reinforced by his macroeconomic apparatus, he observes:

> Thus the reduction in money-wages will have no lasting tendency to increase employment except by virtue of its repercussions either on the propensity to consume for the community as a whole, or on the schedule of marginal efficiencies of capital, or on the rate of interest (p. 262).

From his framework Keynes finds that "the most important repercussions on these factors are likely, in practice, to be the following" (p. 262):

1. A reduction of money-wages will somewhat reduce prices. It will, therefore, involve some redistribution of real income (a) from wage-earners to other factors . . . whose remunera-

tion has not been reduced, and (b) from entrepreneurs to rentiers . . .

What the net result will be . . . is more likely to be adverse than favourable (p. 262).

2. [In an open system, without retaliatory actions from overseas] the change will be favourable to investment, since it will tend to increase the balance of trade (p. 262).

3. [But it] is likely to worsen the terms of trade. Thus, there will be a reduction in real incomes except in the case of the newly employed, which may tend to increase the propensity to consume (p. 263).

4. If the reduction of money-wages is expected to be a *reduction relatively to money-wages in the future,* the change will be favourable to investment . . . (p. 263).

5. The reduction in the wages-bill . . . will diminish the need for cash . . . and . . . this will reduce the rate of interest and thus prove favourable to investments (p. 263).

6. [It] may also produce an optimistic tone in the minds of investors [and raise the marginal efficiency of investments] (p. 264).

7. [But] the depressing influence on entrepreneurs of this greater burden of debt may partly offset any cheerful reactions from reduction of wages (p. 264).

Neutral Equilibrium and the Keynes-Effect

Weighing these considerations Keynes remains skeptical of the "downward" slope of the money wage demand curve for labor. He writes:

It is, therefore, on the effect of a falling wage-and-price level on the demand for money that those who believe in the self-adjusting quality of the economic system must rest the weight of their argument; though I am not aware that they have done so. If the quantity of money is itself a function of the wage- and price-level, there is indeed, nothing to hope in this direction. But if the quantity of money is virtually fixed, it is evident that its quantity in terms of wage-units can be indefinitely increased by a sufficient reduction in money-wages; and that its quantity in proportion to incomes generally can be largely increased, the limit to this increase depending on the proportion of wage-cost to marginal prime cost and on the response of other elements of marginal prime cost to the falling wage-unit.

In these passages, the "Keynes-effect" emerges, involving pressure on interest rates as the real value of the nominal money supply is altered through wage level *and* thereby, price level, changes. There is also the hint, often unperceived, of money supplies varying as an *effect* of price level phenomena, thus removed from any status as a causal agent.[16]

It is in this chapter and these passages that Keynes expresses his doubts on the efficacy of unassisted monetary policy to accomplish full employment and a noninflationary (or nondeflationary, in the 1930s) price level, leading Keynes to favor what now would be called incomes policy.[17]

SOME EVALUATION OF THE THEORY

In this brief evaluation of the theory of derived demand we omit Keynes's points 2–6 which have to do with international ramifications and expectational aspects; both points can be fitted in rather obviously.

Investment Goods

There is a need, first, to distinguish the theory with respect to output sectors. Consider, first, the investment output sector: for capital equipment, the Keynesian concept of the marginal efficiency of capital, grounded in expectational aspects, dominates the demand side; as expected future prices affect the earnings potential the theory of derived demand fits only awkwardly. The theory of I-sector demand thus has only a tenuous "long-run"— induced demand—connection to the Marshallian concept.

Producer's Goods

For intermediate producer's goods Marshall's knives, requiring blades and handles as inputs, remain as the redoubtable illustration of derived demand. The analysis was anticipated earlier by Cournot who described the demand for copper and lead as "derived" from the demand for brass.[18]

The Demand for Labor

Keynes understood very clearly that microeconomic analysis, resting on independent demand and supply functions, was incapable of resolving the theory of *money* wage determination once the interdependence of the *D* and *S* functions was discerned. Money wages would appear on the cost side, as a determinant of the supply curve and, in view of the influence of wage outlays in consumer markets, wages would be a major determinant of the demand side.[19] Changes in money wages would thus engender a parametric effect, shifting both functions (see Chapter 7 below).

Of course, for a localized wage change confined to one industry, especially where the wage earners spend practically nothing on the commodities they help produce, the derived demand analysis suffices: factor prices will depend on the "given" product demand and on the factor supply, and factor substitutionary, forces. But in this day of fairly proportionate wage changes for even heterogeneous labor, this analysis has only a limited validity; the important case is that of general wage increases on the assumption of labor homogeneity in the first telling and then, at the second stage, of proportionate increments in wages for even heterogeneous labor. (A better approximation would include disproportionate wage movements for heterogeneous labor.) [20]

An Aggregate Labor-Demand Curve

As the problem entails aggregate demand in a money, i.e., a wage and price, economy the "correct" approach must be via macroeconomics rather than through Marshallian microtheory. The main point, to repeat, is that a general wage increase must shift product demand curves as well as cost curves; in a money wage-price economy it is simply fallacious to treat factor demand curves as "derived" from product demand, or to assume that money wage changes alter product cost curves but not product demand curves. Once money wages change, there is a chain of reverberations running through both the product demand and the product cost side of microtheory.

ALTERNATIVE CONCEPTIONS

Some of the confusion undoubtedly lies in the diverse conceptions of factor price determination.

On the derived demand theory, either: (1) the analysis was conducted in real terms, so that money wages do not enter, or (2) as Keynes remarked, in seeking to penetrate the mystery, there was the assumption of money supplies or money income, or both, being held constant. Keynes adopted the then heretical third view, namely, that (3) money wages changed exogenously.

We can put (1) aside as simply irrelevant to the money wage economy. Analyses, such as Bailey's or Patinkin's, which write $D_L = S_L$, or labor demand equals supply in real terms, are simply *assuming* full employment: they are eliminating Keynes's unemployment diagnosis even as they profess to be elaborating some Keynesian theory. To assume that adjustments in the labor market are conducted in *real* terms simply ignores the money wage–price level nexus.[21]

View (2) also assumes away the problem. It makes the rather far-fetched assumption that money supplies, and money income, hold firm regardless of whether money wages are 1¢, $1, $10 . . . or whatever per hour. This is an unrealistic supposition no matter how often economists write $M = \overline{M}$. Monetary systems do not—and cannot—operate in this way; money supplies generally change with price movements, with output movements, and with employment movements.[22] We can thus treat this "theory" of $M = \overline{M}$ peremptorily.[23]

On Keynes's view of wages being exogenous, the theoretical issue is a direct one: do wages reflect prices or do prices reflect wages? The former bears the earmarks of the theory of derived demand and embeds, generally, the unreal hypotheses of $M = \bar{M}$ and $V = \bar{V}$ (= the velocity of money). That prices reflect wages is tied to the view of $w = w$, and of wages moving autonomously (or exogenously), while either $M = \bar{M} + \Delta M$, as ΔM varies according to how the monetary authority acts in order to achieve what it regards as politically tolerable employment levels as prices move to reflect money wage changes.

SUMMING UP

If we accept the theory of derived demand with respect to labor, then it is clear that to control the wage rate we need only control the level of final product demand. It follows as a natural corollary that through monetary or fiscal policy, by controlling aggregate consumption outlay (via taxes, say), or by reducing investment or government expenditure, wages will be guided into good balance.

Conversely, once money wages are regarded as exogenous, as Keynes held, then the macroeconomic models based on Marshallian microeconomic reasoning must be scrapped. For changes in money wages must affect, and without any serious time lag, both product demand curves and industry cost curves; *whenever money wages change there is a simultaneous dual force tending to lift prices.*[24]

To cope with undue wage movements, incomes policy has been recommended in recent years—much as Keynes foresaw—to cope with the current experience of excessive wage inflation. On derived demand precepts, in order to combat inflation, tight money alone needs to be invoked. (But to eliminate the simultaneous unemployment, easy money would be in order!)

However valid the theory of derived demand may be in ultimate terms in explaining that the demand curve for products dominates factor demand "in real terms," Keynes regarded it as shorn of explanatory power with respect to wages and prices when applied to events in actual markets. Even in "real terms," changes in money wages which shift cost curves and demand curves will probably have *some* real impact as income is redistributed, say, from rentiers to profit recipients, and perhaps *among* wage earners. Some modification in the underlying "real" demand will be engendered.

NOTES

1. John Stuart Mill, *Principles of Political Economy,* p. 79.

2. Cf. Harry Johnson, "Demand for Commodities Is *Not* Demand for Labour," *Economic Journal,* December 1949.

3. Jevons, *The Theory of Political Economy.*

4. Carl Menger, in *Principles of Economics,* eds. J. Dingwall and B. F. Hoselitz (New York: Free Press, 1950), Chap. 1, Sec. 3: "The Laws Governing Good Character."

5. Leon Walras, *Elements of Pure Economics,* 4th ed., 1900, trans. W. Jaffe (London: Allen and Unwin, 1954), preface.

6. Alfred Marshall, *Principles of Economics,* 8th ed. (London: Macmillan, 1920).

7. J. R. Hicks, *The Theory of Wages* (London: Macmillan, 1932), appendix, pp. 241–246. For his most recent statement, see his article, "Elasticity of Substitution Again: Substitutes and Complements," *Oxford Economic Papers,* November 1970. For some discussion and bibliography on the concept see Martin Bronfenbrenner, *Income Distribution Theory* (Chicago: Aldine Publishing Co., 1971), pp. 142–159.

8. Kenneth E. Boulding, *Microeconomics,* 4th ed., Vol. 1 (New York: Harper & Row, 1966), p. 252. His insightful remarks on wage theory in a macroeconomic context, originally advanced in *A Reconstruction of Economics* (New York: Wiley, 1950), are omitted from *Macroeconomics,* Vol. II.

9. George J. Stigler, *The Theory of Prices,* 3rd ed. (Macmillan, 1966), pp. 242–243.

10. Milton Friedman, *Price Theory: A Provisional Text* (Aldine, 1965).

11. While this is not a criticism of Bailey, if the $f'(N)$ curve is drawn concave to the ON axis it would imply an ultimately decreasing *absolute,* as well as relative, wage share as N advances. Some writers have been careless in their geometry. See Martin J. Bailey, *National*

Income and the Price Level (New York: McGraw-Hill Book Co., 1962).

12. The analytic basis of supply is never really developed in microeconomics. Cf. some remarks of W. Fellner and B. F. Haley, *Readings in the Theory of Income Distribution* (New York: Blakiston Press, 1946), p. viii.

13. Cf. Chapter 5, below.

14. His important Chapter 19 deals only with *effects* of changes in money wages.

15. *General Theory*, Chap. 19, "Changes in Money-Wages."

16. Cf. Chapter 1, "Keynes and the Monetarists," above, where this aspect of Keynes is interpreted in a banking principle context.

17. In view of its contemporary bearing and its implications for derived-demand thinking it is well to quote it in some detail:

> There is, therefore, no ground for the belief that a flexible wage policy is capable of maintaining a state of continuous full employment;—any more than for the belief that an open-market monetary policy is capable, unaided, of achieving this result. The economic system cannot be made self-adjusting along these lines. (p. 267)

This leads Keynes to opt for *Incomes Policy:*

> In the long period, on the other hand, we are still left with the choice between a policy of allowing prices to fall slowly with the progress of technique and equipment whilst keeping wages stable, or of allowing wages to rise slowly whilst keeping prices stable. On the whole my preference is for the latter alternative, on account of the fact that it is easier with an expectation of higher wages in future to keep the actual level of employment within a given range of full employment than with an expectation of lower wages in future, and on account also of the social advantages of gradually diminishing the burden of debt, the greater ease of adjustment from decaying to growing industries, and the psychological encouragement likely to be felt from a moderate tendency for money-wages to increase. (p. 271)

18. Augustin Cournot, *Researches into the Mathematical Principles of the Theory of Wealth*, trans. N. T. Bacon (London: Macmillan, 1897), pp. 100ff.

19. See Chapter 13, below.

20. Cf. my *Approach to the Theory of Income Distribution,* Chap. 1, for some criticism of the theory of derived-demand, and Chap. 16 for an effort to construct a proper theory. Heterogeneous labor is analyzed in Chap. 13.

21. See Chapter 5, below.

22. For some discussion, see Chapter 7, below.

23. For a view of money supplies as endogenous, see Kaldor, "The New Monetarism."

24. For a recent statistical study which is skeptical of the wage "lag" hypotheses, see Thomas F. Cargill, "An Empirical Investigation of the Wage-Lag Hypotheses," *American Economic Review,* 1969.

5 The Full Employment Model: A Critique

with E. Roy Weintraub

Full employment models resembling those which distressed Keynes again proliferate. A new neoclassical synthesis professes optimal labor market results, duly qualified for dynamic, transitional, and informational phenomena.[1]

Yet the facts remain obdurate. Excessive unemployment and immoderate inflation prevail in the U.S. despite the rigor achieved in full employment and stable price level models. Other economies are in the same pathological predicament. The conviction grows that the models and their neoclassical implications are again out of contact with reality.

Although Patinkin's work has earned a certain pride of place in restoring the full employment paradigm, his labor market theory has seldom been examined with the care it deserves. He himself confides that "The labor market as such does not interest us . . . its sole function is to provide the bench mark of full employment" (pp. 204–205). Often he merely *assumes* full employment though he sketches a mechanistic labor market stability *tatonnement*. The more serious criticism, however, is that his labor demand function rests on a marginal productivity theory embodying a flawed price level hypothesis.[2] The explicit concern with unemployment is earmarked outside the formal equilibrium model and ascribed to dynamic and transitional aberrations.[3] In his words: "Equilibrium means full employment, or equivalently, unemployment means disequilibrium" (p. 328). There is the limiting methodological dictum that "involuntary unemployment . . . can have no meaning within the confines of static equilibrium analysis" and that "the essence of dynamic analysis is involuntariness" (p. 323).

Lange's model of a Keynesian (perfectly elastic labor supply curve) unemployment equilibrium may thus be more acceptable analytically despite Patinkin's rejection of it in the course of sharpening the real-balance effect beyond Lange's original "monetary-effect." [4]

To place this article in perspective in capsule form, Patinkin's general equilibrium model requires $N_{sx} = 0$, where N_{sx} denotes the excess supply of labor. Following Keynes, Lange, and the recent probing work of Garegnani, the general condition should be $N_{sx} \geqq 0$. The policy implications of the inequality are substantial.[5]

The Patinkin Labor Market Analysis

Through the metamorphosis of the "real balance effect" into the "wealth effect" (as assets are introduced) and the "net financial claims effect" (with inside money), Patinkin's labor market analysis remains uncluttered. Only the dynamic study (pp. 313 *et seq.*) admits misgivings so that "disequilibrium" points "off" the aggregate supply and demand functions are entered; technically, "adjustment points" off the curve implies a *mis*-specification of functional equilibrium relationships.

Essentially, Patinkin and others write

$$N_d = N_d(w/P; K_o), \text{with } [dN_d/d(w/P)] < 0 \qquad (1)$$

$$N_s = N_s(w/p), \text{with } [dN_s/d(w/P)] > 0,$$

$$\text{but not } [dN_s/d(w/P)] = 0 \quad (2)$$

$$N_s = N_d, \text{but not } N_{sx} > 0. \qquad (3)$$

The Patinkin diagram is reproduced as Figure 5.1. The perfectly elastic N_s function of Lange, permitting Keynes's under-

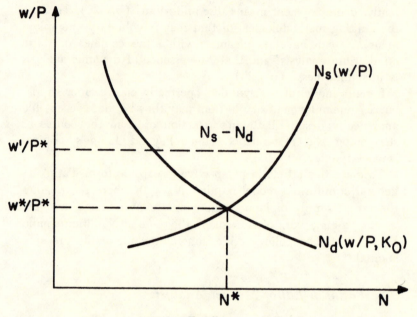

FIG. 5.1

employment equilibria, is rejected (see p. 341). The labor demand function (equation 1) rests on the real-wage (w/P), where w = money wage and P = the price level. To suppress growth complications (and *some* valuation problems) the stock of capital is fixed, denoted as K_o.[6] Further, and this colors part of the argument, Patinkin assumes the money stock (M) as fixed. There are the usual utility functions, productivity relations, and existing financial claims.

The supply curve of labor (equation 2) reflects the response to the real-wage; leisure-dominated labor supply offerings are set aside, for macro simplification.

The demand curve falls and the supply curve rises in Figure 5.1; the equilibrium is stable at "voluntary" full employment.

A student of Keynes's *General Theory* must blink at this fast restoration of the Jevonian—or Pigovian—full employment world. Where the classicists invoked "frictions" to explain unemployment, the Patinkin general equilibrium theory cites "dynamic" adjustments. The distinction may be faint to many.

For Patinkin, and others, the derivation of the demand curve for labor follows directly from elementary marginal productivity theory (p. 203). With one variable factor, we have:

$$P = w/m \quad \text{or} \quad m = w/P \tag{4}$$

where m = marginal product of labor and the w/m ratio is the marginal (variable labor) cost to the firm in augmenting output. Equation (4) embodies the hypothesis of pure competition and profit maximization. (Monopoly, ignored by Patinkin, requires a marginal revenue amendment.) For macroeconomics the relevant "marginal product" must be some composite commodity.

If wage bargains were made in real terms, full employment would be inevitable—as Keynes long ago conceded (*General Theory,* pp. 11–12). Keynes departed from traditional analysis by insisting that wage bargains were made in *money* terms. As prices would reflect the facts of varying money wages "there may exist no expedient by which labor as a whole can reduce its *real-*wage to a given figure by making revised money bargains with the entrepreneurs" (p. 13).

By ignoring Keynes's point, unemployment is permuted into an awkward "frictional" or "disequilibrium" outcome that defies systematic analysis; Keynes (rightly) denied this view; his theory dealt with unemployment equilibria and his work was surely distinctive (revolutionary?) in tracing the money wage–price level nexus which distinguishes the actual economy from the Jevonian or Pigovian barter world of uncomplicated real-wage bargains.[7]

The "Fixed-Price Level" Model

The relevance of this for labor market theory has eluded even some professed Keynesians. For example, along the vertical axis of Figure 5.1 denoting *real*-wages, one might interpret the Patinkin argument as averring that while money wages move, prices hold firm at, say, $P = P^*$. Hypothesizing a "fixed price" model— an anomaly for a *general* equilibrium theory—any changes in labor's money wage will modify real-wages and generate pressures toward full employment so long as the fixed price level prevails. Absent is the recognition that a money wage rise, say, will break the fixed price barrier: at issue is the money wage–price level dependence.

A fixed price model clearly entails a wholesale—and mischievous—reversion to *partial* equilibrium analysis. It implies that whether money wages are $1 an hour or $1,000,000 an hour, prices are unaffected: even though Patinkin's labor force is homogeneous and labor is used in all industrial outputs, any wage-cost pressure on prices is suppressed. In elasticity terms,

$$E_{pw} = w\mathrm{d}P/P\mathrm{d}w = 0. \tag{5}$$

To argue that prices are constant regardless of the money wage constitutes an extreme assumption even for a "mental experiment."

A diagrammatic argument may serve some purpose. In Figure 5.2, D^* and S^* represent demand and supply curves for the economy (or "representative" industry).[8] Both are generated by the *money* wage w^* and the accompanying data, leading to equilibrium output Q^* and the associated employment N^*. As the money wage rises, and assuming a strong wage content embodied in D^*, D' replaces D^* and S' supplants S^* as $w' > w^*$. With P^* firm—the fixed price model—the commodity market will report excess demand, with $Q_d > Q_s$.

The fixed price model is manifestly a disequilibrium system: it would not be worth elaborating if it did not lurk in the background of models built around Figure 5.1. With the price level fixed and output lower, aggregate profits—and the profit rate—must fall. The higher real-wage, however, suggests a greater wage component in aggregate demand, and some shift in income division.

Despite the "excess" commodity demand, the full employment (Q^*, N^*) outcome is rejected by entrepreneurs for the $w'/P^* > w''/P^*$ real-wage dilutes their Q^* profit prospects; the unemployment at Q_s in Figure 5.2 (or at w'/P^* on N_d in Figure 4.1) is attributable to entrepreneurs spurning the full employment goal as entailing too great an inroad on their profits.

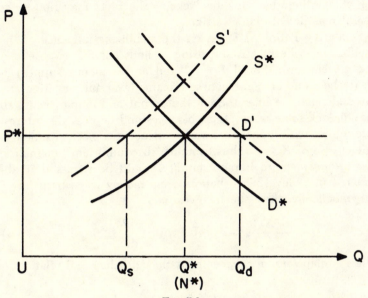

Fig. 5.2

Conceivably, the higher real-wage (w'/P^*) might, sooner or later, promote greater mechanization through encouraging a substitution of capital equipment for labor.[9] Unemployment may thus be mitigated—temporarily—via the burst of investment although it is ultimately enlarged. But these remote consequences of $(K_o + \Delta K)$, or economic growth generally, transcend the Patinkin text.

In sum, the real-wage demand curve for labor traced in Figure 5.1 emerges as a valid locus for a fixed-price level model. But it also represents an unintended excursion into *disequilibrium* analysis, in the sense that the points on its path, with the exception of w^*/P^*, are identified with a price level that is *not* an equilibrium price level for any money wage other than w^*. The D' and S' tracings for w' in Figure 5.2 show that even a *given M* yields a new "full (voluntary) employment" equilibrium at a higher price level and an output (probably) below Q^*.[10]

Excess commodity demand, and possibly excess labor supply, prevails at $w' > w^*$ and $P = P^*$. As argued below, a mechanism for eliminating this may be lacking; the facts may not be as singular as in Patinkin's version.

Pondering Patinkin's stress on the stabilizing influence of the real-balance effect, it is surprising to find that this is absent in the present case. For if $P = P^*$ and M (= money supply) is fixed, the value of real-balances remains invariant, negating any force along these lines though the output and employment fall may unlock some transactions balances and depress the interest rate which, with higher real-wages, encourages mechanization.

The case of $E_{pw} = 0$ thus contains "disequilibrium" anomalies; any *tatonnement* to impart stability would be remiss if it abstracted price level perturbations from money wage bargains.

Symbolically, the issue involves:

$$\frac{d(N_d - N_s)}{dw} < 0 \quad \text{with} \quad \frac{dP}{dw} \geqq 0. \tag{6}$$

The Patinkin *tatonnement* embeds the $(dP/dw) = 0$ relation.

The Wage-Price Proportionality Model

Keynes occupies the other corner by assuming (Book V) that prices move (nearly) proportionately to the wage level, so that $E_{pw} = 1$. From $MC = w/m$, where MC is marginal cost, Keynes equated MC to P in equation 4, concluding thereby that a rise in MC *must* evoke a proportionate response in P. The argument has too frequently been overlooked, even by the Keynesians.[11]

In this case *the Patinkin demand locus of Figure 5.1 degenerates into a point:* the real-wage remains constant regardless of the money wage. If the vertical axis of Figure 5.1 denoted *money* wages, the N_d curve would stand perfectly inelastic. This is identified as the Keynesian labor-demand case.[12]

From his evaluation of $(E_{pw} \approx 1)$, Keynes concluded that there was no way for labor as a whole to *reduce* its real-wage; it could acquiesce to wage cuts but these would be translated into price reductions. In a percipient analysis Keynes noted that lower money wages (and prices) would reduce the demand for money at any N level with the result, with money supply constant, of a fall in interest rates. Wage policy and monetary policy were twins; changing money wages was a roundabout way of altering money supplies and interest rates. To Keynes: "it can only be a foolish person who would prefer a flexible wage policy to a flexible money policy" (*General Theory*, p. 368), since the latter involves less vituperation, villification, and class conflict.

The real-balance effect of a wage-price reduction for Patinkin —as for Pigou—would enrich those owning money; their added real consumption could foster an output expansion and reenforce Keynes's interest rate effect. Obstacles to investment are erected, however, through bankruptcies occasioned by any price level debacle while heavy fixed charges prevail. Insofar as the demand for *inside*-money falls off at a lower wage-price level, and the inside-money supply contracts, the real-balance effect tends to be dimmed—though Keynes's point is unaffected.[13]

In the Keynesian case, therefore, the effect on labor demand of a wage reduction $w' < w^*{}_c$ depends on:

$$\frac{dN_d}{dw} = f\left[\frac{\partial C(Y/P)}{\partial(M/P)}\frac{\partial(M/P)}{\partial P}\frac{dP}{dw} + \frac{\partial(I/Y)}{\partial r}\frac{\partial r}{\partial P}\frac{dP}{dw} - \frac{\partial \sigma}{\partial P}\frac{dP}{dw}\right], \quad (7)$$

where σ represents a "confidence" term associated with bankruptcies and the structure of financial claims. (Distributional effects on C and I following wage and price level changes occupy Keynes's Chapter 19.)

It is thus an easier (or tighter) money policy which *may* stabilize the system to restore an initial (N^*, Q^*) position, given $w' \gtreqless w^*$, with $P \neq P^*$. In the $E_{pw} = 1$ model, the Q^*, N^* system may be *stable* at any initial output-employment level, whether originally full employment or underemployment. The case fits Keynes naturally but it falls outside Patinkin's model.

The Intermediate Case

Most likely is the intermediate case of $0 < E_{pw} < 1$ so long as other costs are included in MC; Keynes recognized indirect taxes while attaching particular prominence to *user* costs, a lead that has hardly been grasped.

Would other costs hold firm? A rise in money wages can stir

expectations of future price rises so that the Hicksian elasticity of expectations might exceed unity. User costs would thus mount and, conceivably, $E_{pw} \geqq 1$.[14]

So long as $E_{pw} > 0$ the implications remain damaging to the neoclassical N_d analysis. "Very large" money wage hikes would entail "large" price rises: the real-wage rise would be tempered. In terms of Figure 5.1 we would settle in the neighborhood of w^*/P^* (with $dP/dw > 0$), so that without specifying whether money supplies alter (as a corrective), and spelling out the regenerative real-balance forces and the changes in σ, the N_d- and N_s-locus remains fairly indeterminate.

In the fixed money supply model, with $w' > w^*$ and $P' > P^*$, tight money would raise interest rates and reduce labor demand; supplemented by the real-balance effect, this would flatten the N_d curve. But then, any stability inherent in the down-to-the-right N_d becomes a consequence not of labor market events but of money market events. With higher money wages, prices, and interest rates, the door is open for monetary policy to restore the Q^* output and N^* employment (and the N_d demand point) whether this is at full employment, as in the Patinkin drawing (Figure 5.1), or some *initial* unemployment position. The "fixed-M" model then becomes a mental experiment rather than a realistic hypothesis.

Given $w \gtrless w^*$, the stability *tatonnement* and the full employment-unemployment theory cannot be divorced from money supplies, price levels, and wage levels. The Patinkin adjustment of w to a fixed P, and never P to a varying w, is a distorted picture of the adaptative process. To (7), therefore, acknowledging changes in the money supply, a fuller description of the *tatonnement* must add:

$$(\partial M/\partial P)/ (\partial P/\partial w), \text{ where } M \text{ denotes the money supply.} \quad (8)$$

The $E_{pw} > 1$ Case

$E_{pw} > 1$ requires brief mention. A higher money wage here leads to a *decline* in real-wages: in Figure 5.1 we are dropped to the

N_d part of the curve *below* the w^*/P^* intersection despite the
money wage rise. The elasticity of N_d in this region would be
diminished by the real-balance erosion *and* the higher interest
rates which militate against an output expansion. With the fall
in real-wages and a curtailed consumption outlay, N_d can be
backward-falling, as in the Giffen case in product markets; this
can cause complications for stability analysis.

Distribution Aspects

Keynes adverted to the distributional aspects of a money wage
change whenever $0 < E_{pw} \leqq 1$. He argued that any shift to wage
earners was likely to be employment stimulating, so N_d would
increase.

That *less* labor will always be demanded at higher real-wages
is itself problematical. For consider the following:

$$\eta A = w/P. \tag{9}$$

In (9) A denotes Q/N, the average product of labor, while η
represents the wage share, the portion of output per head going
to labor.

Suppose now, that $1 > E_{pw} > 0$ so that real-wages rise. If A is
constant at any initial Q^*, N^*, η must immediately rise while
the capitalist share falls. Real *consumption* demand, in the aggregate, should, as in Figure 5.2, rise; while profit-maximizing
decisions lead entrepreneurs to cut back their output, their investment response to their profit erosion can be renewed modernization and mechanization. Labor demand may well expand. In
a disequilibrium model the long-run adaptative wage may run
counter to short-run profit maximization objectives. The N_d
solution of Figure 5.1 may thus be suspect in positing a falling
N_d function in the range $w' \geqq w^*$ and $P = P^*$.

Entrepreneurs may be as eager to traverse the one road, of
technological improvement after a real-wage advance, as to travel
the other, of withdrawal. Hence the Jevonian response is limited
to a short-run profit maximization static model. A modernization
drive would require Patinkin's N_d curve to rise to the right: the

empirical issue is whether industrialists are "drop-outs," or activists striving to neutralize the long-run profit threat.[15]

The N_d Function

Patinkin's N_d curve thus has a logical haven only in a fixed price model of $E_{pw} = 0$. Even then the N_d function is *not* a labor demand curve in the usual sense, for the points along its path are analytically inconsistent with an equilibrium outcome at a real-wage other than w^*/P^*. If N_s intersects N_d at, say, w'/P^*, an equilibrium in the product market (see Figure 5.2) is precluded, for product demand exceeds supply. The output imbalance is manifestly incompatible with equilibrium analysis. The fixed price model is a disequilibrium creation which is out of place in Patinkin's comparative statics analysis. *Ceteris paribus* for the price level must yield to *mutatis mutandis* in a general equilibrium model—which is Patinkin's objective. Mechanization complications also abound. While through Keynes's interest rate repercussions, and the Pigou-Patinkin real-balance effects, the theory of a falling N_d curve *may* be preserved, all this is a far cry from the static real-wage marginal productivity elements basic in Patinkin's approach. Insofar as N_d traces alternate hypothetical equilibrium possibilities, as a demand function should, the full system, rather than merely the marginal productivity features, must be invoked to detail the N_d course. The dominant force shaping N_d may be obscure in this "dynamic" situation. The hypothesis of a "fixed M" also appears strained, for monetary authorities are likely to be compelled to augment M to prevent unemployment growth accompanying the wage-price inflation. This is the sequence that coincides with the modern facts.

The Labor Supply Function

The *stable* Patinkin model invokes forces generated by an excess labor supply to press the real-wage downward to attain full employment. Volitional elements in decision making are not wholly suppressed although the behavior pattern is entirely mechanistic: unemployment fosters an unequivocal willingness to accept a lower real-wage.

Equally plausible even in the classical "real-wage" world of Jevons is the hypothesis that wage earners adhere to, *and only accept*, the real-wage most recently named, say at $w'/P^* > w^*/P^*$. In effect, any upward departure from the w^*/P^* equilibrium in Figure 5.1 instills a sentiment that the *new* real-wage is correct, that as capitalists can pay there is no reason to accept less. Effectively, the most recent experience is regarded as critical, so that at each prevailing real-wage for employed labor, the unemployed abide by it as representative of contemporary income facts.

Graphically, in Figure 5.3 we can redraw the N_s function of Figure 5.1 with a horizontal segment at w^*/P^*. Likewise, at w'/P^* and w''/P^*. Connecting these segments we have a locus that resembles N_s in Figure 5.1. But the interpretation becomes vastly different: if the real-wage demand is w^*/P^*, then the supply function is horizontal at this real-wage, and rising thereafter. Likewise, if we are at w'/P^*, the curve is horizontal at this real-wage; or from w''/P^*, and so forth.

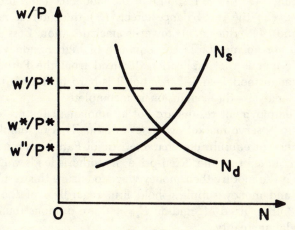

Fɪɢ. 5.3

Involved is a curve perfectly elastic at that rate at which wage earners are hired, and imperfectly elastic thereafter. Whatever the going real-wage, and however it is arrived at, whether fortuitously or through trade union pressure, so long as it prevails for some time interval it is taken as the standard or as the prevailing custom, as Mill and the classicists might contend in arguing that custom as well as competition governed real-wages.[16] It would take some altered attitudes to induce workers, despite unemployment pressures, to permit their real-wage to be cut by accepting lower money wages while prices remained constant (as in the Patinkin model).

On this interpretation of Figure 5.3 (and Figure 5.1) we are back to the Lange-Klein representation of "involuntary" unemployment or underemployment equilibrium.[17] Whatever the level of employment and real-wage (such as w^*/P^*), if w^*/P^* has prevailed (for however long, depending on labor supply behavioral characteristics of the model), the N_s curve may be perfectly elastic. There may, depending on the N_d point, be full employment or "involuntary" unemployment. Further, given any rise in w, and given the concomitant movement in P, the associated N_d point may remain at N^*_d or to the right or left of it, depending on: (1) the response of the monetary (and fiscal) authorities; (2) the real-balance effect; (3) the interest rate outcome; and (4) inducements towards mechanization. Less employment is *not* an inevitable consequence of higher money wages; if the former is the implication deduced from the Patinkin full employment model—and if it is not it is hard to fathom its labor market analysis—the conclusion is incomplete.

Full employment results are not an immanent feature of capitalism, to observe market events even casually. Full employment is an inherent equilibrium characteristic of Patinkin's model only if it is assumed that the "fixed-price" hypothesis leads wage earners always to modify their money wage to ensure this result while prices—and money supplies—hold firm regardless of the money wage. Both a "fixed M" and an $E_{pw} = 0$ are dubious foundations for modeling reality.

Conclusion

Contemporary full employment general equilibrium models, like their pre-1936 antecedents, are contradicted by events and are unconvincing in theory: the automatic full employment outcome is as dubious now as it was for Keynes. A neoclassical revival which presumes that prices will hold (nearly) firm while money wages vary arouses skepticism; the assumption of "fixed money supplies" overlooks the pressures of unemployment on monetary authorities in a democratic regime; their actions to mitigate the anguish of unemployment are more rational than the rigid models imply. Distributional effects, which may affect the slope of N_d, have also been unwittingly neglected.

Further, that "excess" labor supply must drive down the acceptable real-wage is a behavioral oversimplification. So long as wage earners abide by a higher money wage once this is reached, perhaps in resigned acceptance to a union agreement and the emergent facts, entirely apart from any individual money "illusion" the Patinkin labor-market stabilizing *tatonnement* is effectively suspended.

Entrepreneurial real-wage responses are complex. While these belong to growth "dynamics" they add to the perils of extracting serious conclusions from static models; they must be entered so long as policy implications follow from analytic work.

On these grounds, Lange's diagnosis can be sustained: general equilibrium models—meaning a completely interdependent set of structural and behavioral equations—can incorporate involuntary unemployment as well as full employment. Patinkin, himself, can be cited in support of the Lange position, for in his "dynamic" or "disequilibrium" analysis his concern is with "points off the curve." But labor supply points "off" a curve are points "on" some other curve, as on the horizontal segments of Figure 5.3. The "points" must be specified as belonging to *some* function once they are isolated from the "well-behaved" N_s function. Further, the associated demand curve may be inelastic or even rightward-rising—depending on the supporting characteristics of the model.

Although nature may still abhor a vacuum, it is still not certain that the market economy eschews involuntary unemployment. The post-World War II era does not corroborate the robustness of the market mechanism as a full employment restorative; the period can be interpreted as a time in which fiscal and monetary management, under the impetus of enormous government military expenditures, were used consciously to promote *near*-full employment ends. Analytically, we may be taking a small step backward in assuming full employment as a feature of equilibrium and, even worse, in deducing full employment on: (1) limited labor market and (2) limited entrepreneurial behavior premises, and (3) an incomplete analysis of wage-price relations and (4) inaccurate money supply responses.

NOTES

1. Cf. Bent Hansen, *A Survey of General Equilibrium Systems* (New York: McGraw-Hill Book Co., 1970); A. Leijonhufvud, *On Keynesian Economics;* R. Clower, "The Keynesian Counterrevolution: A Theoretical Approach," in *The Theory of Interest Rates* (New York: St. Martin's Press, 1966), eds. F. H. Hahn and F. P. R. Brechling.

2. Patinkin's important work, *Money, Interest, and Prices,* 2nd ed. (New York: Harper and Row, 1965), devotes pp. 199–312 to the workings of the full employment model; involuntary unemployment and other Keynesian conjectures are considered over pp. 313–365; described in a "disequilibrium" context, they involve positions *off* the aggregate labor supply and demand curves (p. 323).

3. A recent article by R. J. Barro and H. I. Grossman, "A General Disequilibrium Model of Income and Employment," *American Economic Review,* March 1970, attempts to generalize Patinkin's *dis*-equilibrium interpretation of Keynes, declaring:

As is now well understood, the key to the Keynesian theory of income determination is the assumption that the vector of prices, wages, and interest rates does not move instantaneously from one full employment equilibrium position to another.

The point of this chapter is just the converse, that prices and interest rates, on Keynes's methods of comparative statics, do adjust "instantaneously" to variations in money wages—which Keynes interpreted as exogenous—and in money supplies. So far as "lags" went, Keynes injected these as qualifying factors for his static equilibrium method, as in modifying the pure theory of the multiplier. See Keynes, *General Theory*, Chap. 19 and pp. 122–125.

4. In what seems to be the same spirit, see Robert Clower, "A Reconsideration of the Microfoundations of Monetary Theory," *Western Economic Journal*, December 1967.

5. Garegnani's work, following Piero Sraffa and Joan Robinson with classical roots in Ricardo, merits attention on all aspects of distribution and full employment theory. See P. Garegnani, "Heterogeneous Capital, the Production Function and the Theory of Distribution," *Review of Economic Studies*, July 1970. Questions raised below on the demand curve for labor are related to the Cambridge criticisms of the derived demand for capital.

6. Although this is not central to our probe, Mrs. Robinson's doubts on capital aggregation are not without relevance. The recent article by Garegnani must call for a reconsideration of the Clark-Ramsey-Samuelson "homogeneous" capital concept with major ramifications into all parts of accepted theory. Garegnani, "Heterogeneous Capital," and Joan Robinson, "The Measure of Capital: The End of the Controversy," *Economic Journal*, 1971.

7. Cf. A. C. Pigou, *Theory of Unemployment* (Macmillan, 1933). Keynes's criticism (pp. 272–279) should be reread. Even Leijonhufvud's excellent book is in this respect often "anti-Keynesian."

8. See Chapter 13 below for an effort to define their analytic base.

9. Mrs. Robinson has argued that this is the common response to higher real-wages. Cf. *Accumulation of Capital*, 2nd ed. (New York: St. Martin's Press, 1965).

10. If the velocity of money is constant, then $P^*Q^* = P'Q'$, with $(P'/P^*) = (Q^*Q')$.

11. An exception is Alvin Hansen, *Monetary Theory and Fiscal Policy* (New York: McGraw-Hill Book Co., 1949). But the interpretation of the labor demand curve, as a macromarginal productivity curve, reduces Hansen's analysis to the disequilibrium "fixed price model" analyzed above.

12. Cf. my *Approach to the Theory of Income Distribution*.

13. "Inside-money deflation" is a normal accompaniment of severe price level declines in an economy where output financing is linked to bank lending.

14. The $E_{pw} > 1$ case may be identified with the modern view that inflation itself is a result of *expectations* of inflation. This is plausible

only in circumstances where wages are rising and forcing prices upward.

15. Cf. Mrs. Robinson on real wages and mechanization, *Accumulation*, Book II.

16. Cf. John Stuart Mill: ". . . wages, like other things, may be regulated either by competition or by custom: but "competition, however, must be regarded, in the present state of society, as the principal regulator of wages. . . ." *Principles of Political Economy*, p. 342. Under modern trade unions the interpretation might be modified.

17. Oscar Lange, *Price Flexibility and Employment* (Principia Press, 1944), and L. R. Klein, *The Keynesian Revolution*, 2nd ed. (New York: Macmillan Co., 1966).

6 Revision and Recantation in Hicksian Economics

WARNING: *Contents on inflation are a hazard to understanding and may leave visible economic and social scars.*

This mental health circular should henceforth be affixed to the proliferation of macroeconomic textbooks and professional writings using the IS-LM techniques originated by Sir John Hicks in 1937.[1]

This is the message emanating from the three Helsinki lectures delivered by Hicks in 1973.[2] In omitting remedial wage policies, the lectures are unlikely to help mitigate the shattering stagflation-slumpflation bouts that have afflicted market economies in recent years. Only a confirmed optimist can think that the work will quickly amend the monumental confusions of the assorted Bastard-Keynesians, castigated by Mrs. Robinson, who have perpetrated the unemployment-inflation hoax on Keynes's great work intended to salvage capitalism and to usher in a stable economy.

CLASSICAL KEYNESIANISM

It is the importance assigned to money wages and their "Spontaneous" (or exogenous) versus their "Induced" (or endogenous) nature—to use Keynes's *Treatise* language[3]—that marks Keynes from most Keynesians. Even Axel Leijonhufvud, who has been so effective in disentangling the two strands, has generally missed the vital money wage ingredient in the inflation story conveying stark real effects.[4] Exempt from this indictment, which largely blankets American Keynesianism and descendent streams, would be Keynesians Joan Robinson, Richard Kahn, Nicholas Kaldor, Roy Harrod, A. P. Lerner, Paul Davidson, Paul Wells, and a handful of others.[5]

Recent years have revealed some egregious Keynesian meanderings. Classical Keynesianism, derived from Hansen and Samuelson and then from Hicks, with the latter reserved at first for only "advanced" students, dominated the 1950s.[6] This apparatus performed the incredible feat of "explaining" inflation in an IS-LM model specified in real terms, where prices were constant: A barter economy was inherently replicated and inflation was "analyzed"! Embedded also was the bland assumption that an economy would exhibit *either* inflation *or* unemployment. That lesser developed economies succumbed to both ailments, well—too bad for them, not the theory. Affluent societies had to suffer the twin ordeal before Keynesians revised their symmetrical model.

Latching on to the empirical Phillips curve display, Keynesians at least acquired a plausible inflation theory: Wages and prices might rise even under unemployment. Small wonder then that in this trade-off milieu the undisguised unemployment policies of monetarists, planned to combat inflation, led to some Keynesian eclipse and converted some of the legion away from their presumed commitment to eradicating unemployment. "Natural" unemployment and "natural" Phillips curve law—and economic folklore—governed the equilibrium economy.

Enter shifting Phillips curves, come Ignore Inflation, meet Indexation Keynesianism, all within about a decade.[7] Each cerebral spin-off was usually hailed within the Keynesian establishment and in their mutual admiration conferences as demonstrating profound insight and "scientific" progress. Consistency and generality were lesser virtues, and promising nonmainstream Keynesian tracks were neither examined nor rejected: They were safely overlooked as threats to "the" model.

Where next? Maybe, considering Hick's initial influence on the group, they will come to admit exogenous (spontaneous) money wage shifts in their taut models, and, unless beholden to labor unions or their political sponsors, they might even contribute to the formulation of a feasible incomes policy to check the ruinous ascent of (mainly) money wages and salaries that spell inflation and, under typical Federal Reserve responses, induce the unemployment that conveys stagflation or slumpflation.

THE "WAGE-THEOREM"

It is in his third and closing lecture that Hicks declares that "it is quite time" to consider money wages and "what Keynes said about wages" and what "ought to have been said" (p. 59).

This emits a scent of Keynes being somehow at fault in misdirecting Keynesians. Yet, he was as adamant as can be, in Chapters 2, 4, and 19–21, on the central part played by money wages and their connection to price level upheavals. (This has been a chronic theme of this reviewer.) To buttress this interpretation there is Hicks's immediate enunciation of "a principle, very important to Keynes, which I shall call the *wage-theorem*" (p. 58, italics in original). Thus: "When there is a general (proportional) rise in money wages . . . the *normal* effect is that all prices rise in the same proportion—provided that the money supply is increased in the same proportion (whence the rate of interest will be unchanged)" (pp. 59–60).

As the "theorem" is likely to gain adherents and invite quotation, it deserves closer scrutiny. To be sure, the tacked on phrase will probably comfort monetarists in their quantity theory predilections, arguing tediously that it is the added money supply that "really ratifies" the price upsweep.

Keynes actually stressed the "cost-unit," comprising mostly money wages, but also including user-costs and indirect taxes.[8] When the cost-unit rose with output, with productivity unchanged, the price level would climb.

With infrequent reference to the degree of competition, Keynes essentially, through all this, premised pure competition and rising supply schedules for industries economy wide: The static laws of return were implicit. Keynes could be faulted for neglecting monopoly and mark-up pricing.

My own version of the price level, consistent with the spirit of Keynes's analysis, has involved a mark-up of unit labor costs consisting of average wages and salaries (inseparable in the data, and in cost evaluation and pricing decisions) to average labor productivity, as conventionally measured. The economy-wide mark-up which is also the reciprocal of the labor share, has been practically constant in Gross Business Product data.[9]

Variability in the money supply is thus stripped of *direct* relevance for the price level. What the money managers do will more obviously and surely affect output and employment, with tight money episodes having a potent real-output clout, in housing especially, over the last quarter of a century. Indirectly, the recession-unemployment phase induced by money restraint, or a "less than proportionate" matching of money supplies to wage-salary hikes, can retard the money wage advance: Blocking investment and the implicit multiplier path comprises the control mechanism, neutralized in small part toward fostering inflation by some lag in productivity gains through the deferral of plant modernization.

This account of the transmission of monetary impulses would be compatible with earlier Phillips curve relations and roomy enough to encompass the modern stagflation-slumpflation genesis wherein money wages and the price level march up despite growing unemployment or even (slightly) declining production.[10]

Hicks, then, may be purveying a false lead by injecting money supply aspects in his rendition of Keynes's "wage-theorem."[11] Also, unless "wages" include salaries—where do we draw the line?—the formulation is too narrow.

A new backtrack to special theories is manifest in Hick's acceptance of the Phillips curve and "demand-pull" inflation under "full employment." Without a money wage-salary upcreep, only a profit inflation, as distinct from a wage-salary (or incomes) inflation, is possible.[12] This would be reflected in a rise in the mark-up term implying an enlargement of the profit share. Evidence of a serious upward drift in the profit share is not revealed in the data of market economies. If it did occur the profit grab could be overcome through higher corporate tax levies or through more active monopoly surveillance.

Largely, the line between "demand-pull" and "cost-push" (or

wage-push) inflation is imaginary. Analytically, it creates special theses rather than a general theory, while obscuring an understanding of the inflation sequence. Clearly, a wage increase places immediate cost pressures under prices, while simultaneously generating higher money incomes that lift demand through the more abundant purchasing power in consumer markets.[13] It is the dual impact that provides the rationale for an incomes policy. Gearing money wage-salary moves to the general productivity improvements would abort both an income or a profit inflation, according to the historical firmness of the employee share in Gross Business Income. Hence, a successful—and acceptable—incomes policy should operate to stabilize the price trend even under "full employment," preventing demand-pull from being translated into higher *money* incomes.[14]

Hicks, as noted, avoids policy advice for coping with the stagflation troubles of our times, contenting himself with some reflections on our era of rising money wage demands (pp. 70–72). Whatever "the" cause, it would be useful, at this late day, to hear of a remedy. One can debate interminably with a physician on the "causes" of cancer—and die. For some it is enough to learn that there are some surgical cures.

THE MULTIPLIER IN A FLEX-PRICE MODEL

The opening lecture in *The Crisis in Keynesian Economics* focuses on the theory of the multiplier from the noncontroversial stance that the concept applies to a process in time. Two points are made: (1) The multiplier momentum depends on stocks of materials on hand, for example, bricks must be available if investment (I) consists of houses, or foreign exchange is indispensable if I denotes equipment containing imported raw materials, and (2) Hicks distinguishes a "fix-price" from a "flex-price" economy, or constant versus varying prices as the multiplier cuts its income swath.

Ultimately the issues hinge on whether the aggregate I is taken gross or net and on whether bottlenecks and inventory decumulation can block an expansion thrust. This is clear enough. Attention to price phenomena (while not entirely novel) was long overdue, but it is mystifying that Hicks sidesteps the more obvious query of whether the *I* outlays are originally stipulated in real or in nominal money terms. Military projects, for example, are often programmed in real terms, while municipal grants for structures and equipment may be budgeted in fixed money sums. While the price level mechanics deserve exploration, the size of the multiplier chain would also depend on the income distribution consequences of price moves, with some potential shift between wage and nonwage shares and between profit and rentier claimants in the nonwage portion. For the size of the average and marginal investment multipliers are dependent on the respective savings propensities and share ratios of the income classes, with the shares likely to be more volatile in the "flex-price" model. Hicks's multiplier scan should at least have paused over the Kalecki-Kaldor-Robinson income distribution theorems.

MONEY AND THE MARGINAL EFFICIENCY OF CAPITAL

The second lecture is devoted to money and the marginal efficiency of capital, with money occupying center stage. There is the apt remark, characterizing much of the American Keynesian family, that "Keynesianism, in practice, has become fiscalism" and that Keynes has been "read to imply that there is nothing to be done with money" (p. 32). Of course, this attitude prompted the ludicrous attack mounted by the monetarists against Keynes, rather than Keynesians, that in his theory "money didn't matter."[15]

Hicks also cites the belief in the late 1930s that changes in the long interest rates were too small, cost wise, to affect investment. This was indeed in the long ago, before double-digit long rates became conventional as against rates hovering about 3 and 4 per cent in that by-gone era, with short rates at fractions of one per cent. Memories are also evoked when Hicks writes that "a theory of money . . . can hardly be centred in the speculative motive in the way that seemed called for in 1936" (p. 37). Nonetheless, "we need something more than a portfolio selection theory; we need a theory of liquidity" (p. 37).

In some lively pages Hicks outlines a monetary theory built around choice, in "a related sequence" over time, wherein money confers flexibility by averting the handicap of firms being "locked in" from exploiting promising new opportunities. Even financial disaster may be threatened by the lack of liquidity. In these pages Hicks strikes a rich lode in extracting unexplored elements already latent in Keynes's precautionary motive; earlier, Kahn and Harrod also perceived the doctrine as undervalued in post-Keynesian interpretation.[16]

Hicks, in candor, draws back from his earlier "expectations" theory of the interdependence of the interest rate structure because of "imperfections" in financial markets. Other Keynesians prefer to overlook these impediments to some grand, if irrelevant, capital market "equilibrium" theories.

Vital passages illuminate money as an input and as a "running asset" for business transactions, an aspect that somehow becomes submerged in the portfolio contemplation of money as only one among near equals as a store of value. There is a depressing irony in the need for Hicks to awaken us to money as a medium of exchange, serving the transactions motive while enhancing flexibility, through liquidity, in filling precautionary objectives. The pages provide a valuable antidote to much superficial profundity in treating money in its stock magnitude, while underplaying its flow dimension.

In linking monetary theory to real investment Hicks sees an avenue of influence through a decline in interest rates entailing a "rise in the price of securities" which "increases the value of reserves . . . thus increasing liquidity" (p. 52). Shades of Keynes of the *Treatise* wherein "purely financial" events have definite real consequences! The observations should finally demolish the contorted concept of "neutral" money. Hicks, however, misses the opportunity to score the erosion of money balances in a wage-induced inflation and to make plain that more money, required *because* prices have risen, can scarcely be alleged to "cause" inflation; they can aid in alleviating unemployment.[17] This is another aspect of the wage-theorem and the employment-sustaining part played by money.

Hicks does have a few lines at the costliness of liquidity under accelerating high inflation rates and hyperinflation. Themes for many lectures abound in chaotic price episodes in which money loses even its temporary store of value attributes.

On Keynes's approach to monetary theory, Hicks writes: "I have come to feel that one of the worst things about Keynes's doctrine . . . is the impression he gives that Liquidity Preference is wholly, and always, bad" (p. 57). Others will undoubtedly feel indebted to Keynes for unearthing a phenomenon to be reckoned with in analysis and policy.

More unease will be engendered by the remarks that, for Keynes, "only investment expenditure is taken into account; the productivity of investment is neglected. (One remembers those pyramids!)" (parentheses in original).

Others, however, will recall the greater social advantage ascribed to two railways from London to York. More baffling in the entire context are the observations that "the social function of liquidity is that it gives time to think" and that "it is socially productive that the form of investment should be wisely chosen" (p. 57).

Aimed at Keynes as even casual criticism these lines miss the target. It would also be well to spell out "socially productive" investment in an enterprise economy with its perplexing uncertainties and financial, and product, market "imperfections."

Hicks's points seem better suited for their shock value as lecture utterances; in print they remain provocative but less defensible.

IS-LM: A PAST WITHOUT A FUTURE?

Robert Clower, in his Foreword, salutes the Nobel laureate: "No living scholar has done more than John Hicks to shape contemporary modes of economic analysis." This is a supreme accolade.

Those who are disenchanted with "contemporary modes" quarrel less with Hicks, who has pioneered many trails, than with the successor generation that has shut its eyes to the dismal inflation-unemployment fiasco that diminishes economists' boasts of scientific acumen. Nowhere is the gap wider than in money wage theory and its price level ramifications which menace our economic, political, and social systems. Many remain content in merely enshrining the theory of *real* wages, confusing it with money wage determination, and perpetuating the account which Hicks developed in making his triumphal world debut some 43 years back. Hicks can hardly be blamed for the contemporary inertia and complacency.

That this review courts the danger of matching the book size is the best compliment that can be paid Hicks for writing a lucid and artistic, stimulating if not wholly persuading, piece. A small book with big themes is worth a library of fat and shallow Keynesian volumes. To be sure, nonmainstream Keynesian writings have eluded Hicks, just as they are habitually by-passed by mainstream Keynesians forever ironing out permanent wrinkles in the think-alike wash.[18]

If the IS-LM curves are decently buried on the inflation pyre, a first telling of the price level and employment theory might invoke aggregate demand and aggregate supply concepts embodying the money wage as a parameter on both sides of the macrosystem.[19] Thereupon: (1) The price level emerges as an endogenous phenomenon, capable of varying even under given money wage and productivity conditions; (2) monetary behavior enters from the start, thereby averting the standard evasion of a constant money supply which, in the nature of events, *cannot* stay fixed when output, employment, and prices follow a wayward course up or down; (3) the micro-macro connection of firms to the economy can be more readily established; (4) an easy transition to the significant Kalecki-Kaldor-Robinson distribution theorems is open; (5) a consistent growth theory can be erected from the static macrotheory;[20] and (6) demand functions for labor, with money wage and employment coordinates chained to price level gyrations, can be extracted.[21] Gone would be the sham that the price level can somehow remain rigid (through monetary maneuvers and without revolution and social chaos) regardless of whether money wages are a penny or a million dollars an hour.

With Hicks's acknowledgment of IS-LM inadequacy it will be interesting to see how other mainstream Keynesians cut their analytic losses; there has been more than a decade of writhing to preserve the fiction of endogenous money wage determination, involving a refusal to accord respectability to doctrines of even partial exogenous factors: Hicks's nod may at last open up some of the heretofore rigid "contemporary" closed minds. Apparently, we must be prepared to weather much mumbo jumbo posturing over "expectations of inflation" as constituting a money wage determinant, although it is no more than a highbrow, heady circumlocution for exogenous or spontaneous money wage changes.

After mainstream Keynesianism recovers from the trauma of having to shed its precious doctrine of endogenous money wages, and textbook revisions are completed, the market economy should benefit from the inevitable ensuing discussion of incomes policy and the outline of viable political options.

Future historians of economic thought may express some astonishment at the 36-year lag in enunciating Keynes's "wage-theorem." It was there, all the time, in the wage-unit, a concept fundamental to Keynes. Maybe other prominent Keynesians will hasten to make their progress reports on "scientific" advance to awe students.

People hurt by unemployment or frustrated by inflation have been the social victims of pretty irrelevant Keynesian models. Since Hicks has written it will be hard for other Keynesians to maintain the composure that everything is as before. Even before policy, the textbooks must come in for some revision. But it is rather late in the century. The market system has suffered, and political and social systems have been damaged.

Mainstream Keynesianism has helped shape some unpleasant history in achieving its academic victory, while silencing in-family dissent on the crucial wage issue.

NOTES

1. J. R. Hicks, "Mr. Keynes and the 'Classics': A Suggested Interpretation,": *Econometrica*, 5 (April 1937), pp. 147–159.

2. Sir John Hicks, *The Crisis in Keynesian Economics* (New York: Basic Books, 1973), p. 85.

3. J. M. Keynes, *A Treatise on Money*, 2 vols. (New York: Harcourt, Brace, 1930), pp. 169–170, 271–272.

4. Axel Leijonhufvud, *On Keynesian Economics and the Economics of Keynes* (New York: Oxford, 1968).

5. I have tried to promote the money wage aspects in Keynes for over 20 years. Samuelson at one time referred to my work on aggregate demand and aggregate supply, with each function embodying the money wage as a parameter, as that of a "lone wolf" Keynesian, P. A. Samuelson, "A Brief Survey of Post-Keynesian Developments," in *Keynes' General Theory, Reports of Three Decades*, Robert Lekachman, ed. (New York: St. Martin's, 1964).

6. Early protests appear in my *Classical Keynesianism, Monetary Theory, and the Price Level* (Philadelphia: Chilton, 1961).

7. The metamorphoses of "the men for all seasons" is traced in Chapter 2 above.

8. J. M. Keynes, *The General Theory of Employment Interest and Money* (New York: Harcourt, Brace, 1936), p. 302.

9. See John Hotson, *International Comparisons of Money Velocity and Wage Mark-Ups* (New York: Augustus M. Kelley); S. Weintraub, *A General Theory of the Price Level* (Philadelphia: Chilton, 1969); and S. Weintraub, *Some Aspects of Wage Theory and Policy* (Philadelphia: Chilton, 1964).

10. For some definition of *stagflation* and *slumpflation,* and the prospect of at least nine different price level and production configurations, see Chapter 9 below.

11. For an interpretation of Keynes and the quantity theory, see Chapter 3 below.

12. Keynes used this classification in *A Treatise On Money*, p. 155.

13. For an elaboration of the theory of the consumer price level, see Chapter 14 below.

14. My own views, with coauthor Henry Wallich, on a compatible, market-oriented incomes policy appear in Chapter 16 below.

15. Compare Chapter 1 above.

16. For an important, modern, nonmainstream Keynesian contribution, see Paul Davidson, *Money and the Real World* (London: Macmillan, 1972), especially Chapter 8.

17. Paul Davidson and Sidney Weintraub, "Money as Cause and Effect," *Economic Journal*, 83 (December 1973), pp. 1117-1132.

18. For some classification of different brands of Keynesianism, see Davidson, *Money and the Real World*, Chapter 1.

19. S. Weintraub, *An Approach to the Theory of Income Distribution* (Philadelphia: Chilton, 1968), Chapter 2.

20. See Davidson, *Money and the Real World*, and S. Weintraub, *A Keynesian Theory of Employment Growth and Income Distribution* (Philadelphia: Chilton, 1965).

21. S. Weintraub, *Theory of Income Distribution,* Chapter 6.

7 Money Supplies and Price-Output Variations: The Friedman Puzzle

WITH HAMID HABIBAGAHI

Monetary doctrine has wavered over time in its assessment of money as cause or effect of economic conditions. In the modern Monetarist revival Professor Friedman, in interpreting the long statistical record, has recognized both aspects of changes in money supplies although the causal attribute dominates the policy recommendations for economic stability.[1]

Countering the New Monetarism has been some growing acceptance of wage-oriented theories of inflation in view of events in the United States in 1969–1971. Infrequently noted, however, are some major monetary implications in this point of view: if excessive wage settlements are culpable in inflation, then changes in money supplies are (largely) divested of price level causality. This culminates in some restoration of Banking Principle doctrine. Concomitantly, as Monetarists and Keynesians acknowledge an output and employment impact of money changes, a Currency School strand adheres.[2]

These issues can be sharpened for some eclectic convergence in analyzing what Friedman declares to be an unresolved problem for Monetarism, namely, the separate effect of changes in the money supply on prices and output. As this study opens up the wider ramifications, it is worth exploring at some length.

THE PRICE-OUTPUT DIVISION

Professor Friedman, as noted earlier, finds the split of money income changes (ΔY) between price variations ($Q\Delta P$) and real output increments ($P\Delta Q$), stemming from money supply changes (ΔM), to be vague and theoretically incomplete.[3] The policy implications of this failure to pin ΔM securely to the separate $Q\Delta P$ and $P\Delta Q$ components of ΔY are enormous: the monetary policy pursued in the United States (and Canada) in 1969–70 succeeded in damping Q and N without leveling P.

For Friedman, the thrust of changes in M upon P and Q filters through the demand equation for money. Given their demand for *real* money balances, once M alters the market actions of economic transactors affect P, Q, and N (employment). Hence, "The conclusion is that substantial changes in prices or nominal income are almost invariably the result of changes in the nominal supply of money." [4]

Keynes was concerned with this very issue although he conceived of the P-process quite differently.[5] Thirty-five years ago he observed:

> For the purpose of the real world it is a great fault in the Quantity Theory that it does not distinguish between changes in prices which are a function of changes in output, and those which are a function of changes in the wage-unit.[6]

Moving upward along industry supply curves under diminishing returns, as Keynes saw it, prices would have to be higher *even if money wages* (and factor prices generally) *were constant.*[7] If wages rose—a changed "wage-unit"—prices must mount. For Keynes, P was largely contingent on the relation of money wages to labor productivity: changes in ΔM might exert an indirect—and probably small—causal influence on P if labor productivity varied through ΔQ increments induced by a ΔM expansion.

Keynes's emphasis on money wages and labor productivity as determining factors for the price level can be embodied in a wage-cost markup equation WCM:

$$P = kw/A. \tag{1}$$

Empirical evidence suggests writing $k = \bar{k}$, for k is practically constant, for most predictive purposes.[8] Manifestly, on this approach, unit labor costs ($U = w/A$) control P so long as the money wage is exogenously determined. If w is treated as an endogenous variable, as in general equilibrium theory and Phillips-curve analysis, it still follows that unit labor costs and prices must be aligned though the causal impetus on this view generally runs from P to w.[9]

On the *WCM* interpretation, and with the constancy of k, the "law" of the price level is, simply and unadorned, prices are governed by unit labor costs. Disproportionate movements in wages relative to labor productivity are the root of inflation.[10]

Wages as Exogenous

Alluding to "Keynesian-Theory," Friedman comments: [11]

> The simple income-expenditure theory adds the equation $P = P_o$; that is, the price level is determined outside the (equational) system . . . It appends to this system . . . an institutional structure that is assumed either to keep prices rigid or to determine changes in prices on the basis of "bargaining power" or some similar set of forces.

He notes "the tendency on the part of many economists to assume implicitly that prices [the price level?] are an institutional datum" (p. 216).

It is possible to embrace the charge that wages are exogenously decided; even though they both reflect and anticipate economic forces their magnitudes of changes are not finely predictable from past facts or the *immediate* P, Q, N, or M variables. Once wages change the price level is *bound* to change—qualified for A (and k) variations.

The remark on an "institutional structure" should be purged of any pejorative ring, as nurturing an inferior theory. Money supplies are also institutionally created. The price level is an institutional phenomenon, substantially, under all plausible theories; a theory must incorporate institutional phenomena which affect economic processes.[12]

The Time Setting

As to the exogenous interpretation of wage phenomena, at any historical P-Q-N-w-r (r = interest rates) setting at time t_0, as a result of collective bargaining actions wages are settled to cover the interval $t_0 \rightarrow t_1$, $t_1 \rightarrow t_2$, $t_2 \rightarrow t_3$, with a not uncommon agreement extending for three years. Given these stylized facts—which parallel real world events—it must be that prices (largely) reflect wages, and not the other way about; it is prices rather than wages that adapt, as derived-demand theory would have it.[13]

The Δw movements are thereby envisaged as autonomous, or (at least partially) exogenous, whether dominated by past or expected price changes, union belligerency, public pressures, and so forth. Whatever the Phillips-curve dependency on unemployment, the connection is imprecise, in a functional sense, as in recent years. Rather than discontinuous jumps in Δw (and ΔP) at any date t_0, t_1, or t_2, wage variations are in fact fairly continuous, rising in one industry today, in another tomorrow, so that the w (and P) series can display a persistent trend.[14]

ΔM AS OUTPUT SUSTAINING

So far the money supply has been stripped of any P-causality; the chief inflationary influence has been assigned to $U(= w/A)$. Once the price level goes up in response to the rising U-tendencies, a central bank will ordinarily have to enlarge M, following $(\Delta P/\Delta w) > 0$, merely to maintain Q. The ΔM augmentation would serve "to meet the needs of trade," to echo the banking principle phrase. The ΔM which buttresses $\bar{Q}$ would be noninflationary for P while constituting an antidote for recessionary Q and N tendencies.

The need for more money to support the Q (and N) level may be put in this way. With the ΔP move realized outside the monetary sphere as a result of an exogenous $\Delta w/w > \Delta A/A$, economic transactors respond by demanding, for an unchanged Q and N position, an unchanged amount of *real*-balances, or an increased amount of nominal money. The enlarged demand for money balances would raise interest rates. The ensuing curb to investment would thereupon depress output and employment. It follows, therefore, that if money wages and prices rise, more money will be required merely to sustain the output-employment level.[15]

ΔM *as Output Causal*

Given the wage level—the wage-unit—Keynes argued that more money has a causal significance for output.[16]

> The primary effect of a change in the quantity of money on the quantity of effective demand is through its influence on the rate of interest [and thereby investment]. *General Theory*, p. 298.

For effective demand we can read money income (Y). Manifestly, for Keynes, Money *Increments* Mattered—but for mainly Q and N levels.

For Keynes the magnitude of the causal impact of ΔM on ΔQ would depend on: (1) the elasticity of the I-function with respect to r; (2) the implicit multiplier, with its dependency on the marginal propensity to consume; (3) the interest-elasticity of the demand for money, so that ΔM affects r rather than being aborted as bondholders exchange less liquid assets for the cash created by the central bank. The degree to which money matters would be contingent on these relations.

The P-*Impact of* ΔM

The theory does not preclude *some* impact of monetary variations on the price level.

First, in the event of a Δw and ΔP rise, tight money, meaning a ΔM variation that is inadequate to sustain Q in the new wage-price circumstances, will signify unemployment, in amount depending on the labor force growth and improving technology.

The resulting unemployment may temper the wage advance. Through this channel, involving the personal anguish and output loss of unemployment, the price level *may* be brought under *indirect* control. Nonetheless, it is worth emphasizing that it is through the money wage—an implicit Incomes Policy—that the monetary anti-inflation counterweight operates.

Second, as ample increments of money can affect output positively, the output-employment enhancement can influence prices: average productivity (A) can change. Interestingly, however, the outcome may be the reverse of some monetary doctrine. For in the realistic time setting in which technology advances so that A rises, a monetary easing to increase ΔN will tend to *lower* prices. The converse also holds: tight money which restrains the Q and N advance, and restrains the A-improvement, has some inflationary implications.

To elaborate this, we posit $w = \bar{w}$ for simplicity and introduce an autonomous ΔM following the implementation of monetary policy. Normally, ΔM will depress r and, as Keynes envisaged it, depending on the multiplier and the sensitivity of I to r, the Q and N magnitudes will advance.

As the WCM-equation contains the A-terms, with $(\Delta Q/\Delta N)$ > 0 there is some incipient P-effect. On the *static* "laws of returns" ΔM thus carries some inflationary overtones: the chain would involve $M\uparrow$, $Q\uparrow$, $N\uparrow$, $A\downarrow$, $P\uparrow$.

Realistically, as ΔM occurs in a time context, advances in technology are likely to raise A as Q and N grow with ΔM: this is the evidence from time series which compromises the static laws of returns.[17] Hence, as the authorities enlarge M to accommodate a larger work force, or to combat excess unemployment, the ΔA move usually meliorates the P-rise.

It is with respect to Q that money lubricates "the wheels of trade" for David Hume, or rotates as the "great wheel of circulation" in Adam Smith. Lacking ample M-sums, market activity would be mired at depressed levels. The causal significance of M for Q (under limited money emissions) comprises some of the substance of Currency School doctrine.

The P-impact of tight money which thwarts full employment

at any given wage level is thus likely to be the *inverse* of the usual conception. Only with respect to its restraint on wage movements can an anti-inflationary influence be assigned to tight money.

A MONEY SUPPLY–OUTPUT VARIATION THEORY

We can now return to the particular theme opened up by Friedman in his concern with the relation of ΔM to $\Delta Y = P\Delta Q + Q\Delta P + \Delta P\Delta Q$. In Friedman's view the magnitudes on the right flow from the interplay of monetary phenomena and the Q-determinants, with their interaction constituting the theoretical secret.

Our argument advances two hypotheses: (1) that the price level is a resultant of wage-average labor productivity relations; (2) that money supplies are *causally* linked to output, and only indirectly linked to prices, often in a way that is contrary to common doctrine. Involved, therefore, is the thought that when prices rise through exogenous wage movements, *merely to keep output constant the money supply will have to increase to support the output level*. Only through the creation of money increments in excess of the sums necessary at $(P + \Delta P)$ can output be affected positively, given some unemployment or excess capacity in the economy. Only the "surplus" or "residual" money can foster a Q and N advance.

ΔM *and* ΔQ

Our basic output model thus entails:

$$(\Delta Q/Q) = f[(\Delta M/M) - (\Delta P/P)]. \qquad (2)$$

The rate of output change is a function of the difference between the rate of change in the money stock and the price level. Only through the residual money beyond that needed to sustain the higher price structure (in an inflationary wage-price advance) can monetary policy be stimulating. To ascertain function (2) is thus the objective of a full employment–labor growth monetary policy.

Friedman's Money Income Elasticity

By drawing on Professor Friedman's work it is possible to push the argument further. Using the following elasticities and definitions:

$$E_{ym} = M\Delta Y/Y\Delta M, \; E_{qm} = M\Delta Q/Q\Delta M, \; E_{pm} = M\Delta P/P\Delta M \quad (3a)$$
$$Y = PQ \text{ and } \Delta Y = P\Delta Q + Q\Delta P + \Delta P\Delta Q \quad (3b)$$
$$P = kw/A \text{ and } P' \equiv P + \Delta P = k'w'/A' \quad (3c)$$

where $k' = k + \Delta k$
$w' = w + \Delta w$
$A' = A + \Delta A.$

After reduction: [18]

$$E_{qm} = (E_{ym} - E_{pm})P/P'. \quad (4)$$

E_{ym} denotes the elasticity of money income to money supplies which Friedman estimates to be 1.84.[19] Obviously, as (4) reports, the output effect of changes in money supplies depends significantly on the price level movement: the "left-over" money will be nil if the parenthesis is zero. On Friedman's estimates this will follow if the price rise is approximately 1.84 times the relative rise in the money supply. That is, if the price level rise is just short of twice the relative rise in money supplies, output will be unaltered.

Thus with a price level rise of the order of 5.5 per cent per annum, as in recent years, a 3 per cent rise in the money supply is a prescription for output stagnation and unemployment. A 4 per cent money increment would be compatible with less than a 2 per cent output expansion, etc.

The Wage-Productivity Relations

We can insert the wage and average productivity elements in order to simulate their separate influence on output growth. Thus:

$$(\Delta Q/Q) = [(A'wk)/(Aw'k')][E_{ym}(\Delta M/M) + 1] - 1. \quad (5)$$

Equation (5) reveals that if wage and productivity changes are synchronized, assuming $k = k'$, then the term in the left bracket becomes unity: the Q-variation depends wholly on the relative money increment and the money-income elasticity. If the wage move outstrips the productivity advance, then $A'w < Aw'$, and the effect of the money increment on output is partially eroded. A strong wage uplift, and a weak productivity response, will negate the real output advance accompanying a steady rate of money enhancement. An undeviating monetary policy set on a target rate of money advance can thus combine a twin disaster, namely, of simultaneous inflation *and* unemployment, with or without output decline. This has an analogy in the "pathological" episode of 1969–1970 where prices and unemployment rates rose, rather than moving along their historically divergent paths.

To consider the monetary measures necessary to hold Q constant in the face of a strong wage advance, we can set $(\Delta Q/Q) = 0$ in (5). Treating $(k/k') = 1$, then:

$$[(Aw')/(A'w)] = (\Delta M E_{ym}/M) + 1. \qquad (6a)$$

Imposing sample values of $(A/A') = (100/103)$ and $E_{ym} = 1.84$:

$$(w'/w) = (1.89 \Delta M/M) + 1.03 \text{ or } (\Delta w/w)$$

$$= 1.89(\Delta M/M) + .03. \qquad (6b)$$

According to (6b), if money wages and productivity both advance by 3 per cent, to hold Q constant the money supply can remain unchanged: no extra money is required to finance either output or income, for both P and Q will be constant. But if money wages rise by 6 per cent, then the money supply required merely to sustain output is of the order of 1.6 per cent. A 9 per cent rise in the money wage would require a money increment over 3 per cent to prevent an output slippage. A falling k-trend can, of course, mitigate the effects of disproportionate wage movements.

SUPPORTING AND STIMULATING MONEY SUPPLIES

The theory of money as cause and effect aimed at in the foregoing analysis has a multidimensional aspect to it. In one direction the monetary authority throws in money supplies in response to a price uplift which it is (largely) powerless to thwart: the provision of funds to set $\Delta Q = 0$, with $\Delta P > 0$, constitutes a defensive or sustaining operation: here the monetary authorities are primarily acting "to meet the needs of trade." A more niggardly monetary provision, entailing $\Delta Q < 0$ with $\Delta P > 0$, marks a *constrictive* posture; this is close to defining the 1970 events. In a second dimension the monetary authority convoys ΔM toward enlarging ΔQ and ΔN, whatever the course of ΔP. This portends a stimulating mission and imparts a causal impact of monetary policy. With higher wages and higher prices in the midst of unemployment, the stimulating and sustaining acts can become joined. Third, even with stable prices and satisfactory employment levels, changes in the demand for money may threaten to undermine Q and N; international influences may provide a case in point. To counter these effects entails a neutralizing stance.

However the operational arena is defined, the upshot of all monetary policy must be to order $\Delta M \gtreqless 0$ over some specified time interval Δt. Regardless of the *ex ante* monetary designs, with every money variation by the authorities, some portion of ΔM will fade off into a supporting, stimulating, or neutralizing mission.

The Art of Monetary Policy

The analysis points up the complexity of monetary policy in an environment of wage inflation. Even large increases in money supplies—by historical standards—may be barely ample to protect production levels; only a scant margin of residual money may remain to induce a Q-expansion.

In formulating policy the monetary authorities must inevitably be guided by some P-expectation for the projected time horizon —the $Q\Delta P$ variation—and the extent to which they plan to nudge Q or N—the $P\Delta Q$ variation. With ΔP and ΔQ both moving, the residual $\Delta P\Delta Q$ magnitude must also be assessed. On a first approximation the mechanistic Quantity Theory hypothesis of $V = \bar{V}$ can yield a clue to the necessary ΔM magnitude. Judgment must thereafter enter, with respect to money magnitudes necessary to compensate for any nonlinear elements in money demand, and any volatility in the money-demand function rendering $\Delta V \neq 0$.[20] Lacking prescience with respect to V, any departure from the hypothesis of $V = \bar{V}$ embodies a "judgment-margin" or discretionary-safeguard: thus in $\bar{V} + \Delta V = V^\circ$, ΔV is the uncertain element with $\bar{V} = $ the past velocity, and V° representing the unknown future velocity.

It is in the context of *ex ante* projections of V° that the art of monetary policy resides, as the monetary authorities execute their policy mandate. So long as ΔV remains imperfectly predictable, discretion must supplement (or supplant) mechanical rules.[21]

MONEY SUPPLY: EXOGENOUS OR ENDOGENOUS?

Variations in M have been envisaged as "exogenous." In contrast, Professor Kaldor has recently described changes in the money supply as an "endogenous" variation, i.e., a response to economic conditions.[22] That is, the real and institutional forces determine output, prices, and money income, and the monetary authorities merely adapt to the facts of economic life, for if they fail to do so, a shift-over to the evolution of money substitutes would develop.

As far as it goes, this view is acceptable. But new costs would inevitably accompany the shift-over; various impediments would be encountered and exchange transactions would be at least partially clogged.

This is, implicitly, an account of higher interest rates. In the usual course these must have some deterrent impact on output.

Apart from semantic nuances perhaps, the position staked out here is not vastly different from that of Kaldor. For with respect to the rise in the price level engendered by disproportionate wage increases, and for which M-increments serve to meet the needs of trade, there is no harm in regarding this part of the M-variation as endogenous, undertaken to prevent an output deterioration and an employment decline: central bankers *must* augment the money supply once P rises. But it would be stretching the use of the term—which has always had ambiguous connotations—to refer to the "residual" money increment as endogenous *unless* it is argued that the monetary measures merely anticipate sure future output prospects without any chance of influencing them.

As the central bank response is imperfectly predictable, the monetary actions can, with equal propriety—or imprecision—be described as exogenous. This has been the usage adopted here.

CONCLUSION

The contribution of monetary policy to halting inflation has been argued to be roundabout, at best. On the theory developed, the future of the price level rests substantially in the laps of businessmen and labor unions rather than the monetary authorities. The settlements of recent years promise continuing inflation. Accompanied by a restrained monetary policy, which proceeds within rates of increase of about 5 per cent, say, unemployment can endure at rates too high for fulfillment of the full employment vision. Unemployment may temper union demands and contain the wage movement; but, then, monetary policy becomes a second stage vehicle for combating the anti-inflation objective.

At this level, perhaps, it is possible to blend the *WCM* inflation theory with the Monetarist view. Under both analyses wage and productivity movements must be aligned for price level stability. The issue, therefore, emerges as one of a *direct* versus an *indirect* approach toward controlling wages for inhibiting inflation.

An efficacious Incomes Policy—if one can be devised—need not run in conflict with Monetarist doctrine.[23] It would free monetary policy of its present dilemma, of tightness to achieve the anti-inflation objectives, and of monetary easing to serve the full employment goal. Incomes Policy could thus complement monetary policy by providing it with an anti-inflation shield, thereby permitting it to make its potent contribution toward providing maximum job opportunities in the enterprise society.

Notes

1. For a short excerpt of the dual views see Milton Friedman, "The New Monetarism," *Lloyds Bank Review*, No. 98 (1970), pp. 52–53.

2. On the historical doctrinal controversy, see Lloyd W. Mints, *A History of Banking Theory* (Chicago: University of Chicago Press, 1945). Also, some remarks in D. H. Robertson, *Money* (New York: Pitman Publishing Corp., reprinted, 1948), pp. 97–102.

3. Milton Friedman, *Optimum Quantity of Money*, p. 279; "Theoretical Framework," pp. 222–223. Also, Anna Schwartz, "Why Money Matters."

4. "Theoretical Framework," p. 195. At other places he remarks:

> For monetary theory, the key question is the process of adjustment to a discrepancy between the nominal quantity of money demanded and the nominal quantity supplied.

> The key insight of the quantity-theory approach is that such a discrepancy will be manifested primarily in attempted spending, thence in the rate of change in nominal income. Put differently, money holders cannot determine the nominal quantity of money . . . but they can make velocity anything they wish. *Optimum Quantity of Money*, p. 225.

In "What Price Guideposts" he observes: "Inflation is always and everywhere a monetary phenomenon."

5. Axel Leijonhufvud makes the same point, *On Keynesian Economics*, p. 132n.

6. Keynes, *General Theory*, p. 209.

7. For an account of Keynes's schematic analysis, cf. Chapter 3 above.

8. Keynes recognized the constancy of the wage share in pondering Kalecki's work. See his "Relative Movements of Real Wages and Output," *Economic Journal*, XLIX (1939).

On the constancy of k, the Council of Economic Advisers, in dropping a monetarist stance, observed:

> One of the best established facts about the American Economy is the long-run tendency for prices on the average to rise at about the same rate as unit labor costs on the average. Put another way, apart from temporary aberrations the general price level tends to

rise by the excess of wage increases over productivity increases. *Inflation Alert #2*, 1970.

Their conclusion derives from GNP data. The relationship is stronger for gross business product, the proper (we think) price level concept.

9. Thus there *is* an incomes policy in the Monetarist position. See my "Incomes Policy in the Monetarist Programme."

10. While this is essentially the Keynes argument, Keynes's "cost-unit" would also include indirect taxes, user costs, and the degree of monopoly power. *General Theory*, pp. 245, 295, 302. For our purposes these elements are subsumed in k.

11. "Theoretical Framework," pp. 219–220.

12. Thus when Friedman writes that "theories of inflation stemming from the Keynesian approach stress institutional, not monetary factors" ("Theoretical Framework," p. 211) the phrase should not be interpreted as a reproof.

13. For Keynes on derived-demand, cf. above.

14. Spillovers to nonunion sectors are not precluded as office staff, say, have their salaries readjusted after union money wage gains are negotiated for factory staff. Changes in w in the auto industry, say, will not only affect costs and prices there but, through higher wage incomes, retail sales in the plant environs will be affected and they will be read as "demand-pull" pressures; retail wage agreements will also be rewritten (as they expire). So it will go, through the system.

15. Cf. Keynes's analogy of changes in money wages to changes in the nominal money supply. *General Theory*, Chap. 19.

16. On the "two-theories" in Keynes, see Chapter 1 above.

17. For an assessment of an older controversy, originally involving Keynes, Dunlop, and Tarshis, cf. Ronald Bodkin, "Real Wages and Cyclical Variations in Employment."

18. From

$$\frac{\Delta Y}{Y} = \frac{\Delta P}{P} + \frac{\Delta Q}{Q} + \frac{\Delta P \Delta Q}{PQ} \text{ then } \frac{M \Delta Y}{Y \Delta M} = \frac{M \Delta P}{P \Delta M} + \frac{M \Delta Q}{Q \Delta P} + \frac{M \Delta P \Delta Q}{PQ \Delta M}.$$

With $\Delta P = (k'w'/A') - (kw/A)$, then (5) follows.

19. *Optimum Quantity of Money*, p. 227.

20. On scale economies in the demand for money, see W. J. Baumol, "The Transactions Demand for Cash: An Inventory Theoretic Approach," *Quarterly Journal of Economics*, LXVI (November 1952); James Tobin, "The Interest Elasticity of Transactions Demand for

Cash," *Review of Economics and Statistics*, XXXVIII (August 1956); Harry G. Johnson, *Essays in Monetary Economics* (London: Allen & Unwin, 1967), Chap. V; Karl Brunner and Allan H. Meltzer, "Economics of Scale in Cash Balance Reconsidered," *Quarterly Journal of Economics*, 81 (August 1967).

21. See Brunner and Meltzer, "Predicting Velocity: Implications for Theory and Policy," *Journal of Finance*, XVIII (May 1963, 1964).

Truistically, velocity estimates are implicit in (2). For from $MV = Y$ and $\Delta Y = \Delta(MV)$:

$$\frac{\Delta M}{M} - \frac{\Delta P}{P} = \frac{\Delta Q}{Q} + \frac{\Delta P \Delta Q}{PQ} - \frac{\Delta V}{V} - \frac{\Delta M \Delta V}{MV}. \tag{7}$$

22. Nicholas Kaldor, "New Monetarism," esp. pp. 6–10.

23. As one proposal, see my "An Incomes Policy to Stop Inflation," Appendix 2, and also Chapter 16.

8 Money As Cause and Effect

WITH PAUL DAVIDSON

A recurring theme in the long evolution of monetary theory is the dispute whether changes in (bank) money supplies play a causal part in influencing economic phenomena or whether their variations are an effect of economic activity, overcoming the obstacles of barter in an interdependent production economy. The view of money as causal represents a Currency School legacy, descending from Lord Overstone and the charter revision of the Bank of England in the 1840s. Money, viewed as an effect, constituted the core of the "real-bills" Banking Principle doctrine espoused at the time by William Tooke. Precursors abound as Marget's careful documentation reveals.[1]

A reconsideration of certain aspects of the causal attributes of money supply is particularly appropriate in a model in which money wages are determined outside a market *tâtonnement* system, either institutionally negotiable via collective bargaining or implemented by government decree as in Nixon's and Heath's Phase I and Phase II economic policies. Despite obvious facts about the determination of money wage rates, macro-models still maintain the fiction that money wage rates are merely "another" price, determined in the market-place as another endogenous variable, unaffected by the confrontation of big labour and big business.

The model presented below embodies the economically realistic position that money wages are determined independently of market *tâtonnements*. Undoubtedly, even for those who dispute its factual relevance—an empirical rather than an *a priori* issue—

139

the case is worth exploration because of certain novel implications for monetary theory and policy.

CAUSALITY AND STATISTICAL LEADS

Professor Friedman has often claimed that the "leads" and "lags" between money supply changes and other series disclose money as both cause and effect of the other series. In short, money supply variations are classed as causes or effects depending on whether the turning points in money supplies come before or after changes in prices, output flows and employment.

Of course, the assignment of causal status by pin-pointing time series dates is perilous.[2] Puzzles arise over the accuracy of data, over events in between if quarterly data are used, over erratic patterns where money leads one series and not another. Further, when "leads" and "lags" vary from a low of one month to a high of 26 months the whole art of dating becomes tenuous.[3] If the underlying economic structure was rigid, and extraneous elements did not intervene, "leads" or "lags" would always be of the same duration; scientific extraction for valid prediction would follow. But when calendar "leads" and "lags" are fitful, there is the awkward possibility that "extraneous" events rather than changes in the money supply are the causes affecting prices and other economic phenomena. Assigning a causal status to money as the key to stabilization could then cause mischief.

Above all, imputing causality by interpreting the fluctuations in the time series suffers crucially from the overlooking of various *anticipations* which can induce a deceptive statistical lead of a money supply series over the G.N.P. series.[4] For example, if businessmen expect an increase in sales some months hence, and begin a phased program of increased equipment installation and inventory expansion, they are likely to borrow in advance of the event. With orders in hand, their capital goods suppliers are also likely to borrow (or obtain a line of credit) to guarantee their working capital needs, *even before extra capital goods are produced*. If the Monetary Authority acquiesces by providing the finance required, then the statistical series will show the money supply increase as *preceding* the output increase. To the casual chart reader, the money growth may appear to cause the investment upturn and the wider multiplier ramifications. Such statistical interpretation overlooks the causal impetus residing in the preparatory business actions, unlike Keynes who construed the finance-motive as embracing an advance monetary demand for increased transactions balances.[5] A naïve interpretation of distributed lag regression analysis may suggest "unidirectional causality," from money to prices and output;[6] a further thought should, in this case, assign causal significance to the prior business decisions fostering subsequent output growth and culminating in larger money supplies to serve as Adam Smith's "wheel of commerce."

If, on the other hand, the Monetary Authority refuses to expand the money supply despite the higher demand for finance, then the rate of interest will rise if, as Keynes noted, "the liquidity-preferences of the public (as distinct from the entrepreneurial investors) and of the banks are unchanged."[7] If the entrepreneurial investors are successful in obtaining finance at a higher rate of interest by drawing off "speculative" money balances, then some increase in output will follow (although somewhat less, *ceteris paribus*, than if the money supply increased and the interest rate level were unchanged). If the ensuing decline in asset prices in security markets induces the Monetary Authority to intervene to maintain "orderliness" in these capital markets, the statistical series may show the money supply series lagging behind output growth, and the chart-reader might then correctly interpret the causality as going from *planned* output growth to money supplies. Hence, if favorable expectations induce an output expansion, the resulting leads or lags in money supply and G.N.P. data will depend on the reactions of the Monetary Authority and the banking system to entrepreneurs' increased demand for finance.[8] Unidirectional causality cannot be determined merely by viewing the leads and lags in time series data.

Of course, in executing its mandate the Monetary Authority can, by means of open market operations, initiate a change in the supply of money, even if entrepreneurial intentions are unchanged. In the ensuing portfolio reshuffle, the banking system absorbs from the public assets which have a negligible elasticity of production—namely securities—by offering bank money on attractive terms as an alternative store of wealth. The lower interest rates and easier money availability can enlarge the demand for resource-using reproducible goods, stimulating an output flow through the familiar Keynesian mechanism involving the schedule of marginal efficiency of capital and the multiplier. Granted some investment sensitivity to lower interest rates and easier availability of money, the exogenous increase in the money supply may justifiably be described as having *caused* the later increase in output.

Considering the diversity of circumstances, chart reading, like calculating a coefficient of correlation, provides an inconclusive guide to what caused what. Observed lags of an output series behind a money supply series may be due either to an anticipatory income-generating finance process, where planned output growth causes an increase in the money supply, or to a portfolio change process where a planned increase in the money supply by the Central Bank causes an increase in demand; consequently, leads and lags in statistical series are poor indicators of the direction of cause and effect.

MONETARIST EVALUATION

In his several attempts at refining monetary theory, involving a metamorphosis from Old to New Quantity Theory, Friedman has repeatedly insisted that changes in the money supply cause changes in money income, after a variable time lag.[9] In familiar symbols with $MV = PT$ in the Old Theory, the direction of causation was from M to P; in the New Quantity Theory with $MV = Y$ (where $Y =$ money income) it is from M to Y. Friedman has even calculated a money income elasticity, estimating that a 1 per cent money variation (on his M_2 definition) creates about a 1.8 per cent steady state ("permanent") money income increase. In assigning policy significance to these calculations, Friedman, and the Monetarists, are propounding what amounts to a causal Currency Principle despite their disclaimers that money supply variations also appear as *effects* of economic conditions.

Friedman has also attached a major reservation to his doctrines which severely limits the significance of his Monetarism:

but unfortunately, this critical qualification has failed to attract the attention that it deserves.

The New Quantity Theory is more tautologous than the Old. In the older, income-velocity version ($MV = PT$) more money could affect *either P, T,* or *V*. In the new theory ($MV = Y$), only Y or V can be affected. Inasmuch as Friedman regards V as a function solely of a set of variables, none of which can depend on the money supply, the direct impact of changes in money supply is after a time lag, not at all on V but entirely on Y. The separate impacts on P and Q where $Y = PQ$, are thus consolidated, never isolated.

This has some far-reaching implications: if Y alone is affected by changes in M in a time series showing positive association between changes of $M(t)$ and $Y(t)$, *the Modern Quantity Theory is devoid of a theory of inflation* despite some airy confident assertions about the dominance of money influences on the price level in the "long run" (of indeterminate calendar time). Money income alone is affected by short-run money supply variations; how much of the money increase runs in the form of price movements, and how much in output and employment, if left obscure.

It makes a vast difference for policy if the prime monetary effect in the short run—in which all of us are compelled to live—is on output (and employment) rather than upon prices. We welcome more output if this can be fostered through the portfolio reshuffles accompanying new money supplies: but as a rule we deplore any associated inflationary phenomena.

Analytically, the inconclusiveness in Monetarist doctrine can be described as follows:

$$\Delta M_t \rightarrow \Delta Y_{t+} = (Q\Delta P + P\Delta Q)_{t+} \quad \text{(approximately)} \quad (1)$$

$$\frac{\Delta M_t}{M} \rightarrow \frac{\Delta Y_{t+}}{Y} = \left(\frac{\Delta Q}{Q} + \frac{\Delta P}{P}\right)_{t+} \quad \text{(approximately)} \quad (2)$$

Monetary injections occur at date (t) and money income increases at a future later date $(t+)$. Clearly, price movements and output movements need not be simultaneous. But Friedman does not distinguish between the separable ΔP and ΔQ components.

Until ΔP and ΔQ are separately accounted for, the Monetarists are bereft of a theory of the effect on the price level of increases in the money supply. In conditions of unemployment, or in a

growth context where the effective labor force is growing unevenly, increased money supply may cause output expansion
rather than inflation. If the price level is determined outside the
monetary sector, by money–wage movements, an abnormal
money growth may be the prelude to a downturn of output, if
the price-level has risen even more. Significantly, there may be
no simple rule on how to expand the money supply so as to maintain steady output–employment growth.

Friedman has been explicit in acknowledging that the New
Quantity Theory has indeed stumbled over the separable price
and output variation.[10] But the significance of this admission for
policy[11] has become submerged in formal debates over side-
issues such as the predictive-efficiency relevance of Monetarist
and "Keynesian" models. The vital distinction between price
effects and output effects has been overlooked despite its central
importance. Examination of the inconclusiveness of matters embodied in equations (1) and (2) is overdue. We thus now suggest a more detailed theory of money, distinguishing the separable effects on price and on output.

GENERAL EQUILIBRIUM MODELS

The assumption in modern mathematical general equilibrium
models that the labor market clears, with the real wage equating
the demand and supply of labor begs an important question in
that the money wage is wholly neglected, as though Keynes
never wrote on the subject.[12]

In terms of Walrasian demand and supply equations the underlying argument is that output, resource allocation, and income division are generated by real processes, modified possibly
by Pigou real balance effects in recognizing the influence of
money supply. Implicitly this "real-economy" theorizing assumes
a barter economy, where agreements to exchange are reconciled,
with money having only a passive clearing influence on con-
summated market transactions already determined. Money's influence is inevitably confined to affecting the price level, whose
absolute height is a matter of indifference since all real phenomena are separately determined.

Friedman, for one, acknowledges the Walrasian foundation in

describing the real phenomena of relative output, prices, and incomes. A "natural" rate of unemployment is also generated by the Walrasian equations. The Old Quantity Theory of the price level in a Fisher or Cambridge cash-balance text is the result. Despite its elegance, the New Theory thus constitutes a tautologous arithmetical appendage to the static equilibrium model. To be sure, the New Theory has more meaning in a growing economy—or one moving from lesser to fuller employment—where output is envisaged as a variable, with one Walrasian equilibrium transformed into another. For output changes, therefore, the New Theory contains a dynamic mechanism for explaining money income growth.

The fictional Walrasian world, where money is superimposed only *after* all the real elements are resolved, presents an impediment to a serious theory of money. The assumptions underlying his equations set up Walrasian producers and consumers free of uncertainty and sure of their tastes, resource productivity, and market conduct. Overall, the models are static, with no yesterday nor tomorrow. Interconnected market events are tied in a timeless setting where market information is universally possessed and "all transactions are carried out at a single date."[13]

Inevitably, in a model cut off from the yesterdays and the uncertainty created by a history still to be made, money is entirely redundant. "Money can play no essential role" in bridging the interval between the time of income receipt and expenditure, or to accumulate "as a temporary abode of purchasing power," or to serve as a short- or longer-run asset.[14] Under full certainty, with all transactions carried out at a single date, it is clearly irrational to hold, as a store of value, money rather than interest-bearing assets timed to mature at the desired expenditure date.

Although some "Keynesians" have also embraced the general equilibrium model in the mistaken opinion that it is compatible with Keynes's arguments, the one crucial hypothesis that vitiates the Walrasian-type analysis is its stipulation that the labor market must clear, with labor-demand determined by marginal productivity and labor supply governed by real wage considerations.[15] *For this imposes full employment by assumption.* Money can then affect only the price level: money-wage levels, in the model, are a by-product.

Curiously, the old and new Walrasian theorists never specifically inquire how any *one* absolute price may emerge as the common numéraire to which other prices are adapted. The unique importance of the price of labor—the money wage—is not acknowledged. In treating the money wage as simply one price in general equilibrium theory, the question of whether the mode of money-wage determination makes any difference is not even raised.

But, suppose the money wage is determined not in the marketplace but around a bargaining table and that as a result of union contracts negotiated in the recent past, money-wage schedules are set up and actually prevail for a *future* contract period, say of three years. Surely, the search for an endogenous market theory of money-wage determination is then both futile and incongruous; it would be more accurate to argue, in this sequence, that as money wages are determined *outside* the theoretical market system to run the forthcoming three-year interval, it must follow that prices will, in the circumstances, adjust to money wages, rather than the converse. Even simultaneous determination of wages and prices would be precluded once *money* wages were already settled outside the demand–supply equations of a Walrasian system. Only real wages would remain to be resolved endogenously.

General equilibrium theorists in their attachment to implausible models of a real economy have, unfortunately, refrained from exploring this situation even as a hypothetical case. They have argued that relative prices, with money-wage rates being "merely" one price, are ground out mechanistically by solving the equations. Not surprisingly, therefore, money variations can, at the most, only modify the absolute price level in this full employment mutually interdependent demand–supply system.

Basically, for monetary theory, the crucial omission by the general equilibrium theorists has been the effects of changes over time, and the uncertainty attached to them. These are the phenomena that push money and contracts to the front, as human institutions devised to mitigate some of the distress of uncertainty in a world where production takes time. The wage contract is undoubtedly the most ubiquitous agreement of all. If it were constantly revised and recontracted, production would be inhibited in a decentralized market economy. The assumption of continuous labor market clearing may imply a contradiction for this model—as Keynes suspected in abandoning the prescription of lower money wages for alleviating unemployment.

Recently, Arrow and Hahn have confirmed the view that in general equilibrium models money cannot play an essential role. They have stated "in a world with a past as well as future in which contracts are made in terms of money, no equilibrium may exist," and "if a serious monetary theory comes to be written, the fact that contracts are written in terms of money will be of considerable importance."[16] This recognition represents an important step forward, but leaves us far short of even a *tentative* "serious monetary theory" to replace the past confidence in general equilibrium analysis.

Thus, if "money matters," its importance may depend on the level of money wages determined in labor contracts. For price level stability it is vain to believe that money wages can be freely flexible as simply one price among many. The money-wage level, as a price entering practically all cost functions and the greater part of consumer demand functions, cannot be left free to move without this affecting practically *all* prices, and thus employment through the demand for money. A change in this "one" price, in the simultaneous system, affects *all* prices in a way scarcely true of any other input or any other income; it cannot be attributed to merely the importance of a rise in the price of peanuts. (To sympathetic interpreters, this view of the pivotal position of the money-wage rate was, of course, the essential element in Keynes's attack on Say's Law and the Old Quantity Theory.)

When on the other hand the money-wage level is taken as mainly an exogenous variable, it may still have endogenous elements operating on it either through past wage, price, or employment events, or future anticipation about these variables. It is safe to posit that the precise level of the money-wage rate is *not* bargained in the competitive market-place in the same way as is the price of peanuts. As a result, the equation system of general equilibrium theory must be changed to allow the possibility of an equilibrium which fails to clear the labor market. Within the matrix of supply equations, money-wage costs of production are obviously determinate, especially in the simple set of equations involving fixed production coefficients. Given profit margins and/or monopoly mark-ups, with labor as the sole variable factor—the simple Keynesian case—the money-price level is now determined.

In this view, a money increase influences output levels if, and only if, it effects a "portfolio adjustment" which, in turn, induces an increase in aggregate demand. Towards the price level, money plays a more passive role though it may exert *some* causal effect on prices, through the increases in output levels because productivity may alter as output and employment expand. Over time, however, this effect is likely to be negligible, and may go in either direction depending on the balance between the static tendency to diminishing returns and the dynamic effects of technological advance.

A QUASI-MATHEMATICAL STATEMENT

A general equilibrium set of equations including the demand and supply of money would surely be lengthy. It would have to cover financial sectors, and intermediate products with monopoly, international flows, and growth factors. Introducing realistic elements such as the divisibility of outputs and input agents, advertising and cultural influences on demand, and varying degrees of monopoly, would add to its intricacy. Finally, to allow for the complete set of equations it would have to cover the full complex of current and *future* markets. All this elaboration would be prolix and inevitably incomplete and contentious. A detailed equational statement thus belongs to the future, and to a weighty tome.

Nevertheless, just for pedagogical purposes, we can indicate some of the changes needed in the simplest Walrasian model. With fixed coefficients, and assuming fully integrated output in each of the firms comprising an industry, we can write:

$$\left(\frac{w}{A} + U + \mu \right)_i = P_i \qquad (3)$$

where:

   w = average money wage
   A = average labor productivity
   U = unit user cost, involving depreciation through use
   μ = other unit costs, such as taxes, interest charges, rents, etc.,
          plus a unit profit margin

for the ith firm (or industry). In (3) unit costs appear on the left, and are equated to price. More concisely:

$$(kw/A)_i = P_i \qquad (4)$$

where k is a (potentially variable) mark-up over unit labor costs in the firm (or industry).

Equation (4) is true in each firm and each industry. Generalizing for the economy we can write:

$$P = kw/A \qquad (5)$$

In (5) the general wage cost mark-up formula appears as some weighted aggregate of individual industry (or firm under monopoly) product prices. The k-term now denotes the average economy-wide mark-up of prices over unit labor costs, or the reciprocal of the wage share. A variety of studies reveals k to be remarkably constant in Gross Business Product data in which the concept of the market price level has bearing, although there may be a secular trend, as shown by Godley and Nordhaus.[17]

Thus Walrasian supply equations can be written as in (3), culminating in (5). In the Walrasian system, too, consumer market demand equations, derived from individual demand functions, can be written as:

$$D_1 = D(P_1, P_2, \ldots P_n, Y) \qquad (6)$$

In (6), the Ps represent individual prices and Y denotes income, money income for our purposes. Aggregating in macroeconomic fashion for the closed system:

$$Y = PQ \qquad (7)$$

where Q = output volume.

Also, since $A = Q/N$, where $N =$ employment, as by (5) and (7) $Y = kwN$, (6) may be written as:

$$D_1 = D(P_1, P_2, \ldots P_n, kwN) \tag{8}$$

Examining (8) we see the macroeconomic interdependence of demand and cost equations: a change in k, w, or N is capable of (1) shifting unit costs, and thus the price level, and (2) affecting the demand equations. If N and k are given, then the (average) money wage emerges as the unique price level parameter without recourse to, or even mention, of money supplies! If employment is a variable (perhaps because money supply varies) the price level depends on variations in average productivity as the level of effective demand varies, as well as on money wages.

THE WAGE AS NUMÉRAIRE

A price dimension in absolute terms is given thus by the height of w, the average money wage. A change in the money wage will change both the cost and the consumer demand function, and thus the various prices and the price level. The money wage, especially if it is resolved not via a market *tâtonnement* but at the bargaining tables or by government decree, is inherently the *numéraire par excellence* in the modern economy. A change upwards in w exerts simultaneously a "cost push" and, in consumer markets where wage and salary compensation explain nearly 90 per cent of consumption purchases, a "demand-pull."

In a more extended analysis the question arises, of course, of whether a change in *any* price is not as vital as a change in money wages in a mutually interdependent system. The difference between the wage levels and other prices is, however, more one of kind than one of degree. Interest charges, and perhaps taxes, are the only other cost elements whose variations directly affect practically *all* costs. Quantitatively, however, the wage cost is far more significant than either of these charges. Even in the nonintegrated model, inputs of unfinished materials are rarely likely to have the universality or the quantitative importance of money wages, except in an open economy (such as the British) highly dependent on some imports of materials and foods.

On this view of the economic process, the price level becomes resolved once the money wage is given. k at the present time may be taken as an empirical constant—it has as a matter of stylized fact been constant for about 70 years. In a more detailed exposition it might be conceived as evolving from the play of market power, in that forces of competition or monopoly determine its magnitude and thereby determine income shares.

A THEORY IN A CLOCK-TIME SETTING

We return now to the original theme of depicting the causal incidence of changes in money supplies, isolating the separable price and output changes. This is the basic problem which Friedman has left as "unfinished business."[18]

There is a grain of truth in the wry jest that time was invented to prevent everything from happening at once. Consider as did Dennis Robertson a "slice of time" between t_0 and t_1, for example between July (t_0) and August (t_1). An intermediate date is labelled t_+.

We suppose a definite variation in the money supply (M_0) to occur at t_0 as a result of monetary policy. Starting with $M_0 = M$ on June 30, we enlarge M to $M_0 + \Delta M$ on July 1. Thereafter, we trace the price level (P), employment (N) and output (Q) over the $t_0 \rightarrow t_1$ interval. There is disequilibrium at t_0, but by t_1, in the absence of any new shock, a new equilibrium state may emerge.[19]

Dennis Robertson described money as constantly "on the wing," rather than "sitting." Monetary analysis should retain the flavor of his image, in contrast to the "sitting" image of the modern portfolio approach which is more apt in a nonflow, final equilibrium setting. Our model is designed also to illustrate how changes in money holdings impinge on the variables of the real sector, and the feedback of these variables on the desired demand for money. Monetary and real sectors are thereby interrelated.

The sequence runs in terms of *nominal* money balances. This is appropriate if we wish to analyse how variations in nominal money supplies affect the economy. Inasmuch as the price level is an explicit variable in our argument, the nominal-money demand function may be translated into real terms so that our procedures merge ultimately with that of Friedman.[20]

As a provisional simplification it is assumed that the money increment (ΔM) provided by the Central Bank at t_0 is transmitted directly to the public either via new loans, or by acquiring second-hand debt contracts from the public via the spot market for such securities. Thus we render irrelevant the vast literature on the money supply-reserve balance multiplier according to which the Central Bank initially affects reserve balances, and after a time lag, the money supply (either M_1 or M_2).[21]

A SIMPLIFIED AUTONOMOUS MONEY SUPPLY MODEL

The analysis can be formalized in a structural equation system (which from initial data traces out the new economic aggregates until they are disturbed by new shocks).

By hypothesis, given the price level, aggregate output, and interest rates for the period just closed, economic agents desire to hold money balances (M^*) at the t_0 date equal to:

$$M^*{}_{t_0} = f_1(P_{t_0}, Q_{t_0}, r_{t_0}, \bar{B}, P_e, r_e) \tag{9}$$

Thus the demand for money depends on current money income (P_{t_0}, Q_{t_0}) and current interest rates (r_{t_0}), bond holdings (B) and currently held expectations of price levels (P_e) and interest rates (r_e).[22] The bar over a symbol indicates that the variable is exogenous.

We now introduce an autonomous change in the supply of money by the Monetary Authority, acting on information of past events, some predictions on the near-future outlook and colored by its ideological policy rules. The key variables are those of equation (9). Thus

$$\Delta M^s = M^s{}_{t+} - M^s{}_{t_0} \tag{10}$$

where superscript s denotes the *planned* money-supply aggregate to be implemented by the Central Bank policy decision.

Since the Monetary Authority can alter the money supply by dealing in debt contracts on organized spot markets it can cause the effective rate of interest (i.e., the spot price of financial assets) to adjust instantaneously to the change in the money supply. Thus, at each instant of time between t_0 and t_1, as the money supply varies the rate of interest may take on different values unless the public's demand for money is simultaneously shifting. Ignoring possible money-demand *shifts* at each point of time, the quantity of desired money balances changes in response to movements in interest rates so that

$$M^*_{t_0} \to t_1 = f_2(P_{t_0}, Q_{t_0}, r'_{t_0} \to t_1) \tag{11}$$

where the $M^*_{t_0} \to t_1$ and $r'_{t_0} \to t_1$ notation denotes an incomplete equilibrium (i.e., disequilibrium) process.

Between t_0 and t_1, we assume exogenous new wage bargains implemented immediately, increasing money wages from w_{t_0} to w_{t_1}. The wage change can be described as an exogenous shock superimposed on the exogenous money-supply change.

Assuming the degree of monopoly unchanged ($k_{t_0} = k_{t_1}$), and assuming a given increase in average labor productivity from A_{t_0} to A_{t_1}, the entrepreneurs stipulate, via the wage cost mark-up considerations of equation (5), the price level (P_{t_1}) which they would be willing to accept for any level Q_{t_1} of output to be offered to the market. The immediate change in the offer-supply price level associated with output flow in the period t_1 is

$$P'_{t_1} - P_{t_0} = f_3(w_{t_1} - w_{t_0}, A_{t_1} - A_{t_0}, k_t) \tag{12}$$

In equation (12), P'_{t_1} denotes the new price level accompanying the new money wage (and new supply of money). If the contractual money-wage increment exceeds the productivity increment, then enterpreneurs, assessing higher production costs for any flow of output, will lift their offer prices.

In the modern mass production economy, production costs are normally incurred, and paid, prior to receiving sales revenue; the costs represent a working capital investment of entrepreneurs. If current production flow costs duplicate the preceding period, the proceeds from past sales could exactly finance the current working capital costs.[23] If, however, wage increases raise production costs, *then even unchanged production schedules* will require more working capital in money terms. Accordingly, entrepreneurs will increase their short-term borrowings from the banks, to coincide with the Monetary Authority's hypothetical increase of the money supply. The increase in money which is necessary because of higher wages is thereby quickly drawn into the income stream.

Assume, initially, that entrepreneurs maintain the production flow. The increase in money necessary to cover the higher working capital requirements may be more than, equal to, or less than, the autonomous increase in money provided by the Monetary Authority. If the finance demand for increased working capital needs exceeds ΔM^s, interest rates will rise ($r'_{t_0} \rightarrow t_1 > r_{t_0}$), and the inflationary wage increase, despite the monetary expansion, will *cause* tight money even if the output flow remains unchanged. At the higher interest rates, however, production will be constrained so that the money-supply increment will fail to sustain the Q_{t_0} output (and employment) at the new price level.

If, on the other hand, the money-supply increase exceeds the additional working capital requirements imposed by the higher production costs, the rate of interest will decline through a "portfolio shuffle" as the Central Bank exchanges money with the public for bonds through open market operations. The resulting fall in interest rates may stimulate higher investment outlays, so that some portion of the exogenous increase in the money supply can admittedly *cause* an enlargement of aggregate demand.

Finally, if the exogenous increase in the money supply just equals the additional working capital requirements for the t_0 production flow, then interest rates will be unchanged and, *ceteris paribus*, $Q_{t_1} = Q_{t_0}$. (Of course, these cases abstract from autonomous changes in entrepreneurial and consumer expectations, and any resultant change in transactions demand and/or liquidity preference.)

Labor productivity in t_1 will usually differ from productivity in t_0. In the static competitive case, more output is associated with diminishing returns. In real life, changes in technology and/or increases in the capital stock will improve labor productivity, so that $A_{t_1} > A_{t_0}$. This can cushion the impact of money-wage increases on costs and price levels.

The desired equilibrium demand for money at the terminal date will emerge as

$$M^*_{t_1} = f_4(P_{t_1}, Q_{t_1}, r_{t_1}, \overline{B}, P_e, r_e) \tag{13}$$

If output is unchanged, $r_{t_1} = r_{t_0}$. If the change in the money supply exceeds the change in money wages relative to productivity, then $r_{t_1} < r_{t_0}$. Hence, changes in the money-wage *numéraire* relative to productivity require equal changes in the money supply, if money is to remain "neutral" with respect to output. Prices, however, will be higher by the excess of average money-wage change over the productivity change.

In the event of a lesser increase in money supplies, *ceteris paribus*, the monetary policy will *be restrictive* with respect to output, even though prices will still increase: a higher increase in money supply will be *expansionary* with respect to output.

Beyond the finance demand for money for transactions purposes, if the nontransactions demand for money (however it may be compartmentalized into speculative, convenience, or precautionary demands) is affected by the pace of changes in M, P, or Q, then there will be further effects on interest rates. Normally, changes in the M, P, Q variables are indeed almost certain to alter expectations and the desired money-demand function.

AN EVALUATION OF MONEY AS CAUSE AND EFFECT

The dynamics of the model originate in the movements of money-supply and money-wage rates which, over time, induce price, output, and interest-rate responses. Once the change in money wages occurs, part of the money-supply increment is deflected to support the higher price level. If the nontransactions demand for money also alters, there are then new effects on interest rates.

Output variations will depend on that part of monetary expansion which is not siphoned off to sustain rising prices. That is, only that part thus left over from support of $Q\Delta P$ (and any nontransactions demands) is available to depress interest rates (stimulate spot security prices) and to transmit a stimulus to economic activity. A condition for a monetary stimulus to output is, therefore, that the increase in money supply must be more than enough to sustain the price rise, plus any increased speculative and precautionary demand for money.

The system is recursive. Once money wages rise (unless offset by increases in productivity), there is a direct *causal* influence on the price level: the money-wage rise nudges price upwards. Only by providing just enough new money merely to hold output constant, with prices thus increased, can the Monetary Authority claim not to exert any influence on the economy. More money, in the "sustaining" case, is properly interpreted as being an *effect* of the higher price level, required to stabilize the real Q, N, and r variables.

In the *stimulating or constrictive cases where* $Q_{t_1} \gtrless Q_{t_0}$, money *primarily influences output,* in the normal case. To the extent that output variations affect productivity, if the policy is output-stimulating with increased productivity rising with increased production, the money expansion can be interpreted as stimulating output and as restraining prices. If, on the other hand, falling productivity accompanies expansion, monetary expansion will stimulate output *and* raise prices. If productivity is unaffected, prices are unaffected. Corresponding relations can be traced for the case of a constrictive policy.

Changes in the money supply always affect output except in the production sustaining case. They may have some effect on price levels if labor productivity varies either way with output. So long as the money wages are determined around a bargaining table, monetary policy can have only limited control over the price level.[24]

In the literature about the Phillips curve, higher output and higher employment tighten labor markets and result in higher wage settlements, so that indirectly, money supply can after all affect the price level. But note, what is decisive is not the level of output, nor the amount of money, nor the movement in interest rates, nor (as a rule) the movement in labor productivity either way but the magnitude of the money-wage rise. The money wage thus remains the crucial and causal price level variable, so long as productivity and the degree of monopoly do not change substantially from year to year. In the long run, the productivity variations tend to lower prices or at least to restrain the price-raising effects of wage rises.

THE COMPLEXITY OF MONETARY THEORY

Our step-by-step account of the effects of disequilibrium suggests some of the complexities of monetary policy, which the Monetary Authority must have in mind in juggling with the many economic variables.[25]

A rise in money wages will almost always induce an increase in money supply unless, for some reason, the Central Bank hopes that a constrictive policy will restrain money-wage rises. In recent years, such hopes have proven illusory.

Ordinarily, if wage increments exceed productivity, and if there is excessive unemployment, more money will have to be provided merely to maintain recent production levels. Public pressure to ameliorate unemployment is likely to prevent a seriously constrictive policy; with the labor force growing, an expansion in money supply will, sooner or later, become unavoidable. To satisfy the public concern to curb unemployment, the immediate growth in money supply will have to exceed that allowed by any "normal" rule.

In sum, where social and political attitudes determine the money wage exogenously, low levels of unemployment are also likely to be a policy aim. So long as the price level, for the most part, is set by wage bargains which are beyond the control of the Central Bank, the Monetary Authority, at best, can ensure ample supplies of money to remove the financial impediments to full employment and growth. It is ill-equipped, however, to exert any effective control over price levels.

For the real phenomena of growth and full employment, monetary policy does remain decisive. With respect to inflation, in an exogenous wage economy, it is badly deficient. It could regain its former dominance but only if it were allowed to make inroads on money wages at a cost in unemployment and human misery which would at present be considered unacceptable to modern *democratic* societies. In such societies some form of incomes policy might be the only effective means for accomplishing price level stability.

NOTES

1. A. Marget, *The Theory of Prices* (New York: Prentice-Hall, 1938).

2. The identification of correlation with causation violates careful econometric usage and evades the profound cognitive issues. Apparently this confusion is being perpetuated by disciples of the Monetarist school, e.g., C. H. Sims, "Money Income and Causality," *American Economic Review* 62 (September 1972), pp. 540–542.

3. M. Friedman, "Have Fiscal-Monetary Policies Failed?" *American Economic Review,* Papers and Proceedings, 62 (May 1972), p. 15.

4. Cf. J. Tobin, "Money and Income: Post Hoc Ergo Propter Hoc?" *Quarterly Journal of Economics* 84 (May 1970), pp. 301–317, and Friedman's reply, "Comment on Tobin," *Quarterly Journal of Economics* 84 (May 1970), pp. 318-327.

5. J. M. Keynes, "The Ex Ante Theory of the Rate of Interest," *Economic Journal* (December 1937), pp. 663–669. For a full discussion of the integration of the finance motive into the IS-LM apparatus, see P. Davidson, "Keynes's Finance Motive," *Oxford Economic Papers* 17 (March 1965), pp. 47–65, and *Money and the Real World* (London: Macmillan, 1972), chapt. 7.

6. Cf. Sims, "Money Income and Causality."

7. Keynes, "The Ex Ante Theory of the Rate of Interest," p. 667.

8. The role of financial intermediaries who "make" security markets is also important. For a detailed analysis of the impact of the "finance" demand on security markets and institutions, see Davidson, *Money and the Real World.*

9. For example, in his newest "superior" theoretical model Friedman notes that the money supply can be regarded as completely exogenous, "A Monetary Theory of Nominal Income," *Journal of Political Economy* 79 (March/April 1971), p. 329.

10. E.g., "A Monetary Theory of Nominal Income," pp. 330, 337.

11. Cf. Chapter 7 below.

12. Cf. Chapter 5 above.

13. F. H. Hahn, "Equilibrium with Transactions Costs," *Econometrica* 39 (May 1971), p. 417.

14. *Ibid.*

15. See Chapter 5 above.

16. K. J. Arrow and F. H. Hahn, *General Competitive Analysis* (San Francisco: Holden-Day, 1971), pp. 357, 361.

17. W. A. Godley and W. D. Nordhaus, "Pricing in the Trade Cycle," *Economic Journal* (September 1972), pp. 853–882.

18. Friedman, "A Monetary Theory of Nominal Income," p. 330.

19. Our procedure thus differs from much modern work. Friedman, for example, emphasizes the *desired* money demand; effectually, his theoretical system is always in equilibrium, responding almost instanteously to money-supply variations. This is the only intelligible interpretation of his statement that money is "a temporary abode of purchasing power." As an abode it is being held "at home," temporarily, to be sure. But as it is in its abode it is not being shuffled about in transactions. If all individuals (or the full economy) are holding the "desired" real balance, then nothing is really happening in the economy: there are neither flows of money moving to any individual, or flowing out from him. Indubitably, the concentration on "desired" money holdings stresses established equilibrium portfolios where individuals are content to hold the prevailing "right" nominal money balances.

20. Cf. W. Smith, who has pointed out that it is not imperative to write the desired money demand function in terms of real balances, "On Some Current Issues in Monetary Economics: An Interpretation," *Journal of Economic Literature* 18 (September 1970), p. 774.

21. As most of this literature frequently employs a linear lag relationship of $\Delta M = m\Delta R$, where ΔR refers to the increment of reserve balances, some expository verbosity is eliminated. In our model, we assume that the Central Bank deals directly with buyers and sellers of debt in financial markets.

22. For expositional simplicity at this stage, we are assuming that planned expenditures during the interval are a function of current money income. The interest rate, r, may be interpreted as some average level of rates; equity prices would have to be stipulated in a more thorough account of the process.

23. Some of last period's sales receipts will be used to pay off last period's short-term bank loans, which were used to finance some of last period's investment in working capital. These same sums are, therefore, available to finance a similar investment in working capital this period.

24. A reservation extends to our hypothesis of a constant k or wage share in Gross Business Product. Empirically, for stable economies such as the U.S., U.K., Canada, etc., this assumption appears warranted. If, however, excess money emissions accompanied a flight from currency—hyperinflation—and important changes in relative shares, then this part of the argument would have to be modified.

25. In our analysis we have ignored the possibility that wage incre-

ments may affect price and interest rate expectations. To the extent that the new wage increments increase inflationary expectations there will be some disgorging of money balances on (1) real goods which were planned to be purchased in the near future and where the additional carrying costs are less than the expected increase in supply price till the date of planned purchase and (2) financial assets, if any, whose future spot price net of carrying costs is expected to keep pace with inflation. To the extent, however, that inflationary expectations raise expections of higher interest rates in the future, the speculative demand for cash balances will increase, thereby at least partially offsetting the disgorging of cash holdings due to expected increases in the supply prices of reproducible goods.

9 A Theory of Monetary Policy Under Wage Inflation*

Those who hold that inflation is a result of too much money relative to the output of goods have an eminently attractive remedy, for it is one that is simple in the extreme. Merely exercise tighter control of the money supply. In the present situation, despite historic high interest rates in the United States, United Kingdom, Canada, Australia, and elsewhere, unmatched in the modern industrial era, and in the face of the reports of a credit squeeze that menaces even strong companies, the proponents of a monetary approach to inflation control are literally begging the central banks to tighten the money noose.

Whatever its success against inflation, we can be sure that it would quickly destruct the employment house. Yet it is doubtful that it would deflect the price surge. This is a lesson that we seem eager to evade in the "stagflation" episodes in the U.S. and U.K., and elsewhere, in recent years. In the U.K. there is talk of "slump-flation," meaning actual declining output, greater unemployment, and rising rates of inflation. It is an article of blind faith to believe that prices would fall if money wages in mining, in the construction industries, and elsewhere, rose by the 55 per cent figures reported as being requested in the British economy.

Once unemployment grew through tight money, we should soon be prescribing easier money for restoring fuller employment in a frivolous stop-go cycle. If the origins of inflation lie not in money largesse but in excessive wage-salary advances, it is an act of economic masochism to suggest tight money remedies.

This is the argument that I have attempted to convey for over

* Lecture prepared, under ANZ Bank auspices, for University of Queensland, Brisbane.

fifteen years; it appears to have gained in credibility now that
money wage (and salary) demands have become so obviously
out-sized, beyond the power of any economy to match with any
semblance of price level stability.[1]

Note, monetary policy is not described as being impotent.
Quite the contrary. It is highly potent. But its main impact is on
output and employment, rather than upon the price level. Its
price level impact is at best indirect and generally inconclusive.
Through creating unemployment it may—a prospect and not an
imperative—slow up the wage ascent. But simultaneously, the
tight money retards investment and so deters the improvements
in productivity that accompany better technology. Which force
is stronger in this tug-of-war will depend on the particular historical circumstances.

Thus if we must endure inflation through our unwillingness to
correct the institutional dereliction in abandoning money incomes
to the whim of unrestricted collective bargaining, or a supine unwillingness to repair the gap in our stabilization armory, then
the better part of wisdom commends the use of the instruments
that we do have to at least maintain full employment. Here
monetary policy retains its supremacy.

Succinctly, if current techniques cannot control inflation, we
should at least perpetuate full employment. It is too costly to
superimpose the ills of unemployment on the ailment of inflation.
So long as our economy is unstable in the price level dimension
we should at least hold it firm on the job front. Institutionally
inspired unemployment should not be heaped on top of the institutional omission of a conscious Incomes Policy. Impaled on
the one instability, we should not inject the double-jeopardy of
an extra destabilizer.

This will be my point of departure here. There is a long history and a monumental literature on monetary policy. If it could
have whipped inflation, it would have done so a long time ago,
to the applause of a grateful mankind in long-suffering inflation-
ridden economies.

THE MONETARIST POLICY PRESCRIPTION

It is not amiss to remind some unreconstructed monetarists that not so long ago it was alleged that only "empirical" issues remained in the realm of monetary theory, that the theoretical differences were only minimal.[2] Shortly thereafter, the proponent of this view, and the widely acclaimed leader of the monetarist sect, participated in a symposium in which some 140 journal pages (maybe a third more book pages) were devoted to conceptual clarification, debate, and extension![3] Apparently, there is more to be said on the subject of money and its place in the workings of the economy. All of it is reminiscent of John Stuart Mill writing in 1848, just before the dawn of the marginal revolution, that: "Happily, there is nothing in the laws of value which remains for the present or any future writer to clear up: the theory of the subject is complete."[4]

Mill's venture in extolling the finished state of the subject should have made the modern monetarists more cautious. Apparently, economists are apt to be carried away by a glow of current success.

Elsewhere, in contradiction to the opinion that all conceptual issues were resolved, an alternate theory of money was presented by the present author in collaboration with Professor Paul Davidson.[5] Augmentations in the money supply were conceived as primarily causal with respect to output and employment, and viewed as a necessary system response, or "effect," of price level changes; that is, once the price level moves, some of the new money created by the monetary authority is drained off to support the price level and to operate to sustain output in the face of inflation.

There is a vast difference in the monetary policy recipes emanating from these opposed money views. Before developing my own suggestions of monetary policy under wage inflation, it is well that their arguments be developed, if only for contrast.

The Monetarist Theory

The Monetarist Theory, despite some modern frills, subtleties, and econometric embellishments, has long been taught in the textbooks. In the Old Quantity Theory, whether in the Fisher Equation of $MV = PQ$, where the terms are familiar (though I take Q = real gross product and P, its price level), or in a Cambridge Cash-balance Equation, the argument was fairly direct, of P tied to M. For the older economists, controlling the money supply would flatten the price trend, reservations for some variation in Q and V notwithstanding.

The Modern Quantity Theorists are apt to insist that the theory is really about $MV = Y$, with $Y = PQ$ (whether net or gross income should make no difference for our purposes here).

It should be apparent that the "New" Quantity Theory is more tautologous than the Old; it is just linked to Y, and not to P and Q as *separate* entities. Actually, there is no theory of the price level at all in the New Theory, if we are to take it seriously. Friedman has admitted as much at several places, saying that as M affects Y, money income, changes in the money supply will affect either or both, *and in indeterminate magnitude,* either prices or quantities. That is:

$$(\Delta M/M) \rightarrow (\Delta Y/Y) = (\Delta P/P) + (\Delta Q/Q) \qquad (1)$$

Friedman has declared that "none of our leading theories has much to say about it."[6]

This is simply in error. Keynes wrestled with this problem, and had something useful to say on it. I have been concerned with this very issue, and like to believe that the ideas are correct.[7]

Despite this gaping hole in the middle of the theory, which is nothing short of a lack of a theory of the price level, Friedman will recommend—and frequently has recommended—monetary policy to stabilize the price level. But the theory is nebulous, on even a generous concession.

It makes a vast difference to policy-makers whether augmentations (or diminutions) in the money supply have their impact on prices or on quantities. We want the extra output and the greater employment induced by increases in the money supply. We want generally to be freed of any price level surge. Yet the New Monetarist Theory is unable to illuminate these major aspects of changes in money supplies. The injunction that "more empirical work needs to be done" is an admission of ignorance—yet not sufficient to deter peremptory recommendations for tighter money even in the under-employment circumstances of the U.S. and the U.K., and for under-developed countries enduring substantial rates of unemployment.

The Rule

On the basis of this inconclusive price-output theory Friedman has frequently suggested that he seeks to supplant the central bankers by a low-level clerk—of utter integrity to be sure—obeying strict instructions to augment the money supply by an undeviating 3 (or 4 or 5) per cent per annum. Discretion would be superseded: an inexorable rule would be mandated. The prescience of central bankers is held in such low esteem that automatism is deemed more conducive toward economic stability than the exercise of human judgment and rational discretion.

Fealty to the "Rule," we are assured, would usher in a stable economy, immune to inflation and verging on full employment. The economy would only be afflicted by a (vague) "natural" amount of unemployment.

These are the awesome themes that will be challenged; it will be contended the promises—and premises—of the Rule are illusory, usually likely to foster unemployment while failing to guide the economy on to a flat price track. Implementation of the Rule is likely to yield grave instabilities rather than inaugurating an era of stability.

Paradoxically, despite its protests to the contrary, the "fixed rule" version of monetarism is rooted in the belief that "money does *not* matter"—except when the money supply (M) alters at an erratic pace. A steady M-trend (write M_1, M_2, or M_3) provides a monetarist anchor for economic stability. Deft intercession by the monetary authority, traditionally hailed as a rational counterweight to the winds of economic instability, is now excoriated as an unwitting hand-maiden of our aberrant economic record.

While merely a steady M-path is often elevated to the status of a unique maxim for economic virtue, the serious message contains two injunctions: (1) steadiness, and (2) at (say) 4 per cent. Despite some inadvertent statements of "the steadiness principle," nobody would really contend that steadfast 100 per cent per week money emissions would impart stability.

The monetarist prescription is thus a two-part rule: steadiness and 4 per cent. The 4 per cent feature devolves from some retrospective averaging of the historical growth path, statistically processed at constant prices. The Rule is thereupon identified as compatible with "normal"(?) "natural"(?) non-inflationary growth. "Normal" or "natural" are undoubtedly elliptical words, as if economic events are independent of human volition—reminiscent of the Physiocratic "natural order."

The stress on 4 per cent rests on Friedman's thesis that inflation is predominantly a monetary phenomenon.[8] We consider the origins of the 4 per cent figure.

ORIGIN OF THE STEADY 4 PER CENT RULE

To understand the validity of the Steady 4 Per Cent Rule it is well to consider the logical base of the projection and what, in my view, is its illicit premise.

Consider the following truism:

$$(\Delta M/M) + (\Delta V/V) = (\Delta P/P) + (\Delta Q/Q), \qquad (2)$$

neglecting $(\Delta M \Delta V/MV$ and $\Delta P \Delta Q/PQ)$, with the letters referring to money supply, money velocity, price level, and output.

Examining the long trend of U.S. statistical data, *and after correcting Q for the price level swings over time*, thereby deriving a series in "constant" prices, Friedman finds:

$$(\Delta Q/Q) = (\Delta A/A) + (\Delta N/N) \pm (\Delta U/U) = 3\%\text{--}5\%, \quad (3)$$

where A = labor productivity, N = employment, U = unemployment.

Thus real growth is estimated in the 3–5 per cent range, interpreted hereafter as 4 per cent.

On this basis, by assuming (from his statistical calculations) that $\Delta V/V = 0.8$, and by eliminating price level phenomena from his estimates, Friedman has decided that if the money supply grows at the steady 4 per cent rate it will be sufficient only to sustain the output advance, that no funds will be available to underwrite price movements, so that the price level will not rise.[9]

The possibility of a price level rise for other than monetary causes is mystically, mythically, and magically, *assumed* away. By not even recognizing the possibility of a price level rise it is confidently asserted that it will not occur.

It is on this faith that the Steady 4 Per Cent Rule is promulgated, and the central bank marked for extinction. On my view of the inflation process, the underlying Friedman price level theory is simply erroneous and the policy recommendation mischievous.

A Premature Dismemberment of the Reserve Bank

On my wage-productivity theory of inflation, it would be premature to dismantle the central bank. Central banking, or the proper exercise of judgment by the Monetary Authority (hereafter, the MA), can enhance economic well-being. While the MA may err, a commitment to a fixed rule can provoke a debacle paralleling the Great Depression when central banks honored the gold standard ritual long after it ceased to be relevant, abandoning it only under duress and after widespread misery.

Setting money wages and labor productivity on center-stage in the inflation drama absolves the MA of culpability for fueling the upward price trend. Obviously, this excludes hyperinflation, and wholesale structural disintegration.[10] In mind, instead, is the cumulative nibbling erosion of the value of money in the Western world where the money wage-productivity imbalance has forged a forty-year Great Inflation ordeal. It is a remarkable distortion of events to allege that the MA has supinely created bank money in an economy of full employment; surely the hyperinflation fears of printing money to meet government deficits have been unfounded.[11]

Parenthetically, it is worth noting that those espousing the proposition that "all inflations are caused by an excess emission of money" have failed abjectly to detail a theory of money wages; despite the omnipresent union-management conflicts, the features of a wage (and salary) trend consonant with price level stability have rarely been explored.

Non-Wage Inflations: A Profit Inflation

Our stress, without detailed elaboration and defence, will be on money wage excesses as the primary ingredient in the cumulative price climb in the (largely) market oriented affluent economies since at least World War II.

An inflation could also occur as business firms lifted prices above unit labor costs to enhance their profit margins. Profit-inflation, however, could be easily countered through invoking the corporate income tax lever to absorb excessive profits.

While a profit-inflation is always a possibility, the theme cannot pass muster for the period of price level distress since 1968.[12]

THE WAGE-COST MARK-UP FORMULAE

A few formulae, which I have been using for many years, offer a compact statement of the elements that provide an alternative view of inflation in this age of excessive wage demands.

The Wage Mark-Up Equation

In lieu of the Quantity Theory Equation $MV = PQ$, consider the Wage Mark-Equation (WCM):[13]

Truism: $PQ = kwN$ with the WCM Equation: $P = kw/A$ (4)

where: P = price level Q = real output
w = average business sector wage and salary
N = business sector employment
$A = Q/N$, average labor productivity
k = average price mark-up, or gross profit margin, or reciprocal of labor income share.

Unless there are revolutionary changes in income distribution in a society undergoing violent changes, k is remarkably stable either year to year or over time, entitling us to largely neglect it so that we can write $k = k$. Of all the ratios in economics—and V is also a ratio, of $PQ/M-k$ is the most stable.[14] In U.S. gross business product data $k \approx 1.9$, for many years now.

Causally, the emphasis is put on the right-hand side: changes in average wages to labor productivity are assigned primal status in price level swings.

The Consumer Price Level

Quite mistakenly, the WCM argument is characterized as a "cost-push" or "wage-push" theory of the price level. This is a misunderstanding, for wages-salaries are not only the major cost elements in the business economy (or in government outlays), they are also the primary ingredients in generating consumption demand, with wage-salary earners responsible for about 90 per cent of all consumption purchases in affluent economies.

Starting wholly from demand considerations, we can write:[15]

$$P_c Q_c = c_w wN + c_r \lambda R + \theta, \tag{5}$$

where $R =$ "gross" profits or non-wage income
   $\theta =$ unemployment and pension, etc. transfers
   $c_w, c_r =$ average consumption propensities
   $\lambda =$ payout ratio.

Dividing through by the wage bill, wN, and by $N_c =$ consumer sector employment:

$$P_c = (w/A_c)(c_w + c_r \lambda R' + \theta')(N/N_c), \tag{6}$$

where $R' = (R/wN)$ and $\theta' = \theta/wN$.

For an open economy a term for consumer-goods exports, minus imports, divided by the wage bill, could be inserted.

Major implications reside in (6). Starting wholly from *demand* elements, the money wage-productivity nexus becomes paramount in determining the consumer price level. All the terms to the right of w/A_c sum up to k_c, which can, like k, be presumed quite constant barring important changes in price margins—or income shares—in the consumer sector. While the parenthesis to the right of w/A_c might create some wiggles in the consumer price level, they are not the stuff out of which, say, price level changes of more than 2–3 per cent, in either a short or long period context, are manufactured. To keep the consumer price level in hand the wage-salary-productivity tie must be observed.

As (5)–(6) rest wholly on demand relations, the formulae should also expose the canard that "cost-push" can be isolated from "demand-pull." Both have a common origin. Both are a manifestation of the interdependence of cost and demand phenomena in the macroeconomic economy.

THE ΔP AND ΔQ MATRIX

On the basis of the *WCM* theory, money supplies are bereft of any direct causal influence on the price level.

The content of this statement should be noted. In a pure exchange economy, *without production,* more money descending from a Friedman helicopter can obviously raise prices. Or in David Hume's parable, where Englishmen awaken to the pleasant discovery of an extra £5 note, more money could raise prices: for Hume was essentially envisaging an economy of *fixed output,* with more money coming in from outer space, in the form of ships laden with gold and silver. My remarks should not be interpreted as denying this sequence.

But our modern industrial economy should not be confused with these conceptions. It is a labor hire-production system that we visualize. Price phenomena—nearly all?—evolve from the fact that labor is hired on the basis of entrepreneurial profit expectations (or government activity), with a money wage or salary paid for the performance of work chores. With the money income derived from work, wage earners—or their households—are able to descend upon the stores in order to make purchases. The income payments establish cost phenomena and provide the wherewithal for purchase behavior.[16]

Monetary Policy and the Price Level

On this conception the monetary authority has, at best, only an *indirect* influence on the price level.

By tight money, the MA can depress output and employment, creating unemployment. The potency of monetary policy thus falls directly, almost entirely upon output and employment, or unemployment.

By creating enough unemployment, the MA may be able to induce some tapering in the money wage-salary rise, imparting an *indirect* hamper on the price level. But the toll in human suffering can be onerous. Even then, under union wage adamancy, it may hardly deflect the price tide.

Contrariwise, by tight money occasioning a deferral of investment, productivity improvements can be retarded by the mechanization slow-down. In the tug-of-war between productivity and wage-salary changes, it becomes hazy to decide whether even the indirect reverberations of monetary policy exert a stabilizing price level influence.

The Price-Output Matrix

Thus the MA may have practically no significant influence on the price level, with its actions clawing only at the Q and N magnitudes. We consider the variety of price-output combinations that can emerge, depending on how monetary policy performs in different $[A(t) \Delta w(t+1)/w(t) \Delta A(t+1)]$ price level circumstances, where t denotes a progression in time.

The nine combinations reported in the ΔP and ΔQ interplay in table 1 depict the potential P and Q path from date t_0; the cross-concatenations reveal the multiple prospects contingent upon MA actions. With the ΔP moves independent of ΔM, ΔQ shoulders the brunt of monetary actions.

Going down the first column, in which $\Delta Q > 0$, the MA actions can be described as expansory or stimulating, for in each case the ΔM augmentation is ample to sustain a ΔQ advance regardless of the ΔP state. The only unsettled issue is whether the ΔQ advance is sufficient to achieve full employment.

TABLE 1.

The ΔP and ΔQ Matrix Pursuant to ΔM Action

ΔP \ ΔQ	+	0	−
+	Growthflation	Stagflation	Slumpflation
0	Growth at constant prices	Stationary state	Recession
−	Deflationary growth	Stationary state deflation	Depression

Column 2, with $\Delta Q = 0$, conveys the stagnant economy; a $\Delta P > 0$ relation denotes the stagflation of recent years. A stationary state is also listed. Monetary policy, in the context of $\Delta Q = 0$, can be termed *neutral*, or *sustaining*, signifying a freezing of Q by the MA.

MA policy is most damaging when the drift in time is to $\Delta Q < 0$: the MA actions can be characterized as *constrictive*, as fostering recession or even depression. "Slumpflation" appears to be the worst of worlds.

The $\Delta P = 0$ and $\Delta Q > 0$ outcome is most nearly optimal, especially if $U \approx 0$. Along this developmental path real-growth occurs at constant prices, as in the macroeconomic textbook idealizations. Full optimality would append $U = 0$ to $\Delta P = 0$ and $\Delta Q > 0$. Our imperfect accomplishment on each front affords a measure of the irrationality of economic policy.

The Theory of Monetary Policy

Monetary policy, therefore, can be linked to the ΔQ outcome in any given time period. Functionally, so far as ΔQ goes, we can write:

$$\Delta Q = Q(\Delta M - \Delta P) \qquad (7)$$
$$= Q(\Delta M, \Delta w, \Delta A)$$

That is, the $\Delta Q(t)$ variation, where t denotes a time variation, is functionally dependent on the size of the MA exogenous $\Delta M(t)$ augmentation, and the coterminous exogenous $\Delta w(t)/\Delta A(t)$ increment culminating in $\Delta P(t)/P(t-1)$. As some portion of the $\Delta M(t)$ augmentation is drained off by the $\Delta P(t)$ movement, only the "excess" of the full $\Delta M(t)$ will determine whether $\Delta Q(t) \gtreqless 0$.

Substantively higher prices require more money to fund merely the prevailing Q-volume. If the "extra" money is not forthcoming, some deterioration in Q will ensue. If the ΔM increment is ample, a stimulative Q impact will be set in motion: it is the "leftover" money of $[(\Delta M/M) - (\Delta P/P)]$, allowing for ΔV, which has an output incidence. If the "left-over" money is nil or negative, ordinarily $\Delta U(t) \geqq 0$.

The Classification of Monetary Policy

Monetary policy, on the basis of the columns of table 1, can be identified as:

Stimulating or Expansive: $(\Delta M/M) + (\Delta V/V) > (\Delta P/P)$ (8a)

Neutral or Sustaining: $(\Delta M/M) + (\Delta V/V) = (\Delta P/P)$ (8b)

Recessionary or
Constrictive: $\qquad (\Delta M/M) + (\Delta V/V) < (\Delta P/P)$ (8c)

Applying a mechanistic Quantity Theory of Money, with $\Delta V = 0$, an expansory money policy would entail money supplies outrunning the P-pace: with a 5 per cent inflation, $\Delta M/M$ would have to exceed 5 per cent, etc. In a sustaining policy, the M-growth would just match the P-move; at a lesser rate the MA actions would be restrictive.

All MA monetary policies which are timid in promoting full employment, ordinarily rationalized by fears of inflation, are inherently restrictive even though $\Delta Q(t) > 0$. To isolate the possibility of $\Delta Q(t) > 0$ concomitantly with $\Delta U(t) > 0$, a double-qualifier might be invoked, as "restrictively stimulating," "restrictively neutral," etc.

Variations in Velocity

On Friedman's estimates of $(\Delta V/V) = 0.8$, a sustaining MA policy would require a money supply increase in excess of one-half the price jump on the Friedman calculation. Failing this, the policy would be constrictive (or neutral).

So long as $(\Delta V/V)$ is not constant, the art of monetary policy entails intelligent surmises of the future velocity magnitudes. At bottom, these will rest on estimates of changes in the future time structure of payments, changes in the shape of the liquidity function, and the sensitivity of investment to interest rates. Volatility in any of these aspects will make predictions hazardous, though in a stable economy, where Δw, ΔA, and ΔN are fairly small, velocity forecasts may be reasonably accurate.

THE RATIONALE OF NONSTEADY M-AUGMENTATIONS

Presumably, if on the full employment growth path the annual $\Delta Q/Q$ rate sums (generally) to 4 per cent, while $\Delta P/P$ lurches by 5 per cent, on a mechanistic $\Delta V = 0$ hypothesis a $(\Delta M/M) = 9$ per cent would be optimal. Qualifications extend only to the best surmise of $(\Delta V/V)$ over the period contemplated by MA policy.

The MA must perforce anticipate $(\Delta P/P)$, as well as $(\Delta Q/Q)$, and order its ΔM emissions to support a maximal Q-position under the emergent ΔP move which it is largely powerless to arrest—or even to thwart—except by a depression antidote involving a cure worse than the inflation disease.

The pursuit of a rigid Monetarist Rule could thus wreak a double disaster: it would fail to control P while having an insidious influence on N and Q. It would be unsuccessful in assaulting the P-trend while imparting some damaging instability to Q and U.

The analysis thus assigns some historical unsteady choppiness to P until a feasible Incomes Policy is either mandated or voluntarily observed.[17] Unemployment, however, may be averted by some countervailing unsteadiness in the M-path. Timid monetary maneuvers designed to combat inflation on erroneous P-theories, have unwittingly succeeded in compounding P-instability with N and Q variability. Full employment has been compromised in the U.S., U.K., and Canada by the MA delusion over its P-capabilities.[18]

If an Incomes Policy was successfully implemented, P-instability could (largely) be obviated and the MA could lend its efforts to maintain the economy on the Q-path of full employment and maximum (feasible) growth. A restrictive MA policy can foster mainly stagflation in an economy undergoing wage inflation.

In the recent climate of double-digit inflation the Monetarist 4 Per cent Steadiness Rule would cause unmitigated unemployment havoc.

Aspects of a Nonsteady $\Delta M/M$ Path

The $\Delta A/A$ ratio contains the well-spring of improved well-being. To finance more output per employee, even at constant prices, would require proportionately more money under mechanistic Quantity Theory notions. With a demand for larger cash balances to accompany higher real income, $\Delta M/M > \Delta A/A$ would prove more nearly optimal.

How much more? The answer is still distressingly vague.[19] As an offset to the effects of affluence, inventory theorizing posits some economies of scale mitigating the demand for real-balances as real income mounts. In the present state of obscurity on these conflicting elements, the MA must exercise its considered judgment on whether to treat $\Delta V \gtreqqless 0$ in each particular circumstance. This, after all, is the function of rational decision-making, to appraise changing circumstances which could prove devastating to slavish adherence to a rigid rule. The prognosis would have to extend to all the components of ΔQ, and their likely aggregated outcome.

Contemplating the raggedy productivity advance in underdeveloped countries, and the income oscillations through swings in foreign trade, a rigid money-rule could provoke deep distress.

Precipitate breaks in the demand for money would render the 4 per cent rule as stultifying as the Great Depression efforts to preserve the gold standard ritual. Keynes aptly observed that if people want more green cheese, an efficient economy would produce the stuff. Likewise, if they clamor to hold more money, the MA must act to provide it. If it is alleged that the funds might be "spent," and are potentially inflationary, the same could be said of any market asset.[20] The Monetarist Rule amounts to a ukase that the economy live with the M-total made available, regardless of the consequences.

A LESS ALARMIST VIEW OF LAGS

Heavy weather has been made by monetarists over lags.

Largely, the bogey is that inflation will follow, after a short or longer interval, if the money augmentation continues to surpass the 4 per cent figure. It is alleged that by going over the line we are doomed to price level excesses, if not quickly, then eventually. And if after a decent time period this does not happen, in the U.S. we are informed that "the lags are longer than expected."

But this alarm is based on the Quantity Theory of Money, after the subtleties are extracted. However, if inflation is attributed to money wage movements, and the money increases are drained off, not to enhance the price level but to sustain output at the new price level, the monetarist fears become muted and far less ominous. The serious concern with lags becomes transformed from trepidations over inflation to matters of how far, and how fast, the MA can edge output on to a full employment path without "overheating," by way of an investment volume proceeding ahead of voluntary savings intentions.

There is implicit a discussion of monetary policy at full employment, a study in itself. But the principle can be stated, running along expected lines, of invoking monetary and fiscal policy to maintain an investment balance, and thus an interest rate structure, that conforms to economy consumption-savings propensities. Otherwise, there can be a (mild) inflationary sequence by way of unbalanced profit rates in the consumption and investment sectors.

So long as lags affect mainly the volume and composition of the Q-stream, they should not occasion the foreboding attached to future inflation being predestined by current monetary maneuvers. The monetarist threat of pernicious lagged consequences can serve as effectively as superstition in precluding current action to achieve desirable goals.

Invoking doleful distant attributes as ensuing from any effort to improve the content of economic life can be an artful prescription for laissez-faire.

Policies for full employment should be viable in the long, as well as the short, run. Where consequences differ over time, the optimum selection would be that which is best when appraised in all time dimensions. But inflation is hardly a significant lagged phenomenon if the price move emanates from non-monetary causes.

THE OPEN ECONOMY

Amendments for the open economy seem to provide no exception to the theory of a nonsteady monetary augmentation staked out above. Exports, like any form of investment comprising the Q-aggregate, require to be financed, as part of the total money supply required to float the output volume priced according to WCM criteria. Imports, likewise, require financing out of the total balance of payments, and exchange rate considerations motivating internal and external economic policy. Although intricacies abound in the light of capital account, current account, and exchange rate interplay, none of the elements appear conducive to implementation of a Steady 4 Per Cent Rule. The arena of discretion, instead, seems to undergo an inflation itself, by the need for the exercise of monetary judgment.

The on-going New Cambridge debate, among Kaldor-Neild-Godley-Cripps et al. on the one side, with Kahn-Posner on the other, does not appear to affect the main view presented here. The argument for recognition of the budget to "determine" the foreign balance and the exchange rate to "determine" the level of activity seems to have been conducted in real, not price level, terms.[21]

When all this is sorted out, it may be less "revolutionary" than at first sight. In any event arguments for fiscal discretion and exchange rate adjustment make a point for monetary discretion, i.e., money supply unsteadiness.

SOME OTHER INFLATION THEMES

As a sub-variant of the monetarist theme, or to reinforce it, there appears the frequent assertion that we suffer from "inflationary expectations," which, one way or the other, become translated by an acquiescent monetary policy into the real thing, inflation.[22]

Ultimately, whatever esoteric words we employ to describe the relations between ideas and events, if we perennially *expect* prices to go up it is because we see the wage-salary incomes of bricklayers, carpenters, plumbers, electricians, office staff, public employees, tool makers, repair men, etc. climbing inordinately. It is the wage-salary hikes that feed our beliefs. And it is the roundabout, interlocked process of income-cost payments and consumer demand outlays that sustains the price bulge and fortifies reiterated belief of inflation.

"Expectations of inflation" must ultimately derive its legitimacy from income facts. Once these are brought into reasonable balance the inflation-expectations will evaporate into conviction of price level stability. Expectations cannot alter price events without an underlying base of substantial income facts.

Wages as Merely Another Price

In the rare and fleeting moments when monetarists devote a passage to wage theories of inflation they are apt to deride wages (and salaries) as "merely another price," no more important than any other price.[23]

There are two points to make: (1) money wage costs enter into the cost side more heavily and more frequently than any other element of cost; the difference of degree can be more of a difference in kind; (2) on the income side, it is myopic to deny the importance of wage-salary recipients as comprising the overwhelming bulk of consumption sector purchasers.

CONCLUSION

Under wage-salary price level inflation, the central bank is primarily a bystander in the price play. It can mainly determine whether we will have output instability superimposed on price level instability. To maintain output levels under an unsteady price level path will mean that the optimal trend of money augmentation will follow a ragged course. With full foresight, and by ascribing inflation to "natural" forces beyond its orbit, the MA augmentation would (with $\Delta V/V = 0$) equal the percentage sum of the potential price and output move.

Given the current fascination with "indexation" schemes, not to exorcise inflation but "to live with it," or to follow the will-o-wisp of "corrections," the "indexation" is likely to inspire inflation under government sanction. A consciously "unsteady" monetary policy involving irregular ΔM variations will have to be enforced in order to maintain full employment, given the price level as "corrected" by "indexation." Unless the Reserve Bank includes an ample price level estimate in its money supply policy projections, monetary policy will be too tight. Interest rates, because of price level allowances, will probably shoot to exorbitant heights to reflect the certain price leap.

Curiously, the Monetarist and Wage-Productivity views could be reconciled in an economy where, either voluntarily, or under legislative duress, or just through fortuitous happenstance, income movements were properly geared to productivity advances.

In such circumstances, with $\Delta P = 0$, and the $(\Delta Q/Q)$ advance being of the order of 4 per cent per annum, the money augmentation could match the Monetarist Rule.

Monetarists should thus welcome Incomes Policy in order to render their monetary recipes a sure-fire success. It can only be an antagonism to any new ideas that leads them to even reject consideration of measures to validate their rigid Steady Rule.

But a *WCM* theorist is also apt to prefer some judgment, and some deviations, in enforcing the Steady Rule under price stability through Incomes Policy. In the main, however, the rule should then prove serviceable. In any event, until we stabilize the price level it would be foolhardy to dismantle the central bank. For the impending chaos would drive us quickly to restore it, after needless confusion and political harassment in debating wrong issues.

NOTES

1. For an early schematic statement, though not my earliest expression of the wage-price nexus, see my *General Theory of the Price Level* (Westport, Conn.: Greenwood Press, 1959 reprint).

2. Milton Friedman remarked: "One purpose of setting forth this framework as I have is to document my belief that the basic differences among economists are empirical, not theoretical." See his "A Theoretical Framework for Monetary Analysis," *Journal of Political Economy* (March/April 1970).

3. See the "Symposium on Friedman's Theoretical Framework," *Journal of Political Economy* (September/October 1972), with Friedman, Brunner-Meltzer, Tobin, and Davidson as participants. "Empirical" material is notable mainly by its omission.

4. John Stuart Mill, *Principles of Political Economy* (Ashley edition, 1909 reprint), p. 436.

5. Cf. Paul Davidson and Sidney Weintraub, "Money as Cause and Effect," Chapter 8 above. See also Nicholas Kaldor, "The New Monetarism," *Lloyds Bank Review* (1972).

6. For one reference, see Milton Friedman's "A Theoretical Framework," pp. 223–224. He has made the same statement in other places.

7. Cf. "Keynes and the Quantity Theory Elasticities," Chapter 3 above. Also Chapter 7, "The Friedman Puzzle."

8. This statement should not require documentation. See, e.g., his "A Theoretical Framework," p. 195. Or: "Inflation is always and everywhere a monetary phenomenon . . ." in "What Price Guideposts" in George Shultz and Robert Aliber, eds., *Guidelines, Informal Controls, and the Market Place* (Chicago: University of Chicago Press, 1966), p. 18.

9. Rather than assuming $\Delta V = 0$, as in the Old and mechanistic Quantity Theory, in a new mechanistic slant, which treats liquidity-demands as invariable, Friedman holds $(\Delta V/V) = 0.8$, a constant. In proof, his money income elasticity $(\Delta Y/V)/(\Delta M/M) = 1.8$. Thus: $EYM = [(M\Delta Y)/(Y\Delta M)] = 1 + (M\Delta V)/V(\Delta M)$. Hence, with $(\Delta M/M) = 1\%$, $(\Delta V/V) = 0.82$.

10. Even in hyperinflation the accelerating price trend would stop unless money incomes, especially wages and salaries, kept mounting disproportionately to productivity. Mrs. Robinson points out that in the great German inflation wages were adjusted hourly, according to a "cost-of-living" index. She observes that the significance of this was lost on Bresciani-Turroni in his book on *The Economics of Inflation.* Her pithy brief review in *Economic Journal* (1938), p. 150, is still a valuable contribution to the inflation literature.

11. Since 1930, there have been only about nine years of U.S. budget surpluses, and some of very meager size. Yet for most of the period the price level performed quite well. Even the $80 billions of Nixon deficits are paltry compared to the GNP. In the 1930s there were *falling* prices amid deficits of 50 per cent. Thus it is a distortion to assign inflation to recent deficits.

12. Peter Wiles, arguing from U.K. experience, points to *dwindling* profit margins. His article, a lament for the failure of economists to apprehend the money wage-price level connection in their stupefaction with Quantity Theory preconceptions, embodies the general theoretical position advanced here. See his "Cost Inflation and the State of Economic Theory," *Economic Journal* (June 1973).

13. See my *General Theory of the Price Level.*

14. Cf. Richard Kosobud and Lawrence Klein, "Some Econometrics of Growth: Great Ratios of Economics," *Quarterly Journal of Economics* (May 1961). For international comparisons of k and V, see John Hotson, *International Comparisons of Money Velocity and Wage Mark-Ups* (Clifton, N.J.: A. Kelley, 1968).

15. See my "Comment" on cost inflation, Chapter 14 below. For an earlier statement, see my *Classical Keynesianism, Monetary Theory and the Price Level* (Westport, Conn.: Greenwood Press, 1960 reprint). The latter, it might be noted, is a criticism of American Keynesian models, calling for their abandonment, many years before the work of Axel Leijonhufvud.

16. Curiously, it was this conception that Frank Hahn derided in a review of my *A Keynesian Theory of Employment Growth and In-*

come Distribution (Philadelphia: Chilton, 1965). See *American Economic Review* (1965). I have seen no reason to alter my views.

17. For one effort to design a market-oriented Incomes Policy by using the tax mechanism, see "A Tax Based Incomes Policy," Chapter 16 below.

18. Kenneth Arrow has remarked that "the recurrent periods of unemployment which have characterized the history of capitalism are scarcely compatible with a neoclassical model of market equilibrium." See his "Limited Knowledge and Economics Analysis," *American Economic Review* (March 1974), p. 2. My position here is that the major bouts of unemployment, at least since World War II, are attributable to the misguided tight money ventures invoked to combat inflation.

19. Cf. the estimates in Milton Friedman, *The Optimum Quantity of Money and Other Essays* (Chicago: Aldine, 1969), Chapter 1. Also Keynes, *Economic Journal* (1937).

20. On the entire theory, see Paul Davidson, *Money in the Real World* (London: Macmillan, 1973).

21. Cf. *The Economist* (London, April 27, 1974), pp. 13–14, and Richard Kahn and Michael Posner, *Times* (London, May 18, 1974).

22. See my "Inflation and Incomes Policy: Closing the Institutional Gap," *Economic Forum* (Economic Society of Australia and New Zealand, Western Australian Branch, July 2, 1974, Perth, W. A.)

23. *Ibid.*

10 The Price Level in the Open Economy*

In practically every country economists and policy officials are apt to blame their price troubles on "imported" inflation.[1] Inflation thus appears as a unique phenomenon which everybody imports and nobody exports. Even U.S. officials, with less warrant than elsewhere, draw visions of "global" inflation to deflect criticism of their own price level failures.

Of course, the doctrine of "imported inflation" furnishes a comforting rationalization for do-little public policies; if the problem is "global!" then the ball is tapped into the courts of other countries; the corollary is that the rescue must await an international conference rich in vague communiques but short of concrete steps to bank the price fires. To be sure, economic analysis stemming from the classical economics of Hume and Ricardo, and an older gold standard world, or even the more recent Bretton Woods commitment to (relatively) fixed exchange rates, lends some plausibility to the theme of imported inflation. Nonetheless, ideas on sheltered industries, with the frequency of exchange rate variations over the last quarter century, and the more recent departures toward exchange rate "floating," must invite some revision in the older theories. As a recent survey article (by economists sympathetic to the doctrine of global inflation) observed: "Nevertheless major discrepancies between the inflation rates experienced by different countries persisted . . . and these divergences need explaining."[2]

* I thank W. Ethier for comments on an earlier draft of this paper.

Essentially, the present paper is concerned with this problem. Its aim is three-fold: (1) to consider the determinants of the domestic price level in an open economy; (2) to classify economies by their "degree of price level openness"; and (3) to assess the domestic price level impact of external price movements on any particular economy, whether the higher import prices are attributable to higher prices abroad under fixed exchange rates or due to some appreciation of foreign currencies.

Some concreteness is imparted to the theory by simple calculations from readily accessible data. A prefatory word is appropriate on the definition of "openness." Our perspective involves price level interdependence. Other criteria might be invoked for other purposes: in other contexts the relative size of migration, interest rate interdependence, capital flows, the international transmission of knowledge, technological absorption, literary communication, or external political influences might receive singular attention as a test of the open society. Our focus is solely on the internal price level impact of external price changes in imported goods.

The conclusion that will emerge is that the world inflation is unlikely to be allayed until the major trading nations act, mainly independently, to control their own price levels. Most countries, it will be argued, can determine their own price level fortunes though a tougher policy stance will be imperative when other countries are remiss in their performance. A concerted international program can undoubtedly be mutually reinforcing, permitting more moderate domestic price level initiatives by any one country. Without the wider world joint participation more stringent domestic action will be required, sustained indirectly (after some time lag) by domestic exchange rate appreciation as a resolute price level course is pursued despite external complacency which refuses to confront the inflation disorder.

PRICE LEVEL EQUATIONS
FOR THE CLOSED ECONOMY

Though my own partiality is to a price level theory that stresses the relation of money incomes to output, and especially the money wage-productivity ratio, the classification of open economies adopted is neutral in this respect, being equally at home with doctrines that depict money as the root of all inflation.[3] Thus the analysis will proceed (unevenly) from both points of view; the same "coefficient" of openness can be entertained on monetarist or money income precepts for domestic price level control.

We recite first some of the more familiar price level equations usually applied to the *closed* economy. Monetary, and money income, theories of price level determination and control, despite individual variations and attendant subtleties, operate essentially through one or the other thought scheme as the wider model is elaborated.

First, the equation which makes money incomes prominent in the price level formulation:

$$P = Y/Q, \text{ from } PQ = Y \qquad (1)$$

where Y = money income
P = price level
Q = real output.

From (1), the Wage-Cost Mark-Up equation (*WCM*):

$$P = kw/A, \text{ from } PQ = kwN = Y \qquad (2)$$

where w = average wage and salary
N = employment level
$A = Q/N$ = average labor product
k = average mark-up of price over unit labor costs, or the reciprocal of the wage share.

Largely, it is the substantial fact of $k = \bar{k}$—involving a high degree of labor share constancy—with causality from unit labor costs w/A to P, that is at the bottom of the *WCM* theories of inflation. The theory leads to the position that incomes policies must be devised to stem the inflation tide.

Relation (1) reveals that whenever the money income rise surpasses the pace of output, the price level will mount. In (2) there is recognition of k, and w, where the latter denotes the average level of money wages and salaries; work-incomes (embodied in w) constitute 70 to 75 per cent of money income in most affluent market economies. In talking about inflation in the market economy, it would be nice to have as the appropriate measured income concept for Y the data on the *Gross Business Product*, relating the quantity of market output at market prices. Unfortunately, international GBP data are not easy to come by so that we shall interpret Y as Gross National Product.

Those of a monetarist persuasion will prefer, as a price level equation, either a form reminiscent of Irving Fisher, or a Marshallian Cambridge cash-balance variety.[4] For simplicity, a Fisher-type will be used:

$$MV = PQ, \text{ or } P = MV/Q \tag{3}$$

where $M =$ money supply (whether M_1, M_2, M_3 . . .)
$V =$ money velocity.

Dividing (3) by N elicits a parallel, and contrast, between the Equation of Exchange (EOE) and the WCM:

$$P = M'V/A \tag{4}$$

where $M' =$ money supply per employee.

In (2) it thus becomes necessary mainly to predict w and k; in (4), M' and V. To avoid polemical digression off our main line, this distinction will not be pressed. One view leads to monetary prescriptions to control the price level, the other to some mechanism to taper movements in money incomes, especially in average wages and salaries.[5]

THE PRICE EQUATIONS IN THE OPEN ECONOMY

One or the other set of equations would have to be applied for the price level analysis in the closed economy: the ultimate "victory" will depend more on operational success than on either logic or a torrent of words.

In the open economy the new complication is that both exports and imports affect the quantities of goods available for sale domestically and thus, the home market price level. Yet the injection of the external influences may be less formidable, and less ambiguous (at least within bounds) than previous work has suggested.

Suppose we visualize the economy as having for sale domestically the entire range of final goods and services bought by consumers (C), by firms as investment goods (I), which includes new houses, and by government (G). Further, there are exports (X), which sell domestically—as C, I, or G items—for the same price as is yielded by the unit proceeds rendered after conversion from foreign currencies. Embodied in all these goods, too, is the import content (F), as either raw and semi-finished materials in C, I, G, X, or final C-output. From usual Gross National Product (GNP) accounting it follows that:

$$C + I + G + X - F = \text{GNP} \equiv P_d Q_d \qquad (5a)$$

$$C + I + G + X = \text{GNP} + F \equiv PQ = P_d Q_d + P_f Q_f \quad (5b)$$

$$(5c)$$

$$\frac{(C + I + G + X - F)}{(C + I + G + X)}(C + I + G + X) \equiv \text{GNP} = nPQ$$

where $P_f Q_f$ = import prices and quantities

$P_d Q_d$ = prices and quantities of domestic output content

P, Q = prices and quantities in the open economy, embodying import content

$n \quad \leqq 1$ = domestic content of each money unit of $C + I + G + X$.

Running down the equational sequence, the first relation (5a) conveys the GNP aggregate, which is equal to the multiple of domestic prices and domestic outputs *after* imports are eliminated. Relation (5b) restates this relation to embrace both the domestic and import price-quantity set: P denotes the price level inclusive of imports. In (5c) the sales value of output, gross of import content, is explicitly stated before reduction by the n-term to domestic content.

It is the size of the n-term, we shall find, that enables us to classify economies according to the degree of "open" or "closed"-ness. As its value shifts the home price level becomes more, or less, buffeted by external price winds.

The alternative forms of the *WCM* and *EOE* price level relations for the "open" economy thus become:

$$nPQ = Y, \text{ or } P = Y/nQ, \text{ or } (P_d + P_f Q_f/Q_d) = Y/nQ_d \quad (6a)$$

where P_f, P_d = prices of imported and domestic outputs, Q_f, Q_d = quantities of imported and domestic output.

$$(6b)$$
$$nPQ = kwN, \text{ or } P = kw/nA, \text{ or } (P_d + P_f Q_f/Q_d) = kw/nA_d$$

where $A = Q/N$ and $A_d = Q_d/N$.

$$(6c)$$
$$nPQ = MV, \text{ or } P = M'V/nA, \text{ or } (P_d + P_f Q_f/Q_d) = M'V/nA_d$$

In (6a–c) n conveys the domestic component of gross internal output, including import content. Thus if $n = 0.9$, then 90 per cent of every dollar of $(C + I + G + X)$ consists of domestic output (and income), with 10 per cent $(1 - n = n')$ being the import content in each gross domestic sales dollar.

SOME CALCULATIONS OF THE DOMESTIC CONTENT OF MARKET OUTPUT

In the *fully* closed economy $F = 0 = X$. Conceivably, $F = 0$, with $X > 0$, where the exports are paid for in international reserves or financed through loans or capital grants. In any event, with $F = 0$, then $n = 1$ so that the pertinent price level theory is that of the closed economy. Either through incomes policy or monetary maneuvers the price level should be, according to the theoretical conjectures, amenable to domestic control: "imported-inflation" would be precluded.

At the other extreme, $Y = F$, and $n = 0$, so that *all* goods (and services) are "imported." This is a rather far-fetched instance; conceivably, it would cover nil domestic production where all goods are sold at the exact import price—maybe at dock-side—with domestic incomes nil. This would be "openness" indeed, with the country's price level "manufactured abroad." In descending from $1 \geqq n \geqq 0$ the door of the economy becomes unhinged to "openness". A sample of world economies, developed and developing, places n commonly in a range of 0.6 to 0.9. As n shifts the degree of "openness" alters.

From (6a–6c), it follows that to control its price level, so long as $n < 1$, with external prices rising, a country will either have to run a more taut money policy, or place tighter clamps on money income than in the closed economy of $n = 1$. Clearly, a falling n works to reduce A: either Y, or w, or M', must be more firmly compressed to yield price level stability whenever n descends.[6]

Leaving the analytical terrain some illustrative n-values can be computed from data published by the International Monetary Fund, covering 1970–1974. In all cases Gross National Product statistics were used (in domestic currencies), together with the accompanying information on imports. Results are gathered in Table 1 where economies are classified as "Almost Closed," "Amply Closed," "Moderately Closed," "More Open," etc. Others may hit on better descriptive labels.

Examining the table, the chief surprise (for the author) was to note India as the most closed economy of all. Undoubtedly, this is part illusion, a statistical artifact in view of the relatively large amount of imputed nonmarket—maybe about half—GNP output in Indian statistics.[7] As imports belong to the market price system, India would drop to a more open setting, maybe with $n = 0.85$ or so. For other less developed economies on the list, a parallel distortion probably also taints the n-values based on uncorrected GNP statistics which contain varying amounts of imputed non-market output in each case.

Obviously, the U.S. classifies as a highly closed economy; Japan and Australia are also up on the list; refinement of the GNP totals, to confine them to market transactions, may lead to some change in the enumeration. In the raw GNP data, however, both countries class as more, not less, closed than the U.K., or Canada, over the period covered. Germany and France are fairly high on the closed list, listing moderately to openness.

The openness of the smaller democratic economies is also apparent in the size of n for the Scandinavian and Low countries. Israel and Luxembourg are prime instances of openness for "westernized" market economies.

PRICE LEVEL INDEPENDENCE
AND INTERACTION IN THE OPEN ECONOMY

Let us consider the elements that would have to be considered if a country tried to pursue an independent price level policy in an open economy, whether the objective be a flat trend or a controlled pace of movement. As part of the analysis we consider the impact of discrepancies in external world prices (or price events in trading partners) on the domestic price level. The latter involves, of course, the issue of the degree of "imported inflation." Initially, we adopt the strong assumption that the "real" import-content is unchanged, that n is unaltered despite the rise in import prices, including price swings due to exchange rate fluctuations.

Using subscripts 1 and 2 for dates t_1 and t_2, and recalling earlier relations, we have:

$$(P_2/P_1) = (n_1 Y_2 Q_1)/(n_2 Y_1 Q_2) \qquad (7a)$$

$$(P_2/P_1) = (n_1 k_2 w_2 A_1)/(n_2 k_1 w_1 A_2) \qquad (7b)$$

$$(P_2/P_1) = (n_1 A_1)(M'_2 V_2)/(n_2 A_2)(M'_1 V_1) \qquad (7c)$$

For a first approximation, on the heroic assumption of "other things unchanged," the price rise will turn on:

$$(P_2/P_1) = (n_1/n_2) \qquad (8)$$

In words, the price move will equal the reciprocal of the fall in domestic content: if n drops from 0.9 to 0.8, meaning a doubling of foreign content from 0.1 to 0.2, the upward price pressure will be of the order of $\frac{1}{8}$, or $12\frac{1}{2}$ per cent. That is, a 100 per cent increase in import prices will yield a limited price level move. If $n = 0.8$, and then falls to 0.6, the price rise will be $33\frac{1}{3}$ per cent.

"Other things," of course, will not be unchanged. One not uninteresting supposition is that the Q's will be unchanged (neglecting import substitution) as the monetary authority endeavors to maintain employment. Then we have:

$$(P_2 Y_1)/(P_1 Y_2) = n_1/n_2 \qquad (9a)$$

$$(P_2/P_1) = n_1 Y_2/n_2 Y_1 \qquad (9b)$$

TABLE 10.1

Domestic Content of One Currency Unit of Gross
Domestic Product, 1970–1974

	High	Average	Low
"Almost" Closed Economies: $1 > n > 0.9$			
India (1968–1971)	0.978	0.958	0.945
United States	0.948	0.938	0.919
Argentina (1970–1973)	0.942	0.928	0.919
Brazil (1970–1973)	0.934	0.924	0.915
Turkey (1970–1972)	0.922	0.909	0.902
Mexico	0.917	0.909	0.895
"Amply" Closed Economies: $0.9 > n > 0.85$			
Japan	0.916	0.899	0.864
Uruguay (1970–1973)	0.901	0.888	0.876
Chile (1970–1972)	0.893	0.886	0.873
Australia	0.885	0.870	0.861
Spain (1970–1973)	0.866	0.857	0.843
"Moderately" Closed Economies: $0.85 > n > 0.80$			
France	0.863	0.848	0.807
Greece	0.847	0.827	0.801
Germany	0.835	0.827	0.804
Venezuela	0.836	0.825	0.815
Italy	0.842	0.823	0.770
Canada	0.827	0.815	0.792
United Kingdom	0.828	0.806	0.755
New Zealand (1970–1973)	0.812	0.803	0.795

If $n_1 \approx n_2$, then the price move hinges on the *domestic* money income development, of (Y_2/Y_1). Over the sample years, for several countries listed in Table 1, a strong case can thus be made for domestic rather than imported inflation: the inflation source would be in the domestic Y magnitudes, either through money or money income tolerance.

If we write $P_1 = 100 = Y_1$ (as index numbers for t_1), then:

$$(P_2/Y_2) = n_1/n_2 \qquad (10)$$

TABLE 1 (continued)

Domestic Content of One Currency Unit of Gross
Domestic Product, 1970–1974

	High	Average	Low
"More Open" Economies: $0.80 > n > 0.75$			
South Africa	0.813	0.795	0.764
Sweden	0.811	0.794	0.748
Finland	0.783	0.771	0.742
Denmark	0.788	0.768	0.741
"Substantially" Open Economies: $0.75 > n > 0.70$			
Austria	0.763	0.748	0.729
Switzerland	0.758	0.748	0.739
Costa Rica	0.730	0.715	0.677
"Extremely" Open Economies: $0.70 > n > 0.65$			
Belgium	0.713	0.693	0.650
Iceland	0.713	0.682	0.677
Norway	0.712	0.691	0.663
Ireland	0.713	0.692	0.677
Netherlands	0.695	0.673	0.646
"Practically" Open Economies: $0.65 > n > 0.55$			
Israel (1970–1973)	0.654	0.638	0.601
Luxembourg (1970–1973)	0.563	0.559	0.556

Source: *International Monetary Statistics,* International Monetary Fund,
December 1975.

The prime move, and money income moves, will be proportionate
to the reciprocal of the n-ratios: if $n_1 \approx n_2$, then prices and money
incomes jump in unison.

If $Y_1 = Y_2$, so that the GNP is constant, it follows that:

$$(P_2 Q_2)/(P_1 Q_1) = n_1/n_2 \qquad (11)$$

Thus if the price of imports rises from 10 to 20 cents, with
$n_2 = 0.8$ from $n_1 = 0.9$, and if the price rise is held to 10 per cent,
with $P_2 = 110$ and $P_1 = 100$, then:

$$(0.9/0.8) = (100/110)/(Q_1Q_2) \qquad (12)$$

The output ratio (Q_1/Q_2) will be $(88/90)$, involving a drop of about 2 per cent in the previous output volume. This rests on a shift to substantial openness, and an adamant monetary (and money income) position in repressing the domestic money income aggregate.

Ruling out an enormous rise in import prices, of the order of 100 per cent outbreaks, with $n_1 \approx n_2$, (and allowing for import substitution and possible exchange rate appreciation), the price level, money income, and output-employment results are scaled down to less scary figures. Of course, a fall in n always means more "imported" inflation.

PRICE-MAKING ELEMENTS AFFECTED
BY IMPORTED INFLATION

While a full tracing would carry us into all of international trade theory, complicated by still unresolved micro-macro aspects of price levels, employment, money wages, money supplies, etc., it is possible to do a bit more to stake out the price-making elements touched off by imported inflation.

From earlier considerations:

$$P = P_d(Q_d/Q) + P_f(Q_f/Q) \qquad (13a)$$

Differentiating (dP/dP_f), and reducing terms to elasticity forms by injecting suitable (unity) terms, we thus have:

$$E_p = nE_{pd} + nE_{qd} - nE_q + n' + n'E_{qf} - n'E_q \qquad (13b)$$

where the E's are elasticities of domestic and imported quantities (qd, qf) and gross and domestic prices (p, pd), all with respect to variations in import prices (pf).

If we take total output as constant, thus $E_q = 0$, then two terms drop out: this is tantamount to assuming gross output constant and inquiring into the price level effect of imported inflation. Likewise, there appears no obvious reason why P_d should vary with P_f other than, perhaps, as domestic output replaces some of the import content. Assuming $E_{pd} = 0$, then

$$E_p = nE_{qd} + n'(1 + E_{qf}) \qquad (13c)$$

$$E_p = n'(1 + E_{qf}) + E_{qd}(1 - n')$$

If $\Delta Q_d = 0 = \Delta Q_f$, so that import and domestic content hold rigid, then $E_p = n'$. Otherwise, with import substitution, the price rise will be more limited. In (13c) it follows that $E_{qf} < 0$. Also, in absolute value it is most certain that $E_{qd} < E_{qf}$. Thus the reduction in n', compared to the $\Delta Q_d = 0$ case, is only partly augmented by the nE_{qd} value.

So long as import prices rise faster than home output prices, substitution phenomena should work to relieve the price havoc of imported inflation. Countries able to replace foreign wares after just a slight switch in relative prices will best cope, and mitigate imported inflation.[8] Overall, by containing the domestic price level, exchange rate appreciation should over time contribute further to moderate the internal net impact of external inflation.

Using the price equation of $(P_d + P_f Q_f / Q_d) = kw/nA_d$, and differentiating this with respect to a change in P_f, while on the proviso that $\Delta P_d = \Delta k = \Delta A_d = 0$, then after reduction:

$$E_n = \frac{n-1}{n}(E_{qd} - E_{qf} - 1) \qquad (14a)$$

where the E's are elasticities of the subscripts with respect to changes in P_f. Generally, $E_{qd} > 0 < E_{qf}$. If $E_{qd} = 0$, the relation is condensed to:

$$E_n = [(1-n)/n](1 + E_{qf}) \qquad (14b)$$

SOME CONCLUDING REMARKS

On a WCM theory, effective control over w should be enough to direct the domestic price path at practically any pace that a country would desire—in principle, if Archimedes had an Incomes Policy lever he could maintain a domestic price *plateau*. As the n-term qualifies A, w must be more severely contained to prevent inflation in the open economy where $n < 1$. Supplementing Incomes Policy, ensuing exchange rate appreciation and import substitution, would also work to safeguard the domestic price level from world forces.

On a monetarist version, a tight enough money policy should depress aggregate demand and depress imports, thereby serving to elevate n. The sequence leads to the same general conclusion of domestic monitoring and control of the price level despite external world influences.

On monetarist reasoning (I think) unemployment would be entailed, even invited, to accomplish the price level stabilization objective: total imports would fall and a decline in Q would be operative. On WCM thinking, Q could (under underemployment) increase so long as the w/A ratio is restrained; total imports could conceivably also go up.

Our analysis thus suggests, at least for the major western economies, that even with world price movements, say in the 15 per cent range, leverage to thwart inflation resides substantially in domestic hands. Imported inflation appears mainly to be a comforting apologetic supporting inaction by political leaders reluctant to antagonize political supporters, often labor groups, frequently deceived between money and real wage gains, and tolerably acquiescent to the ensuing job inroads induced by conventional monetary and fiscal measures while firmly adamant against money wage concessions.

One-crop, or one-mineral, or one-commodity, underdeveloped lands are undoubtedly likely to have a tougher time in exercising domestic price level control mainly because of the lack of stabilization instruments, or ineptness in their use, or political instability, or apathy. Imported, and much non-imported, inflation is but one price of economic and political backwardness. Some relief from imported inflation would follow from a better record in affluent countries. Exchange rate depreciation and proliferating trade controls would, in the future as in the past, be the price paid for chronic "banana republic" inflation even in a world in which the affluent market economies achieved reasonably stable price level norms.

NOTES

1. In visits to about 27 countries, including all major trading nations, the complaint of imported inflation is as prevalent as the common cold. Part of the analysis was developed in the course of a study

on Incomes Policy prepared for the *Economic Council of Canada,* published as a discussion paper, April 1976.

2. D. E. W. Laidler and J. M. Parkin, "Inflation: A Survey," *Economic Journal,* Vol. 85 (1975), p. 783.

3. Cf. "Keynes and the Monetarists," Chapter 1 above.

4. Milton Friedman expresses a preference for a Cambridge cash-balance version. See his "A Theoretical Framework for Monetary Analysis," *Journal of Political Economy,* Vol. 78 (1970). I trust this use of the $MV = PQ$ formulation will not provoke some irrelevant controversy. After more than a decade's confusion by monetarists of an equation for the demand for money with a price level relationship, discussion has reverted back to square 1 and old price level formulae. Cf. the sardonic comments of Lawrence Ritter, in a review of the reprinted article, *Journal of Economic Literature,* Vol. 13 (1975).

5. Cf. the TIP incomes policy developed in collaboration with Henry Wallich, Chapter 16.

6. The interpretation of A might be noted to prevent confusion. As Q (in P) is interpreted gross of import content, to compute A we have:

$$A = (Q_c + Q_i + Q_g + Q_x)/N \qquad (16)$$

That is, the average labor product (A) embeds the import content of real output marketed as C, I, G, and X goods and services. When forms involving $(P_d + P_f Q_f/Q_d)$ are used, A_d represents the usual GNP calculation of average productivity.

7. Some years ago I made some attempt to place the statistics on a market basis. See *Growth Without Inflation in India,* Delhi, National Council of Applied Economic Research, 165.

8. Domestic substitutes which must meet import prices have, at any given w/A_d ratio, restricted ability to decide their k-markup.

11 A Macro Theory of Pricing, Income Distribution and Employment

INTRODUCTION

Investment largely governs profits, and profits largely comprise the savings magnitude. The low savings propensities of wage earners, and the high savings ratios associated with profit incomes, enter in a crucial way in determining employment, income, and income growth.

These seem to be the main inferences to be drawn from the important recent writings of Professors Joan Robinson and Nicholas Kaldor, supplemented by Luigi Pasinetti.[1] Once exploited, these insights promise to alter our understanding of the macroeconomic process and the enterprise system itself.[2]

It may be that their work accords too little attention to the price mechanism through which income shares are determined. In any event, the dependence of distributive shares on pricing will be the theme of this paper. With income shares resolved through pricing decisions, the income and employment levels rest upon: (1) investment, (2) income shares, and (3) the respective savings ratios.

This is a turnabout in Keynesian analysis where pricing has generally been suppressed while the argument has been conducted in real terms.[3] The importance of income distribution for macroeconomics, moreover, had practically dropped from view until the seminal Kaldor-Robinson writings opened up the subject.[4]

Undoubtedly, the mainstream of macro theory will be revised by the new views on distribution. New attention will be accorded monopoly and competition once it is perceived that pricing practices dominate income division and, thereby, the income and employment level, and the growth process itself.

THE PRICE LEVEL AND INCOME DISTRIBUTION

An easy way of showing the connection of prices to income distribution is through a general formula for the price level, involving the wage cost–markup (WCM) equation. Thus:

$$P = kw/A = w/A\Theta. \tag{1}$$

One can argue, of course, that k is a structural constant so that with given unit labor costs, w/A, the structural or institutional facts control the price level. Or it might be averred that k is an endogenous outcome of the market facts of competition and monopoly, so that income shares are molded in the market processes. In any event, so long as k is subject to minor variations in the normal circumstances, the price level is a consequence of money wage and productivity forces.

THE "ALL AND NOTHING" HYPOTHESIS

For a good part of the way we can adopt the ingenious simplifying assumption, often invoked by Mrs. Robinson and Mr. Kaldor, that wage earners spend all their income and save nothing, while capitalists save all and consume nothing. That is, $c_w = 1$ and $s_w = 0$ and $c_r = 0$ and $s_r = 1$, where the c-terms and the s-terms refer to the respective average propensities to consume and to save.

Obviously, the realism of this assumption can be derided but few would doubt that it is close to the mark in economies with low living standards, with a small very wealthy class as even in England and the United States in the not too distant past. After all, a modified "All and Nothing" hypothesis has a long ancestry in economics, from Cantillon and Hume, through Malthus, not to omit Marx and, in a latter day, Kalecki.

For analytic convenience the unqualified hypothesis will be employed initially. Even after it is watered down, it provides powerful illumination.

Income Definitions

Familiar income terms and definitions will be required: C = consumption output, I = investment output, $W = wN$ = the wage bill, $R = gross$ profits, or more accurately, the nonwage share in gross business product, involving *all* distributive allocations other than wages. Government outlays and taxes will be temporarily excluded. Subscripts identify the C and I outputs in the two sector model that we shall diagnose.

$$C \equiv P_c Q_c \equiv W_c + R_c \tag{2}$$

$$I \equiv P_i Q_i \equiv W_i + R_i \tag{3}$$

$$Z \equiv C + I \equiv W + R \equiv (W_c + W_i) + (R_c + R_i). \tag{4}$$

Further, $\Pi + \Theta = 1$, where Π and Θ represent the "profit" (or nonwage) and wage shares, respectively, in gross business product.

A two sector system entails at least two separate "commodities," Q_c and Q_i. Throughout, as a simplification, it will be supposed that $w_c = w_i$, or that average wage levels are equal in each of the sectors.

Profit and Consumption Relations

From the Keynesian identity of $I \equiv S$, where S denotes the savings magnitude, the All and Nothing hypothesis entails:

$$I = S = R \tag{5}$$

$$C = W = W_c + W_i \tag{6}$$

$$R_c = W_i. \tag{7}$$

Relations (5–7) are the "obvious" outcomes of the All and Nothing hypothesis. They contain a residue of explanatory insight even when the hypothesis is modified. Their content was not so obvious until the Kaldor-Robinson work appeared.

The Income Split in the I-Sector

Examining (5), once we are given any I-value, then R is immediately settled. But in relation (3), what determines W_i and thus R_i? And thereafter, W_c? It is at this stage, that is, in determining the income split in the I-sector consequent upon any level of I-outlay, that a theory of pricing, or a separate theory of income shares is imperative. Let us pursue this.

From (3), given the money I-outlay, how is the I-sum split between the two claimants? As in (1) we can write: [5]

$$P_i = (wN_i/Q_i) + (R_i/Q_i) = (w/A_i) + (R_i/Q_i) \quad (1a)$$

$$= (k_i w/A_i) = w/\Theta_i A_i. \quad (1b)$$

Given a price markup ratio $k_i (= 1/\Theta_i)$, the system is closed. The income split in the I-sector is fixed up, the profit magnitude in the C-sector is decided, and thus, with a pricing mechanism in the C-sector deciding the income split there, relative income shares and absolute income magnitudes are determined.[6]

C-Sector Activity

In an economy where income is saved—the actual economy—investment is the indispensable ingredient for the maintenance of consumption activity, for otherwise sales receipts in the C-sector would always fall below income payments. Investment activity thus performs the vital task of shoaling up the economy, in carrying it to high levels of employment and, through enlarging capacity, to growth.[7]

The Kahn-Keynes "multiplier" described how a "dollar" of investment could lead to a multiple increase of income, in both consumption *and* investment volume. It is superfluous to repeat this familiar tool of macrotheory here. Instead, what will be done, on the All and Nothing premise, is to show how the income magnitude in the consumption sector is uniquely tied to the investment magnitude, *and to the distributive phenomena in I and C,* and thus implicitly, to the underlying pricing mechanism. Thus:

$$C \equiv P_c Q_c = R_c + W_c$$

$$= W_i + W_c$$

$$= \Theta_i I + \Theta_c(\Theta_i I) + \cdots + \Theta_c^{\infty}(\Theta_i I) \tag{8a}$$

$$= \Theta_i I/(1 - \Theta_c) = I(\Theta_i/\Pi_c). \tag{8}$$

Equation (8) is of major interest.[8] It reveals that in the All or Nothing world the C-volume depends wholly on distributive phenomena and the investment magnitude. If $\Theta_i = \Pi_c$, then $C = I$: both sectors are of equal size. If $\Theta_i > \Pi_c$, the C-sector will be the larger.

Employment and Resource Allocation

Some simple derivations throw added light on the All and Nothing economy. The results retain some interest even on more realistic assumptions.

$$\text{Wage Bill: } W = P_c Q_c = I(\Theta_i/\Pi_c) \tag{9}$$

$$\text{Income: } Z = P_c Q_c + P_i Q_i = I(1 + \Theta_i/\Pi_c) \tag{10}$$

$$\text{Employment: } N = (I/w)(\Theta_i/\Pi_c) \tag{11}$$

$$\text{Relative Sector Size: } (N_c/N_i) = (\Theta_c/\Pi_c) \tag{12}$$

$$\text{Resource Use: } (N_c/N) = \Theta_c \tag{13}$$

On the proviso that $\Theta = \Pi$, or that shares are equal in each sector, with each amounting to $\frac{1}{2}$, the wage bill would equal investment, income would be twice I, employment would equal I/w, and sector size $C = I$.

THE "ALL AND SOMETHING" HYPOTHESIS

Greater realism follows from an "All and Something" hypothesis, involving the view that wage earners save nothing while capitalists devote a small part of their income to consumption. Manifestly, with high per capita profit income, per capita capitalist consumption may be high, despite the low c_r ratios. If the capitalist class is small it may be that $c_w W > c_r R$, where $c_r R/C \approx 0$, and $c_w W/C \approx 1$. This situation may describe some underdeveloped regions of the world with huge populations, such as India, where the ordinary standard of living is low but where there exists substantial conspicuous per capita consumption of a small group of wealthy individuals which is dwarfed, in the aggregate, by the sum of the meager consumption intakes of ordinary wage earners.

Profit and Consumption Relations

In this model the definitional relationships are as follows:

$$I = S = s_r R \tag{14}$$

$$C = W + c_r R \tag{15}$$

$$R_c = W_i + c_r R. \tag{16}$$

Further, if $W = R$, so that the income split is equal, then $C = W(1 + c_r)$, which approaches W as c_r approaches zero.

C-Sector Activity

Given the investment magnitude, let us consider the elements governing the size of C-activity. Thus:

$$P_c Q_c = W_i + c_{ri} R_i + W_c + c_{rc} R_c \tag{17a}$$

$$= (\Theta_i + c_{ri}\Pi_i)I + (\Theta_c + c_{rc}\Pi_c)(\Theta_i + c_{ri}\Pi_i)I +$$

$$\cdots (\Theta_c + c_{rc}\Pi_c)^\infty (\Theta_i + c_{ri}\Pi_i)I \tag{17b}$$

$$= I(\Theta_i + c_{ri}\Pi_i)/[1 - (\Theta_c + c_{rc}\Pi_c)]$$

$$= I(1 - s_{ri}\Pi_i)/(s_{rc}\Theta_c). \tag{17}$$

From (17) it follows that high profit shares in the separate sectors, and high savings propensities of the capitalist group, will restrain the volume of C-sector activity.[9] With $s_{rc} = s_{ri} = 1$, we revert back to (8). As an extreme result, with unity savings ratios and unity profit shares, C-activity would grind to a halt.

Employment and Resource Allocation

Writing $\mu = (1 - s_{ir}\Pi_i)/s_{cr}\Pi_c$, the other major characteristics of the All and Something economy can be developed.

Wage Bill: $W = (\Theta_c\mu + \Theta_i)I$ (18)

Employment: $N = [(\Theta_c\mu + \Theta_i)I]/w$ (19)

Relative Sector Size: $(N_c/N_i) = (\Theta_c\mu)/\Theta_i$ (20)

Relative Resource Use: $(N_c/N) = (\Theta_c\mu)/(\Theta_c\mu + \Theta_i)$ (21)

Thus income distribution, the investment level, and the capitalist savings ratio, determine the wage bill; the wage rate must be introduced for the employment level. The relative size of the C- and I-sectors is entirely a resultant of the savings ratio and the facts on relative shares.

Implicit, therefore, is the pricing mechanism through which income distribution in the separate sectors is determined. Hence Keynesian employment and income analysis must be supplemented by a theory of price making and, thereupon, income distribution.[10]

Some Simplifications

In the All and Something analysis some of the important relations can be approximated by assuming $\Theta_c = \Theta_i$, and $\Pi_i = \Pi_c$, and $s_{rc} = s_{ri}$. That is, that the income split in each sector is the same, and that savings out of nonwage income is unrelated to the sector in which profits are earned. Both assumptions are plausible.

On this basis $C = I[(1 - s_r\Pi)/s_r\Pi] = \mu'I$. Thereafter, we could write as approximations:

Wage Bill: $W = I(\Theta/s_r\Pi)$ (18a)

Relative Sector Size: $(N_c/N_i) = \mu'$ (20a)

Relative Resource Use: $(N_c/N) = \mu'/(\mu' + 1)$ (21a)

Thus the wage bill depends wholly on distributive phenomena, the savings ratio, and the investment volume; the employment level entails, in addition, the wage rate. Sector size depends entirely upon distributive phenomena and the savings ratio. A high nonwage share will enlarge the I-sector relative to C, especially if the consumption propensity of the nonwage group is low.

THE "LARGELY AND SOMETHING" HYPOTHESIS

A giant step toward reality follows a "Largely and Something" hypothesis. That is, wage earners are conceived to save something but still, to spend *most* of their income, perhaps 90 per cent of it, on consumption goods and services. While they save 10 per cent of their income, their chief use of income is in consumption outlays. Nonwage earners display opposite income allocation propensities, saving most of their income, spending a smaller part. The full step to reality would involve exact specification of the c- and s-ratios and, of course, the size of income shares.

Profit and Consumption Relations

In the Largely and Something universe we find the following relations:

$$I = S = s_wW + s_rR, \qquad \text{with } s_r > s_w \tag{22}$$

$$C = c_wW + c_rR \qquad \text{with } c_w > c_r \tag{23}$$

$$R_c = c_rR + c_wW_i - s_wW_c = c_rR + W_i - s_w(W_i + W_c). \tag{24}$$

Thus capitalist consumption augments C-profits, and wage earner savings reduce C-profits.[11]

C-*Sector Activity*

Expanding (25) as was done earlier in (8) and (17), we find:

$$P_cQ_c = \frac{c_{wi} + \Pi_i(c_{ri} - c_{wi})}{s_{rc} + \Theta_c(c_{rc} - c_{wc})} I = \frac{c_{wi}(1 - m\Pi_i)}{s_{rc}(1 - n\Theta_c)} I = \nu I. \quad (25)$$

In (25), $m < 1 > n$.

From (25) it follows that a high profit share in the *I*-sector, with a low consumption proclivity for profit recipients, will curtail *C*-sector activity. A high savings propensity for capitalists in the *C*-sector, and a high profit share, spells the same outcome. A high wage share in the consumption sector would lift *C*-activity.

Assuming $m\Pi_i = n\Theta_c$, or that they are *nearly* equal, we have the interesting result that $C = I(c_{wi}/s_{rc})$. That is, that the consumption ratio of workers in capital goods, and the nonwage consumption ratio in the *C*-sector, along with the *I*-magnitude, fix the extent of *C*-activity. This seems to be the major conclusion for the more realistic Largely and Something case.

Employment and Resource Allocation

On the Largely and Something hypothesis:

Wage Bill: $W = I(\Theta_c\nu + \Theta_i) \approx \Theta I(\nu + 1)$ (26)

Relative Sector Size: $(N_c/N_i) = \Theta_c\nu/\Theta_i \approx \nu$ (27)

Relative Resource Use: $(N_c/N) = (\Theta_c\nu)/(\Theta_c\nu + \Theta_i)$

$$\approx \nu/(\nu + 1) \quad (28)$$

The approximations here are based on the supposition of $\Theta_c = \Theta_i$. Adopting the $m\Pi_i = n\Theta_c$ hypothesis, the decisive importance of the c_w/s_r relation emerges.

In sum, savings propensities and relative shares, and the investment volume and the money wage, determine the basic economic phenomena. The price mechanism, through which shares are decided, looms in the background as an arbiter of activity and of the relative size of the *C*- and *I*-sectors: pricing decisions cannot be ignored in determining the macroeconomic variables in view of their impact on distributive shares.

A RECAPITULATION

The several results can be combined for ready reference. The tabular presentation (Table 11.1) indicates the major relations that have been deduced.[12] If we assume $\Theta_c = \Theta_i$ and thus $\Pi_c = \Pi_i$, the Keynesian multipliers yielding $Z \equiv C + I$ emerge simply as:

(1) All and Nothing: $Z = I/\Pi$
(2) All and Something: $Z = I/s_r\Pi$
(3) Largely and Something: $Z = I/(s_w\Theta + s_r\Pi)$

TABLE 11.1

A Recapitulation of Relationships

Variable or Ratio \ Assumption	All and Nothing	All and Something	Largely and Something
(1) Investment and Profits: $I = S =$	R	$s_r R$	$s_w W + s_r R$
(2) C-sector Profits: $R_c = \ldots$	W_i	$W_i + c_r R$	$W_i + c_r R - s_w(W_i + W_c)$
(3) Value of C-output: $C = \ldots$	$W = I(\theta_i/\Pi_c)$	$W + c_r R = \mu I$	$c_w W + c_r R = \nu I$
(4) Wage Bill: $\ldots$	$I(\theta_i/\Pi_c)$	$I(\theta_c\mu + \theta_i)$	$I(\theta_c\nu + \theta_i)$
(5) Employment Structure: $N_c/N_i = \ldots$	(θ_c/Π_c)	$\theta_c\mu/(\theta_c\mu + \theta_i)$	$\theta_c\nu/(\theta_c\nu + \theta_i)$
(6) Relative Size of C-sector: $N_c/N =$	θ_c	$\theta_c\mu/\theta_i$	$\theta_c\nu/\theta_i$

Note: In $(3) - (6)$, $\mu = (1 - s_{ri}\Pi_i)/s_{rc}\Pi_c$ and $\nu = c_{wi}(1 - m\Pi_i)/s_{rc}(1 - n\theta_c)$. Also, $mc_{wi} = c_{wi} - c_{ri}$, and $ns_{rc} = s_{rc} - s_{wc}$.

MONOPOLY, MONETARY POLICY,
THE MONEY WAGE, AND GOVERNMENT

We now consider some further aspects of the economy omitted until now, specifically the influence of: (1) monopoly pricing, (2) monetary policy, (3) money wage changes, and (4) government tax and expenditure policy.

Monopoly Power

Consider, first, the effect of a rise in prices through monopoly pricing and, to begin with, assume that it occurs in the I-sector. It will simplify matters to consider this solely in the Largely and Something model.

We are faced with two alternatives here. We can assume that the money-I level is constant, or that the "real"-I is constant; in the latter event the money-I rises with a rise in monopoly power in the I-sector. To analyze the latter case involves study of two forces, a price force and an incremental money-I force. Hence it is easier, with no loss in generality, to hold money-I constant.

A rise in monopoly power will involve an increase in k_i and, thus, a fall in the wage share Θ_i. Examining (25), this must portend a fall in C-sector activity, as well as a fall in N_i. Thus total employment will be lower, but the fall in money income will be confined to the C-sector by virtue of the hypothesis of money-I unchanged. According to (27), however, the size of the I-sector should shrink by more than C. In the All and Nothing model the relative sector size would not alter while in the All and Something circumstances the C-sector would grow relatively.

A heightened degree of monopoly power in the C-sector, involving a lower wage share there, would, in the All and Nothing world, lower income and employment, and reduce the relative size of C. With All and Something, the wage bill would be reduced in C, employment would fall, and the relative C-size would diminish. In the Largely and Something situation, more or less the same effects follow: employment, wage bill, and the relative C-size would be cut.

A rise in monopoly power always moves us closer to the All and Nothing world in that it shifts income in favor of profit recipients with high savings propensities, and away from workers whose spending ratios are larger. Monopoly power, therefore, whether emanating in the C- or I-industries, requires a higher investment volume to offset its damaging employment consequences. The size of the money-I increment required will be mitigated to the extent that the propensity to consume of nonwage recipients approaches that of wage earners. Insofar as $c_r \to 0$, and $c_w \to 1$, the necessary investment load increases.[13]

Examining the case most vulnerable to unemployment under monopoly pricing tactics, the All and Nothing situation, if initially $\Theta_i = \Pi_c = .5$, and if monopoly pricing shifts the shares to $\Theta_i = .48$ and $\Pi_c = .52$, the effect would be to reduce employment by 1.5 million if $I = \$100$ billions and $w = \$5,000$. Small distributive changes can thus inflict substantial unemployment damage. (See formula (11), above.)

Monetary Mischief

Suppose that either C-sector or I-sector prices go up as a consequence of monopoly power, exemplified by an increase in the k markup. In these circumstances, with money wages constant at w, unless the monetary authority can somehow accomplish a rise in A—the average productivity of labor—any effort on its part to fight inflation will entail sorry consequences for the economy. Tight money to combat inflation—and central banks seem always to be on a nontriumphal crusade against inflation—must operate to cut the I-volume. Yet unemployment engendered by monopoly pricing requires a *greater* investment volume, not a smaller volume of investment. Thus in an economy where monopoly power is increasing, inflation can scarcely be countered by monetary policy.[14] Tighter money can only compound the mischief, and may be disastrous in the final outcome.

Insofar as tight money *cuts* investment, and delays the introduction of cost-saving equipment, it must over time tend to *raise* prices. The only circumstance in which money policy can thus be effective in restraining the price trend—for it is doubtful if in the modern world of rigid wages it is likely to accomplish a price downturn—is by creating enough unemployment to institute some restraint on the money wage upsweep. The consequences on employment may be frightful, especially compared to a policy which has a more direct impact on money wages.[15]

Money Wage Changes

A rigid money wage level has been premised thus far. Assuming that the money wage rises, either exogenously or through Phillips curve relationships as unemployment narrows, the general macroeconomic effects can be traced. First, the price level will be affected, other things unchanged. If the I-sum is unchanged, the only effect is on employment, for the wage level also enters into this relationship. On the other hand, if the I-magnitude changes to reflect the higher prices, and to maintain real investment constant, then C, W and R will also alter. Total money income, comprised of $C + I$, will of course be higher.

Given an increase in the average money wage level w, if prices rise proportionately with wages, and the real output level is unchanged, then the relative increase in profits will equal the relative wage increase.

Higher money wages and a higher sum of money profits, in an economy in which continuing I-outlays are contingent upon realized profits, can have important effects over time on money I, *and on real I*. For in a more realistic setting the higher prices shift income from rentiers to profit recipients, thereby lightening the debt burden. Further, the stock market need not be free of money illusion; higher money profits can affect equity prices disproportionately, thereby influencing the course of real-I in subsequent time intervals.[16]

One further observation on the treatment of money wages as largely an exogenous variable. In the modern economy it is not uncommon for money wages to be fixed ahead by collective bargaining agreements, for one to three year periods. Under these circumstances it is not unreasonable to treat w as settled for the unfolding months according to outside forces, namely, the prevailing contractual agreements.

Government

Government outlays and tax policies have been overlooked. We can indicate briefly how they may be incorporated into the argument.

1. Government, in implementing its programs, buys some goods from the *I*-sector. Insofar as it does so, these purchases belong under the *I*-category as "honorary investment," as D. H. Robertson once termed these outlays.[17]

2. Government hires civil servants and pays them wages (W_g). These aggregate amounts can also be regarded as a form of honorary investment, but *one on which profits are not earned*. The effects of W_g are thus transmitted to the *C*-sector through civil servant consumption intake.

3. Government buys ordinary *C*-goods for its own "household" needs (G_c). It also undertakes transfer payments to an assorted group of income recipients. These sums, too, have a "*C*-multiplier" effect on the *C*-output level analogous to wages in the *I*-sector.

4. Government levies income taxes on wage and profit incomes. Interpreting W and R as *before tax* magnitudes, the effect of income taxes is to reduce the *c*- and *s*-ratios in our formulae for the wage and profit recipients involved.

5. Insofar as Government levies sales and excise taxes, the simplest way to deal with these is to utilize an income concept *net* of such taxes, so that we can still write $\Theta + \Pi = 1$. Otherwise, we have a new income share to contend with, namely that accruing to Government as a sort of monopoly income with proceeds redounding to the Treasury in a 3-way income split.[18]

WAGE EARNERS AND CAPITALISTS?

The personification of income recipients as either wage earners or capitalists has not been evaluated in the foregoing pages.

Undoubtedly, many will feel uncomfortable with the characterization of income recipients as "workers," or wage earners, and "capitalists," or profit recipients. Perhaps the designation was fairly apt not so long ago in England and the United States; it is not accurate now (though it may fit some lesser developed economies).

Largely, the argument could be maintained if the behavior of those receiving both wage *and* profit income was of the nature outlined: that is, if each individual compartmentalized his income into one or the other, and followed one or the other of the behavior patterns outlined.[19] Needless to say, many would reject this as an artificial description of income behavior. Especially serious would be its omission of the corporation as a source of income retention or saving.[20]

On the other hand, it is not implausible to characterize income recipients as belonging to a "low" income group or to a "high" income group, with the former substituted for wage earners in the foregoing analysis, and the latter displacing the profit group. High incomes and low incomes do conform to modern versions of capitalists and wage earners. Further, in recognition that in our economic world a good part of gross business product (netted for excise and sales taxes) adheres to corporate entities and institutions, the latter bodies would have to be counted in the high income group. For through undistributed profits and depreciation allowances, most of the gross savings in our economy—and these are linked to the investment volume—are performed by corporate entities rather than by individuals.[21]

What is the cutoff? How high is a "high" income? A "low" income? Undoubtedly, we are faced with an arbitrary classification, though not necessarily more arbitrary than characterizing individuals as workers or capitalists. For the United States at the present time, a figure of $10,000 of income might serve as the bench mark for classifying individuals and institutions up or down. Whatever the exact height of the income cutoff selected, the analytic apparatus outlined can then be brought into play for macroeconomics.[22]

A RECONCILIATION OF MARGINAL PRODUCTIVITY AND MACRODISTRIBUTION THEORIES?

Possibly, the foregoing pages offer some means of reconciling the older marginal productivity theories of distribution, and the new macro theories promulgated by Mrs. Robinson and Mr. Kaldor. For insofar as the distribution of shares has its origin in the pricing mechanism the door is opened to the older theories. For the k-magnitudes in either the C- or I-sectors will be determined by the forces of competition and monopoly, and the facts on profit maximization. If pure competition and profit maximization hold true for commodity markets, then k will reflect this set of facts as firms equate, at each market price, the marginal value product of labor to the money wage. If monopoly profit maximization occurs, it will be the marginal revenue product relations that will prevail in the firms as they adjust labor's marginal revenue contribution to the money wage. If profit maximization is rejected, this, too, will be reflected in the ruling k-magnitudes.

Simultaneously, the analysis stresses the crucial role of investment, income distribution, and savings propensities in deciding the magnitude of total activity, the C- and I-profit levels, the wage bill, employment, and the relative sector size.

If this reconciliation is rejected by those who hold fast to one view or the other, what could be insisted on is that the theory of price making, and the theory of income distribution, cannot be excluded from macroeconomic models of income determination and employment.

NOTES

1. Nicholas Kaldor, "Alternative Theories of Distribution," *The Review of Economic Studies,* 1955–56; *idem,* "Economic Growth and Inflation"; *idem,* "A Rejoinder to Mr. Findlay," *The Review of Economic Studies,* 1959–60; *idem,* "Marginal Productivity and the Macro-Economic Theories of Distribution, Comment on Samuelson and Modigliani," *ibid.,* 1966; *idem,* with James A. Mirrlees, "A New Model of Economic Growth," *ibid.,* 1961–62; Luigi L. Pasinetti, "Rate of Profit and Income Distribution in Relation to the Rate of Economic Growth," *ibid.;* "New Results in an Old Framework," *ibid.,* 1966; Joan Robinson, "Comment on Samuelson and Modigliani," *ibid,* 1966 and

Collected Economic Papers, Vol. 2 (Oxford: the University Press, 1960).

2. Their arguments are very general. They dispense with assumptions of linear and homogeneous production functions, or of factor divisibility or homogeneity, long the bane of capital theory. The analysis is independent of the assumption of profit maximization, the supposition of pure competition, or of the need for identification of the elusive entrepreneur for the attribution of profits. See Kaldor, "Marginal Productivity," p. 309.

3. Cf. Lawrence Klein's remarks on "the need to close the system by extending it in such a way that the price level is explained." Lawrence R. Klein, *The Keynesian Revolution,* pp. 194, 217ff.

4. In my own experience, when I came to write on this subject over ten years ago, I was unable to find any significant guidance in the macroeconomic literature. See my *Approach to the Theory of Income Distribution.* For some recognition of the problem see K. R. Boulding, *Reconstruction of Economics,* Chap. 14.

5. The markup $k_i = (1 + R/wN) = 1/\theta_i$.

6. Kaldor avoided this in his earlier article by *assuming* full employment or, thus, a predetermined income level. Considering the income and employment variability of Keynesian analysis, this is too restrictive a hypothesis. See Kaldor, "Alternative Theories of Distribution," p. 95. As Mrs. Robinson remarked (*Collected Economic Papers,* Vol. 2, p. 149): "The proposition that the share of profits in income is a function of the ratio of investment to income is perfectly correct, but capacity and the degree of monopoly have to be brought in to determine what income it is that profits are a share of, and investment is a ratio to."

7. As Kaldor remarks, the Keynesian revolution was substantially one of recognizing the dominating position of investment. Thus he writes: "Keynes's theory of income generation—which can be summed up by saying . . . that it is investment which determines savings, and not savings which determine investment—was the really novel feature of his *General Theory.*" Kaldor, "Economic Growth," p. 214. Also: *idem* and Mirrlees, "A New Model," p. 175. Kaldor, "Marginal Productivity," p. 312n.

8. The derivation of (8) should be obvious: the expenditure of W_i leads to a "multiplier" chain of additional income and wage-earner consumption outlay in the C-sector.

9. The terms in (8) and (17), exclusive of I, might be called a

"truncated" multiplier, for unlike the Kahn-Keynes multiplier, it includes only the income chain in the C-sector, rather than the entire income chain in C *and* I.

10. Cf. Klein, *Keynesian Revolution,* pp. 217ff.

11. It is from relation (22) that Kaldor derives his well-known formula for the profit share, namely, that:

$$(R/Y) = [1/(s_r - s_w)][I/Y] - [s_w/(s_r - s_w)]$$

where Y, in Kaldor's formulation, denotes full employment income. Thus Kaldor is assuming that not only is I given but that C is predetermined, independently of pricing and the income split in the C-sector. Treating Y as a variable requires the theory of the "truncated" C-sector multiplier as in (8), (17), or (25). Cf. Kaldor, "Alternative Theories of Distribution," p. 95.

12. The profit share Π ($\equiv R/Z$) can be formed from $I = R$, $I = s_r R$, and $I = s_w W + s_r R$ on line (1) by dividing through by Z, and transposing the W- and s-terms. For the rate of profit (R/K), where K denotes the value of capital, the same equations can be used. These are the important results emphasized by Professors Kaldor and Robinson.

13. Analytically, with $I = \bar{I}$ so the money-I level is maintained, monopoly power in the I-sector will lower W_i, and thus the numerator of our "truncated"-C multipliers by an amount $\Delta R_i(c_{wi} - c_{ri})$, where $\Delta R_i = w\Delta N_i$. Monopoly in the consumer sector will lower Θ_c to $\lambda\Theta_c$, where $\lambda < 1$, and raise Π_c to $\epsilon\Pi_c$, where $\epsilon > 1$. All the formulae can be modified in this way.

14. On all this, see the valuable recent analysis of Abba P. Lerner, "Employment Theory and Employment Policy," *The American Economic Review,* 1967.

15. Thus if an incomes policy could command a fair degree of assent, keeping government intervention to a minimum, it would be far more instrumental for inflation control than the clumsy maneuvers in monetary policy which always tend to have a negative output-employment incidence.

16. Cf. my *Employment Growth and Income Distribution,* Chap. 9. Kaldor observes ("Economic Growth," p. 290) that "a slow and steady rate of inflation provides a most powerful aid to the attainment of a steady rate of economic progress." On "inflation breeding inflation" through shifting Phillips curves as a price level rise is anticipated, see Edmund S. Phelps, "Phillips Curves, Expectations of Inflation and Optimal Unemployment Over Time," *Economica,* 1967.

17. D. H. Robertson, "Mr. Clark and the Foreign Trade Multiplier," *Economic Journal*, 1939, p. 354, n. 3.

18. On excise taxes likened to "monopoly" price, with the Treasury as the beneficiary of the higher price, see Joan Robinson. *The Economics of Imperfect Competition* (London: Macmillan Co., 1933), p. 164. Writing C_{net} to refer to C-output net of excise taxes, and I_{p+g} to denote private and Government I-outlays, with c' and s' to represent the ratios after income taxes, for the "Largely and Something" case we have:

$$C_{net} = \frac{(c'_{wi}\Theta_i + c'_{ri}\Pi_i)I_{p+g} + c'_g W_g + G_c}{s'_{wc}\Theta_c + s'_{rc}\Pi_c}. \qquad (29)$$

19. Pasinetti ("Rate of Profit and Income Distribution," p. 273) comes near to saying this in the remark that "savings out of wages always turn out to be equal to workers' extra consumption out of profits."

20. Working wholly in terms of *personal* income, by wage or non-wage types, Burmeister and Taubman find "that s_r is twice the size of s_w," in the 10–17 per cent and 23–30 per cent range respectively. See Edwin Burmeister and Paul Taubman, "Labor and Non-Labor Income-Saving Propensities," *The Canadian Journal of Economics* (1970). For the "low-high" income classification suggested, these figures would probably be too high for the low-income group, and too low for the high-income part of the total.

21. For example, in the United States in 1967, personal savings amounted to $40.2 billions, capital consumption allowances were $69.2 billions, and undistributed profits were $25.2 billions. Thus even if all personal savings were performed by wage earners, 70 per cent of the total gross savings would have been contributed by corporate entities. The latter are the modern "capitalists." See *Survey of Current Business*, August 1968.

22. This approach would have the further advantage of aligning macroeconomics with the theory of personal (rather than functional) distribution where good data are available. The c- and s-ratios would have to be computed as averages for the aggregate of total income by each "group." For the corporate gross income consisting entirely of undistributed profits before taxes and depreciation allowances, the savings ratio would be unity. This would apply to a share (in gross business production in 1967) as large as 19 per cent of total business sector income.

12 Marginal Productivity and Macrodistribution Theory

It may be time to acknowledge the Kaldor-Kalecki-Robinson revolution in distribution theory.[1] If the new order prevails it will be because of extra insights conferred by the new approach, compared to some formidable obstacles for marginal productivity theory (*MPT*), which Bronfenbrenner has termed the Good Old Theory.[2] Some account of the issues is in order.

To evade the complexities of growth theory it will be assumed generally that investment takes place with a gestation period beyond the current interval so that the new capital goods are not engaged in immediate consumption (*C*) or investment (*I*) output. Staying within the Marshallian short period puts the best complexion on marginal productivity reasoning. Marshall, to be sure, expounded the principles not so much as a theory of distribution but as a means of exploring significant phenomena at the equilibrium margin. Later theory abandoned his caution on this.[3]

For J. B. Clark the *MPT* also contained some agreeable ethical overtones.[4] While they will not be pressed here some sociopolitical implications of distributive theory are inescapable.

Reference will be made to relative shares, especially the wage share. The implicit income concept is that of gross business product (*GBP*), for the economist's explanations generally pertain to the enterprise sector of the economy.[5]

SOME COMPLICATIONS FOR
MARGINAL PRODUCTIVITY THEORY

A theory of macrodistribution should illuminate: (a) movements in real wages; (b) income shifts as the size of the employed and unemployed groups vary; (c) relative wage and nonwage shares; (d) the absolute profit magnitude and the rate of return; and (e) any rentier-profit reshuffle.

Judged by the needs of theory, as the purpose here is not to praise but to condemn the *MPT,* a catalog of shortcomings follows. Bias will be apparent; but it comes only after having attempted to preserve the *MPT.*

Distributive Feedbacks

Keynes's theory has largely been transformed (by Keynesians) into an output (Q) or employment (N) theory.[6] Price level (P-theory) aspects implicit in Keynes's decision to work in terms of wage units have been virtually suppressed. The Q and N variations are ordered by shifts in the C and I functions, and in the liquidity function and money supply.

Suppose that in the usual macromodel $\Delta Q > 0 < \Delta N$. In the final outcome there is the prediction that under pure competition, following the static law of diminishing returns, the real wage will fall. For the theory of relative shares, however, the a priori *MPT* becomes vague, for the wage share depends on variations in the MP/AP ratio of marginal to average product of (homogeneous) labor.[7] That MP declines in the N advance discloses nothing about the ratio without embedding some special empirical assumptions: the absolute real-wage bill may even fall under sharply diminishing returns.[8] Labor's total share may thus be jeopardized—a possibility rarely mentioned.

While the theory is informative on real-wages it omits the feedback influences running from income distribution itself, and affecting the actual size of the ΔN variation in the comparative macrostatic theory. To take a simple case, suppose investment outlay (at constant prices) increases while interest rates are firm. Then:

$$\Delta Q = \Delta I / (s_w \Theta + s_r \Pi), \tag{1}$$

where the s-terms denote the average propensity to save of wage and nonwage earners, and Θ and Π are the respective wage and nonwage shares.

Clearly, a higher wage share and a lower savings propensity for labor will enlarge the "multiplier" and the real output expansion, thereby affecting the real-wage and, possibly, relative shares. The repercussions from shares and separate savings propensities have been overlooked in the Old Theory. Income distribution itself is thus a determinant of the MP relationship. As Marshall was wont to say, MPT does not provide a full explanation of distributive phenomena; by their own spending behavior income recipients are able to influence their own real income, shares, and the employment volume.

Consumer Sector Productivity

Although the MPT seems so sure-footed in its prediction for the course of real-wages in the competitive model, the significance of the Pigovian "wage-good" has frequently been ignored in the comparative statics covering a Keynesian Q-variation.

Sometimes the MPT visualizes the economy as a gigantic farm or factory harvesting a unique (composite) good: this is implicit in the contemporary recourse to Cobb-Douglas functions.[9] Of course, the forced homogeneity must yield *some* invalid answers. In a conventional two sector C and I model, an increase in I must, through the "multiplier," advance C-output. But if labor bargains for real wages, the facility with which investment can banish unemployment and minimize voluntary unemployment depends on the supply elasticity of "wage-goods" and the consumption ratios of income recipients. The course of declining marginal productivity curves in individual firms, on the other hand, can influence only the maximum profit adaptations: aggregate employment is not merely dependent on the course of "the" MP curve. Cobb-Douglas functions have oversimplified the analysis to the point of eliminating vital considerations.

The issue is not without relevance for underdeveloped economies differing in the size and extent of ostentatious capitalist consumption. Implicit are aspects of relative shares—an MPT weakness—and the dependence of labor supplies on real-wages. Analogous complications perplexed Ricardo and Pigou: the Sraffa-

Robinson writings also wrestle with these vital matters.[10] They have become lost somewhere in the n-firm general equilibrium theories which focus on maximum profit–marginal productivity relations.

"Wage-Goods" and Luxury Consumption

To follow on, suppose we subdivide $C = C_w + C_r$ on the supposition that distinct goods cater to each income class, with wage earners absorbing "wage-goods" and nonwage recipients deflected (mainly) to luxury items, perhaps overpriced through monopoly presence so that resource use is not commensurate to relative consumption outlay.

The greater the differentiation in the respective commodity bundles the less significant are diminishing returns as an employment barrier: the real-wage will hold up better in a ΔN expansion especially if productivity is advancing in the C_w sector. Involuntary unemployment is thus even more costly and irksome than when the consumption bundles are more nearly alike. Soirees and safaris, mink coats and motor boats, do not compete with wage earner meat and beer. Ordinary MPT thinking misses this facet in treating C-output as homogeneous.

Distributive theory is thus linked to the sociology of income classes, as Veblen understood long ago in stressing the structure of tastes. Earlier, for Malthus, luxury outlay sustained employment as a form of abortive investment which facilitated a higher utility-disutility balance than if the same outlays were deflected to wage-goods.[11]

Monopoly and Oligopoly

Monopoly and oligopoly erect almost insuperable barriers to a determinate MPT; at a minimum they preclude any pretense of a simple theory.

On profit maximization criteria we can equate marginal revenue products to factor prices so that $\epsilon MP/AP$, with $1 > \epsilon > 0$, thereby inhibiting the wage share. Unfortunately, even in the most determinate case we can say nothing about real-wages and relative shares without information on ϵ, the degree of monopoly power interpreted as the reciprocal of some generalized elasticity of demand. To confound matters, how ϵ moves in a Q and N advance is still obscure: there is the Harrod view of a diminishing elasticity of demand as real income rises, and the Kalecki position that monopoly practices are intensified in a slump.[12] Empirical evidence is lacking; the problem has been blotted out despite more facts on the economy and stronger techniques to distill meaning from them.

Under monopoly and oligopoly our confidence in the validity of the short or long run profit hypothesis has always been tempered: vagueness on the magnitude of monopoly power follows, to unsettle the good old theory.

More damaging still to the theory, even if the degree of monopoly power were isolated, is the fact that the commodity bundle under monopoly differs from that under pure competition. Index number problems obtrude to taint any *MPT* illumination on welfare significance: how compare different shares of different commodities?

The complexities of monopoly cumulate further in that the final degree of monopoly power also depends on the degree of vertical integration in the system, with monopoly and monopsony contributing to the separation of production phases. In the competitive model the degree of integration is quite incidental.[13] Integration may even *reduce* monopoly power compared to n-stage monopoly. Under monopoly, sales outlays also enter the model, with a new income claimant in the advertising field, with puzzling short and long run distributive incidence. Some imitative cross advertising cancels demand effects but influences the income configuration. Advertising also undermines the comfortable rationalization of resources pliantly adapted to consumer tastes in a regime of consumer sovereignty; where profitable, tastes are directed toward favoring products that firms are intent on producing. Astride the entire conception of the process is the fact that sales outlays support all the communications media, with inevitable distributive effects emanating from the sociological, political, and economic power thereby amassed and wielded.

How the distributive consequences are unraveled by the *MPT* remains obscure, for little attention has been given to the formal dimensions of the problem since some of the elements of the monopoly problem were spotted by Chamberlin a generation back.

Product Variation and Technical Change

In the same vein it would be good to have some consideration of the distributive consequences of the Chamberlinian product variations which impart a dynamism to the system even in conditions of "given" tastes and productivity. Real income and well-being are affected by efforts of firms to improve their market position; distributional changes must result from this despite their neglect in models which stipulate an unchanging array of *m*-products.

Technical progress is generally assigned most weight in enhancing real wages though Mrs. Robinson has rendered respectable the uncommon view that real-wages influence the search for techniques to maintain or improve the capitalist share. Neither the finely competitive model nor the minor monopoly-oligopoly departures prepare us for predicting the distributive influences of technical change; at best we have definitions of "Harrod-neutral" and "Hicks-neutral." They permit us to be wise in explanation, *ex post*, but *ex ante* all seems obscure.

Institutional Elements and Services

Overlooked so far is some indeterminacy, even for the competitive model, inherent in the production function concept. In the elemental macromodel where the valuation of capital stock does not plague us, we are still not home free by simply writing $Q = Q(N)$.

First, how well has labor been fed? What is the state of its health, education, training? Supervision? Hiring bias? Morale? How much real income does labor expect in the short and longer run from its work participation? What are the laws regulating work practices? Also, in a ΔN expansion do new organizational and specialization possibilities emerge: is there some "learning by doing"?

All of these matters have been noted by institutional economists, efficiency experts, or in the context of X-efficiency. The ideas compromise production function and MPT approaches, which maintain a calm facade despite the implication of a theory consistent with a range of outcomes rather than with a unique result. Excluded, too, are the long-run arguments of Mrs. Robinson, that higher real-wages, by influencing capital formation, affect productivity rather than the other way about, of productivity determining real-wages.[14]

The various points may be accepted as providing some necessary supplements or background specifications for the MPT; in some respects this may be admissible. But when one assays the possible applicability of the theory it becomes very apparent that a good part of the labor force cannot be identified with any tangible output, as the good old theory presumes: no stretching and forcing can preserve the theory intact.

What is the marginal productivity of an economist? Keynes? A college president? A baseball player, golfer, tennis pro? A State Department employee, or soldier or general?

There is no need to extend the list. In some cases some support might be found for the theory, though utility theory might generally afford a better explanation. As direct consumer services grow relatively, the MPT may be left with memories of that past day dominated by agriculture and rural life.

Heterogeneous Capital and Reswitching

The end of the controversy on capital measurement means the demise of the J. B. Clark notion of homogeneous capital and the imputation of a unique marginal product to capital.[15] MPT can never be quite so simple again.

The "switching" controversy contributes another dimension of indeterminateness: a lower rate of interest may promote *or* retard more capital-using techniques so that the effect of interest rate variations on income shares becomes theoretically vague.[16] *MPT* must teach that anything can happen—a scientifically nihilistic insight.

Government

Along the march to the welfare state, government expenditures and tax revenues must have profound distributive consequences. Their variety and magnitude influence, globally, resource use, commodity varieties and quantities, and the output and employment level. The progressivity of the income tax has ramifications for income shares and real earnings. The pervasive influence of the State cannot be omitted from distributive theory without reducing it in scope and relevance.

Indivisibilities

Indivisible items have long posed a hard test for *MPT*, itself regarded as an exercise in the differential calculus. Capital formation invokes concepts of marginal efficiency; *ex post* installation imputation constitutes the essence of quasi rents. Whether the lumpy items of equipment exist in contemplation or in actual use their productivity contribution depends substantially on the precise mode of variation in conjunction with other discrete factors.

As the production process becomes more robotlike, with limited substitution of component pieces and heterogeneity in the set of machines used by the firm, the more hopeless it becomes to impute separable productivities to each element. As Mrs. Robinson long ago remarked (following Gerald Shove), with heterogeneous lumpy factors resource organization resembles a complicated jigsaw puzzle, whose marginal productivity distributive pieces may never match.[17]

Price Levels and Forced Savings

There may be some solace in a reproach to both old and new theories in that neither has integrated the distributive effects of inflation into the main corpus of analysis, though there are banalities aplenty in the Old Theory on inflation aiding creditors and injuring debtors.

Inflation now covers the last forty years; we should not have to wait longer before the distributive consequences occupy a prominent place in the exposition of the theory of shares and real income.

In some theories (such as my own) the wage share and the money wage relative to output per head dominate the inflation analysis so that distribution and inflation are not really separated.[18] Inflations, though, can have many shades: there can be rising profits and prices, with money wages constant, or money wages and prices in step, or money wages moving disproportionately as in recent years. Distributive implications, of course, differ. By dropping the unrealistic labor homogeneity hypothesis the door is opened to the important shifts among wage earning groups as well as between wage and nonwage incomes. Distributional and allocational aspects abound.

The venerable concept of forced-savings, referring to the decline of real consumption of fixed income groups when prices rise, also finds its niche in the inflation analysis. It is properly supplanted by a more generic concept of forced real income changes.

There are those who sometimes say, privately though properly reticent publicly, that inflation does not matter, that its distributional consequences can either be disregarded or corrected by public policy. It would be interesting to have this in print, that distributional inequities are beneath notice by economists, or to read the ingenious proposals of how to "correct" for the distributive inroads. The writing might add another chapter in useless economics.[19]

Factor Payments: The MPT Evisceration of Profits

In any realistic account of the economic process we are compelled to distinguish between *MPT* as a theory, at best, of imputational significance as compared to the facts of income payments: the association may be tenuous.

For productivity imputations there are really only two productive agents, personal labor services and the services of instruments, whether land or equipment. Distributive payments, however, emanate out of the contractual arrangements between entrepreneurs who organize resource use and resource owners. At a minimum three income *payment* categories must be recognized: for personal services, for the use of money or things, and a residual of "gross" profits accruing to the firm for which the contractual decisions for the other services are made. Without this classification marginal productivity theory is bereft of a theory of profits so that, in describing income division under capitalism, it has effectively eliminated the unique profit component which distinguishes capitalistic institutions for resource organization from socialist counterparts.

Marginal productivity theory can, of course, cover the contractual phenomena in some summing up of its relevance. Unfortunately, this stage is generally forgotten, with the result that *MPT* has severed its institutional linkage. The eagerness to display the parallel imputational forces in all social orders is an exercise in analytic depth which obscures the income process under which we happen to live.

Derived Demand

Coloring *MPT* thinking is the theory of derived demand. Jevons, Walras, Menger, and then Marshall, hailed this as the big departure from the classical argument that costs determined prices. For the revolutionaries of the 1870s, it was the demand for products that conferred importance on factors of production capable of producing goods: factor costs were incurred because goods had value, not the other way around. Marshall's demand for knives, and the derived demand for blades and handles, has been a sturdy *MPT* pillar since then.

Once we take money wages as (at least partly) exogenous the theory of derived demand must be revised. Changes in money wages shift both cost curves *and* demand curves in consumer markets; it is mischievous to assume consumer demand curves unchanged despite movements in money wages. The frequent assumption that product demand curves hold rigid or, even worse, that market prices are constant, in deriving the demand curve for a factor of production—for labor, say—is an error that distorts our views on public policy: it commits us to the untenable position that changes in money wage lift the cost curves but are devoid of any demand significance. This *cannot* be correct. Further, it perpetrates the widespread confusion that monetary policy has its primary effect on product prices and then, after some lag, on money wages, rather than on employment immediately and money wages not at all.

While real wages are arbited in the full economic process, and "real" consumer demand curves may shift only slightly or not at all after a money wage change, it cannot be that market demand curves or cost curves, reflecting money outlays at money prices, are unchanged after the money wage rise. On this, despite Keynes's despair some thirty-six years ago, and some comments of my own fourteen years ago, our textbooks and journal articles perpetuate the confusion, as if stale repetition will validate it.[20] If the defense is that the analysis is conducted in real terms (in constant dollars), then it has little direct bearing on market price phenomena. If it is intended to apply to market phenomena and price determination, then it is guilty of evading the interdependence of cost and demand facts.

THE NEW MACRODISTRIBUTIVE THEORIES

Regardless of the ultimate fate of the good old theory it is doubtful if we will want to dispense with the insights gleaned from the new work. The implications for macroeconomics are substantial; distributive elements help shape the outcome but are also themselves governed by the macro determinants. The distribution of property ownership and the decisions of the corporation—institutional phenomena both—assume a new and more realistic prominence in the theory.

First, for the price level we can write $P = (kw/A) = w/\circledcirc A$, where k is average markup of prices over unit labor costs or the reciprocal of the wage share $\circledcirc$, with w the average money wage and A output per employee. The constancy of the wage share ($\odot$) assures that prices will rise whenever money wages forge ahead faster than average productivity.

Kaldor has argued that under full employment and in the "capitalists mainly save, wage earners wholly spend" situation, the profit share is contingent upon the investment level and capitalists' savings propensity.[21]

It is possible, instead, to argue that the wage share is decided in the pricing process, that it is the resultant of the price-making decisions of firms. Further, if savings ratios differ among wage and nonwage earners, this can only be attributable to inequalities in initial wealth positions. Realistically, if we are to emphasize savings attributes then the vital distinction is between wage earners, or personal income recipients generally, and the corporation, for the latter is the vehicle for pricing and the major instrumentality for gross savings as the offset of income disposal to gross investment. A theory that overlooks the corporation scarcely comprehends our market economy. Though the fact itself is so obvious it is a virtue of the new theories to insist on including the corporation, and it is a defect of *MPT* that it argues as if landlords and farm workers were alone involved. The corporation can seldom be offstage in the distributive process. Its price making, its withholdings, and its investment decisions practically dominate the distributive mechanism, and the macro magnitudes. It should be obligatory for marginal productivity theory to explain the impact of the corporation on income division rather than viewing it as a mere transmission belt without an impact of its own.

Of course, neither the theory of price making, nor the stress on savings ratios and the investment volume, really prepares us for explaining the reported "near-constancy" of the wage share. A theory is ordinarily invoked to explain change, not constancy; an explanation is fairly superfluous unless we seek to alter the income division. The fascinating issue that begs explanation is, rather, how did the wage share in the United States become stuck at approximately one-half of the *GBP* and absorb the momentous economic, social, and political changes in this century?

Mrs. Robinson has employed the "wage earner spends—capitalists save" thesis to open up some new vistas for profit theory. Writing the linear consumption function:

$$C = \alpha w N, \qquad (2)$$

on the Robinson hypothesis, $\alpha = 1$. In the United States in recent years consumption expenditures have approximated 1.05 of the wage bill (= compensation of employees). Currently, the surmise of $\alpha = 1$ is thus not too wide of the mark, at least for opening up the analysis.[22] For other countries the estimate may be even better, especially if the wage earning class is large and the consumption of capitalists comprises a very minor part of the total. The unity approximation for the United States implies that the taxes and savings out of wages and salaries are slightly over-compensated by nonwage consumption, which includes not only capitalists but transfer recipients.

From (2), if employment movements are limited, as they are from month to month, or even over the annual period, movements in money wages control consumer outlay. Cost-push inflation is simultaneously demand-pull inflation in consumer markets; this would not be worth mentioning if it were not so often overlooked. Reality is advanced by (2) compared to the obfuscation emanating from discussions of "the" consumption function as if wages and wage earners had only some nebulous connection to phenomena in consumer markets.

For the average propensity to consume, and for relative sector size:

$$(C/Y) = \alpha\Theta. \qquad (3)$$

The wage share is crucial in determining this important ratio.

From (2), if $\Delta w = \Delta\alpha = 0$, the marginal propensity to consume is simply $\alpha w \Delta N$, with the money wage decisive in governing the slope of the consumer outlay function.

For the *average* multiplier:

$$Y = I'/(1 - \alpha\Theta), \text{ where } I' = I + G. \qquad (4)$$

The wage share is again prominent in deciding the income aggregate accompanying the I' outlay. If $\Delta\Theta = \Delta\alpha = 0$, the marginal multiplier accompanying any $\Delta I'$ will coincide with the average multiplier.

For consumer sector profits (R_c):

$$R_c = \alpha\Theta[wN(\alpha - 1) + I'], \qquad (5)$$

so that with $\alpha = 1$, then:

$$R_c = \Theta I'. \qquad (6)$$

Total profits (R), if $\alpha = 1$ and sector income division is uniform, is:

$$R = I + \Theta G. \qquad (7)$$

The wage bill, with $\alpha = 1$, is equal to $\Theta I'/\pi$, where $\pi =$ the profit share. Employment requires the insertion of w, the average wage, into the denominator. If $\Theta = \pi$, as is "nearly" the case in United States GBP data, the relations are simplified further.

CONCLUSION

The formulae reveal that the new theories are capable of accomplishing some new understanding, on income distribution in the macroeconomic process, and on the determinants and the quantification of profits. Supplanted are commonplaces on "normal" profits and the demand and supply of entrepreneurial effort. Price-making and monopoly practices have obvious influences on income shares. The theory, in the light of its simplifications, imparts a good deal of the "truth," though not the whole truth. One can argue that this is the function of good theory, to unravel the major ingredients of a problem.

Predictably, there will be the usual protests that the new results emanate from truisms. This is a good place at which to close, amid some bafflement on how ideas can be otherwise derived. Mathematicians, who also pride themselves on being logicians, seem not to raise this issue. But then, of course, they are not economists.

NOTES

1. A partial bibliography would include: Nicholas Kaldor, "Alternative Theories of Distribution," *Review of Economic Studies,* 1955–56, and "Marginal Productivity and the Macro-Economic Theories of Distribution," *ibid.,* 1966; L. L. Pasinetti, "Rate of Profit and Income Distribution in Relation to the Rate of Economic Growth," *ibid.,* 1962, and "New Results in an Old Framework," *ibid.,* 1966; Joan Robinson, "Comment on Samuelson and Modigliani," *ibid.,* 1966; also, *Economic Heresies,* and *Accumulation;* M. Kalecki, *Essays in the Theory of Economic Fluctuations;* P. Garegnani, "Heterogeneous Capital."

2. Martin Bronfenbrenner, *Income Distribution Theory,* pp. 407–8.

3. Marshall wrote:

The part played by the net product at the margin of production in the modern doctrine of Distribution is apt to be misunderstood. In particular many able writers have supposed that it represents the marginal use of a thing as governing the value of the whole. It is not so; the doctrine says we must *go to the margin to study the action of those forces which govern* the value of the whole: and that is a very different affair.

See Alfred Marshall, *Principles of Economics,* p. 410, italics in original; also see p. 518.

4. In the very first sentence to the preface of his work Clark wrote:

It is the purpose of this work to show that the distribution of the income of society is controlled by a natural law, and that this law, if it worked without friction, would give to every agent of production the amount of wealth which that agent creates.

See J. B. Clark, *The Distribution of Wealth* (New York: The Macmillan Co. (1899), p. v.

5. For some evidence on the limited variability of the wage share, see my *Wage Theory and Policy* (1963), Chaps. 3, 4.

6. For discussion, see Chapter 1 above.

7. Cf. my *Approach to the Theory of Income Distribution,* p. 51.

8. *Ibid.,* pp. 61–62. This result can be derived from the smooth bell-shaped curves often drawn in price theory textbooks.

9. Theorizing from aggregate production functions must come in for revision in the light of F. M. Fisher's work. See his "Aggregate Production Functions and the Explanation of Wages."

10. A. C. Pigou, *The Theory of Unemployment,* p. 21f.; Piero Sraffa,

Production of Commodities by Means of Commodities (1960); Joan Robinson, *Economic Heresies.*

11. T. R. Malthus, *Principles of Political Economy* (1836), p. 398.

12. See my *Approach,* pp. 66–68.

13. *Ibid.,* pp. 71–75.

14. Joan Robinson, *Accumulation,* p. 130.

15. Joan Robinson, "The Measure of Capital."

16. Cf. P. Garegnani, "Switching of Techniques," and L. Pasinetti, "Changes in the Rate of Profit and Switches of Techniques," *Quarterly Journal of Economics,* November 1966.

17. Joan Robinson, *Economics of Imperfect Competition,* p. 107.

18. Cf. A. P. Lerner, "Employment Theory and Employment Policy," and Chapters 1 and 11 above.

19. I have heard this view expressed privately and in some newspaper reports of talks by economists. It seems to be confined to some Keynesians who simply appear unable to comprehend inflation with unemployment and, obviously, are without any plan for coping with the phenomena.

20. Cf. Chapter 4 above.

21. Kaldor, "Alternative Theories," p. 97.

22. Since 1949 the highest figure for α was 1.25 in that year. Thereafter it has descended closer to a unity value. Between 1960 and 1968 it fell from 1.105 to 1.045. Over the full period 1949–68 the average was 1.117 with an average deviation of 0.014. (I am indebted to Hamid Habibagahi for the calculations.)

13 Rising Demand Curves in Price Level Theory *

Geometry still retains some persuasive power in economics; usually the same underlying ideas permeate the more general mathematical models. It appears, however, that contrary to a fairly common practice the demand curve proper for consumer price level theory can run partly the "wrong way," rising from left to right, rather than following the normal "law" of price theory.[1] It thus partakes a "Giffen" form with its slope strongly contingent on the elasticity of supply. The analysis carries some overtones for policy as well as for theory.

Characteristics of the Model

Modelwise, what is posited is a money supply response that is accommodating to: (1) the wage level (w), and (2) the output (Q) and employment (N) level, while (3) through the combined play of money and fiscal policy nonconsumption sector incomes are held firm. Consequences of abandoning these assumptions will be alluded to, briefly.

That money supplies do in fact vary positively with w, Q, and N provides ample warrant for hypotheses (1) and (2) despite the more usual model stipulation of a constant money supply. Assumption (3) serves merely to restrict the study to the consumption subsector of the system. Still, despite the partly perverse demand curve uncovered, the stability of equilibrium need not be

* I have benefitted from comments by Paul Davidson, Hamid Habibagahi, and E. R. Weintraub on an earlier version of this paper.

threatened. In a way the analysis is linked to what the late Oscar Lange once described as a *"negative" monetary effect* with destabilizing overtones; Lange interpreted traditional theory to involve a constant money supply, while observing that "if the nominal quantity of money . . . increases in the same proportion as or in greater proportion than prices" (and output?), then "the conclusion of traditional theory [does] not apply." [2]

To pursue the Lange trail would lead us beyond the consumer market to the full system, opening up a bag of perplexing issues· in a labor–capital growth context under varying money wages. Our aim is more modest and the case more nearly static; even under these restrictions the model conveys a possible source of dynamic mischief under plausible monetary patterns.

The Prevailing Geometry and Analysis

In the price level diagrammatics the axes must refer to some index of prices and of output. In the prevailing accounts the concept of a "composite good" (real output) is usually injected as if all the diverse productions moved uniformly; accepting this fiction the index number complications are bypassed. Undoubtedly, it is better to work with at least a two-sector model, involving both consumer goods and capital goods; for consumer demand is subject to the income constraint, while, for investment goods, this bind is relaxed—unless it is stipulated that money supplies are rigidly controlled and total activity is thereby constrained.

The subsequent argument will thus interpret Figure 13.1 as applying to the *consumer* price level. This is not an unreasonable restriction on the analysis, for even in the United States consumer output comprises 60–65 per cent of the *GNP*. The ratio would often be larger in other countries.

The Demand Curve

The demand curve in Figure 13.1 has been drawn as highly inflexible over most of its course except in the nether regions. A

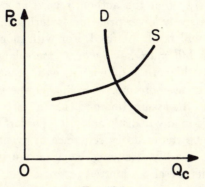

Fig. 13.1

concise explanation of its path appears in the valuable survey article by Bronfenbrenner-Holzman. They state: "Aggregate demand curves D are drawn downward. This slope illustrates Patinkin real-balance effects with a constant nominal money supply and static price expectations." [3]

Patinkin, in developing a comparable demand curve, also assumes that the money supply is fixed and money income is also specified. In his "mental experiment" to display the potency of the real-balance effect he assumes that "the absolute level of money prices is, say, lower" where "during the *tâtonnement,* all commodities can be considered as a single composite good with the price p." [4]

Issues in Assumptions

Perhaps this suffices to set the theoretical basis of the D-curve in Figure 13.1. Money supply and money income are constant *despite output variations in the consumer goods sector* involving movements along the supply curve.

But this is a dubious hypothesis in macro theory where supply and demand functions are interdependent, so that if there is an output variation along a supply curve, there must generally be a money income variation and thus a demand impact. As we move rightward along the horizontal axis, with the rise in output (and employment) that the authors regard as being "demand-priced" at successively lower price levels during the *tâtonnement,* money income will rarely be fixed. For with money wages constant, *the wage bill must be higher* as more labor is hired for more output. With more employment, entrepreneurs will go to the banks to borrow more money to finance the greater production flow, so that the assumption of a "given" money supply must be contradicted—in any realistic analysis.[5] For large output movements this will be the ordinary sequence of events.

Money wage rigidity has long been recognized. Exogenous wage movements are also admitted in this era of "cost-push" inflation and the entry of incomes policy into the arsenal of inflation control. There is thus good warrant to consider the price level outcome in terms of constant (or rising) money wages as output advances. Manifestly, the attitude with respect to money wages also affects the construction of the supply curve.

The C-sector Supply Function

Clearly, the *D–S* curves of price level theory are not mere macro blow-ups of micro tracings: their supporting base is substantively different. We consider first the less controversial supply function.

The Aggregate C-sector Supply Function

All expositors lean heavily on Marshallian-type industry supply curves. While references to the *S*-curve in Figure 13.1 brand it as an "aggregate" supply function, Keynes reserved this modifier for a function denoting *total* factor outlays for a price–output set, and not for the average cost outlays (or supply price) at the given output level. An extended nomenclature may dispel minor confusion in reference.

For Keynes, "aggregate supply" (Z) was a function of employment (N), with the wage rate (w), the stock of equipment, and the degree of competition stipulated. In terms of factor payments, the Z-function can be defined as: [6]

$$CAS \equiv [Z \equiv \Sigma PQ = wN + F + R]_c^{P_0, Q_0}. \qquad (1)$$

P = price level
Q = output level
F = fixed or rentier incomes
R = gross profits, including depreciation allowances and corporate taxes.

The subscript (c) after the bracket ties the concept to consumer markets, while the superscripts identify the *expected* prices for the *intended* consumer outputs (P_0, Q_0).

Average Aggregate Consumption Supply

The unit supply-price required by all consumer sector firms (and industries) to evoke each output volume (Q_c) is simply $[Z/Q]_c^{Q_0}$. Thus:

$$CaS \equiv [Z/Q]_c^{Q_0} = [(wN/Q) + (F + R)/Q]_c^{Q_0} \qquad (2a)$$

$$= [(w/A) + (F + R)/Q]_c^{Q_0}. \qquad (2b)$$

In (2b), the A-term denotes the average product of labor (Q/N).

Relation (2) yields the supply-price curve (CaS) appropriate for price level theory, for it reveals the path of necessary proceeds per unit of output as Q_c varies.

The C-sector Demand Function

Aggregate demand outlays on consumer goods (CAD), in the closed economy, emanate from incomes earned in the consumption sector (Z_c), the investment sector (Z_i), and from wages in the government sector (W_g).[7] Expenditures also derive from transfer incomes and from dissavers, lumped together in θ.

Aggregate Consumption Demand

The aggregate consumption demand function (CAD) to subtend against the CAS curve must contain the intended (= hypothetical) volume of consumption expenditure outlays at each Q_c-level, *given the expected* Q_c *supply price* (P_c). That is to say, with each Q_c and the P_c that evokes it, we inquire whether demand intake $\lessgtr$ the supply quantity. The CAD^* notation signifies that the concept comprehends the *desired* outlays.

$$[CAD^* = c_c Z_c + c_i Z_i + c_w W_g + \theta]_c^{P_c \cdot Q_c}. \tag{3}$$

In (3) the Z-terms refer to the expected sales proceeds in the C and I sectors; their inclusion reveals the dependence of consumer outlays on cost and production phenomena, or the basic interdependence of the macroeconomic process. The c-coefficients denote the respective average propensities to consume. Decomposing the Z-terms into their wage, rentier, and profit components serves to underscore the dependence of consumer demand outlays on factor incomes.[8]

$$[CAD^* = c_w W + c_f F + c_r \lambda R + \theta]_c^{P_0 Q_0} \tag{4}$$

In (4), the λ-term signifies that only a fraction of "gross profits" are paid out: the withholdings include depreciation allowances, taxes, and undistributed profits.

Comparing either (3) or (4) with (1), if the Z_c-magnitude at any tentative supply price is small while Z_i, W_g, and θ are relatively large, then the desired consumption-intake must inevitably surpass the available supply. This will be examined at more length below.

Average Aggregate Outlay

From the CAD^* function it is easy to extract the demand curve (CaD^*) to suspend against the "supply" curve of Figure 13.1.

CaS, as derived in (2), specifies the necessary unit proceeds for each output volume. To construct the demand function we do a turnaround: by *knowing* the Q_c and P_c along the CaS function we can elicit the *desired demand* quantities.

Essentially this follows the Walrasian practice.[9] Walras's sellers "cry out" the prices they would be willing to take for their offerings; equilibrium occurs when the buyers' desired intake equals the quantities offered. Our procedure resembles this: sellers produce a volume of consumer goods, while nonconsumption output occurs simultaneously. At the supply prices that C-sellers envisage as necessary for their output (Q_c), we ask: what is the desired intake? The answer constitutes the relevant demand quantity point at the "announced" (or intended) supply price.

To derive the CaD^* function, equation (3) or (4) must be deflated by the $P_c{}^0$ accompanying $Q_c{}^0$. That is, (3) or (4) reports the aggregate desired outlay (CAD^*); dividing through by P_c the desired $Q^*{}_c$ thus shakes out instantly.

$$[CAD^*/P_c{}^0] \equiv [CaD^* = (c_c Z_c + c_e E)/P_c{}^0]^{P_c{}^0, Q_c{}^0} \qquad (5a)$$

$$= [(c_w wN)/P_c{}^0 + R']^{P_c{}^0, Q_c{}^0}. \qquad (5b)$$

In (5a), E denotes the consumption demand potential from the Z_i, W_g, θ sources in (3), while in (5b) the several (price deflated) nonwage consumption outlay terms of (4) are denoted by R'.

According to (5b), the demand-intake at each $P_c{}^0$ depends (substantially) on the real wage (w/P_c) and on the wage earner's average propensity to consume (c_w). The employment volume will also be crucial, as well as the real-demand of nonwage earners.[10]

The money wage (w) is a parameter in both the CaS and the CaD^* functions (2 and 5). Inevitably the D and S curves appropriate for price level theory (as in Figure 13.1) will shift simultaneously and interdependently with variations in the money wage.

Equilibrium and Stability

With the CaS and CaD functions in hand we can consider some implications of equilibrium as well as some aspects of stability.

Market Clearing

Equilibrium depends on the balance of (desired) demand quantities $(Q^*{}_c)$ to the supply quantities offered $(Q'{}_c)$ at each price. Thus from (5a):

$$(c_c Z_c + c_e E)/P_c \equiv CaD^* \lesseqgtr CaS \equiv Q'_c. \qquad (6a)$$

Dividing through by Q_c:

$$(c_c + c_e \bar{E}) \lesseqgtr 1. \qquad (6b)$$

In (6a–b), the E term is as before, while $\bar{E} = E/Z_c$.[11]

In (6b), almost invariably $1 > c_c > c_e \bar{E}$. If $c_c = 1$, capital formation would be precluded by the denial of consumer goods to I and G sector income recipients. With $c_c \sim 0$, high investment goals are achievable; in fact without massive I and G programs unemployment and depression will ensue. $\bar{E}$, the ratio of I and G sector outlays to Z_c outlays, plays a vital part in determining the Q_c equilibrium.

The Slope of CaS and CaD*

The prospects of price-level equilibrium, and its stability, involve some comparison of the slopes of the CaS and CaD^* functions. Thus from (2):

$$[d(CaS)/dQ_c] = \left[\frac{w(A - M)}{Q_c AM} + \frac{1}{Q_c}(R_M - R_A) \right] \qquad (7)$$
$$= [MC - AC]/Q_c.$$

In (7) it is assumed that money wages are constant.[12] While MC = marginal cost, and AC = average cost, A and M refer to the average and marginal products of labor, respectively. R_M denotes the *marginal* user cost, or marginal profit rate, while $R_A \equiv (F_c + R_c)/Q_c$, the *average* nonwage income. As under pure competition $A > M$, and generally $R_M > R_A$, the CaS curve will be positively sloped. When $MC = AC$, the CaS curve will be flat or perfectly elastic.[13]

For the change in demand price, as $CaD^* = Q_c(c_c + c_e \bar{E})$ in (6a), then

$$\frac{d(CaD^*)}{dQ_c} = \frac{\partial(CaD^*)}{\partial P_c} \frac{dP_c}{dQ_c} + \frac{\partial(CaD^*)}{\partial Q_c}. \qquad (7a)$$

On the proviso that $\Delta c_c = \Delta c_e = \Delta E = 0$, then

$$\frac{d(CaD^*)}{dQ_c} = \{c_c - [(c_cE)/Z_c][1/\epsilon]\} = c_c - c_e\bar{E}/\epsilon. \quad (7b)$$

In (7b), $\epsilon = (P_c dQ_c)/(Q_c dP_c)$ = the elasticity of supply, while $\bar{E} = \frac{2}{3}$—if consumption approximates 60 per cent of gross output.

Examining (7b), when supply is very highly elastic $(\epsilon \rightarrow \infty)$ the slope of CaD^* is *positive* and equal to c_c. As ϵ falls the *positive* CaD^* slope is somewhat reduced. When $\epsilon = \bar{E}$ and with $c_c = c_e$, the CaD^* curve turns horizontal. With highly inelastic supply $(\epsilon \rightarrow 0)$ the CaD^* curve tends to become vertical.

A "Giffen"-Shaped Demand Function

This is the interesting and important result: *the supply elasticity in the C-sector is a major determinant of C-sector demand.* The shape—and site—of CaS thus affects the shape—and site—of CaD^*.

A CaD^* curve drawn on this argument is mapped in Figure 13.2. Its features are reminiscent of the *"Giffen"* case of price theory though it is cusped and, perhaps, discontinuous. The arrows indicate the direction of the demand path, moving from

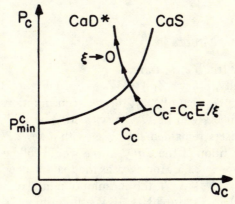

FIG. 13.2

low supply prices to high prices. So long as the demand curve does fall to the right for part of its course the equilibrium is likely to be stable; we return to this issue below.

Marginal CaS and CaD* Functions?

Curves marginal to CaS and CaD^* can be easily derived. But a curve marginal to CaD^* would be relevant only if the consumer supply sector was fully monopolized and under unitary control. Similarly, a curve marginal to CaS would only pertain to a situation in which an overall consumer-sector monopsonist bought output from the C-sector array of firms.[14]

"ACCELERATOR" THEORY AND "REAL-BALANCE" EFFECTS

That the CaS curve—the "supply curve" of price level theory—will rise seems assured. That the CaD^*—the "demand curve" of the theory—always falls to the right is doubtful. Yet, assessing the possible CaD^* slope reversal at high Q_c levels a price-output equilibrium should ensue.

Equilibrium results, however, follow most surely only from the restrictions that the E and c terms are constant. This requires closer scrutiny, for there are some destabilizing elements implicit here.

Real-balance Effects

Consider, first, the $(c_e \bar{E})$ term.

Definitionally, $c_e E = c_i Z_i + c_w W_g + \theta$. In Figure 13.3a, at the minimum supply price $(P_c^{\min})$, the real-consumption intake from the E components will be Q_c^i. If with ΔP_c the real intake from the E purchasers remained intact as with $(\Delta c_e / \Delta P_c) > 0$, then the CaD^*_i partition of the CaD^* curve would follow the vertical line (1) in Figure 13.3a. However, as the real income implicit in E is eroded at $(P_c^{\min} + \Delta P_c)$, the consumption intake should fall off, as in line (2) in Figure 13.3a. If Pigou-Patinkin "real-balance" effects are also operative, this result should be reinforced so that

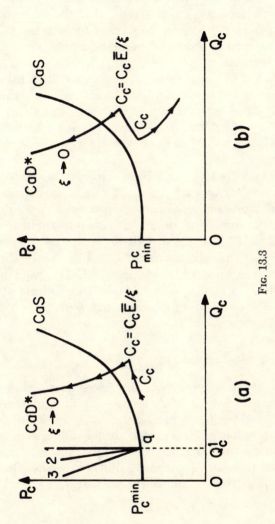

Fig. 13.3

the CaD^*_i curve may trace a path such as (3) in the diagram even though $(\Delta c_e/\Delta P_c) > 0$. Hence, that the "demand curve" emanating from the nonconsumption sector will be of "normal" form ensues directly from the "constant money income" stipulation of this sector.[15]

The odd Giffen shape of CaD^* is thus wholly attributable to the consumption propensities of C-sector income recipients. At P_c^{min}, a ΔP_c move fosters a large ΔQ_c advance, and a magnification in W_c (as $\epsilon \to \infty$).[16] Thus CaD^* tends to rise to the right. As the supply elasticity wanes, and a shift to profits sets in, c_c is likely to diminish.[17]

"Real-balance" effects have been subsumed within the c coefficients in the above analysis: as P_c rises, "real-balance" effects should cut consumption. Consider, however, a move downward from P_c^{min}. Presumably, consumption *output* would dry up; C-sector income (Z_c) would dwindle to zero. As a "mental-experiment" we could ask about *desired* Q_c and, on "real-balance" considerations, the broken line segment of CaD^* could be tacked on as a tail, as in Figure 13.3b. "Real-balance" effects would thus impart a new direction to the curve but, with $Q_c = 0$, their significance seems muted.[18]

Accelerator Influences

Variations in the E-term, containing investment and government outlays, introduce new complications. Outlays in these sectors may be geared positively to advances in Q_c. In the long run they must be, according to "accelerator" theory where, over time, capital formation is tethered to output expansion in all sectors, including the C-sector. Government outlays are also likely to rise with consumer goods employment, at least over time. Thus:

$$E = E(Z_c) = \alpha\Delta Z_c. \qquad (8)$$

In (8), E is denoted as a function of Z_c and, for concreteness, as a linear multiple (α) of changes in Z_c.

Hicks has accustomed us to "explosive" phenomena in trade cycle theory through high accelerator values, following the earlier work of Harrod and Samuelson. In price level theory we may encounter the same phenomenon: a term such as $(c_e/P_c)\Delta E > 0$, added on to (7b), buttresses the theory of a positive CaD^* slope. Curve (2) in Figure 13.3a, for example, could rise to the right from point q, rather than being negatively sloped.

It follows that the CaD^* curve will rise to the right, given high ϵ values and $\Delta E > 0$. Hence there may be: (1) a failure of price level equilibrium, or (2) the equilibrium balance will occur only at a high P_c (and Q_c).

Conclusions

A rising demand curve in the macroeconomic theory of the consumer price level cannot, therefore, be dismissed on *a priori* grounds.[19] A Marshallian-type demand curve is sustainable only as a special case.

The foregoing arguments can be given a dynamic character. They would lend themselves to cyclical and growth extensions; obviously, in the more realistic price level dynamics, movements in money wages would have to be assigned a major role. Partial neutralization would follow from improvements in productivity as new techniques entered the economy.[20]

Although attention has been riveted on the consumer price level, the general approach seems suitable for the price level of *I*-goods. With a variable money supply it is doubtful that the appropriate demand curve will always track the downward path of Figure 13.1. "Explosive" outcomes cannot be precluded. Also, while monopoly aspects have been ignored in our analysis (as is the fashion), market imperfection can enter more prominently into the argument through the (dR_c/dQ_c) term in (7): a higher degree of monopoly will raise this magnitude. Income distribution and demand would be affected and the economy-wide supply curve would become steeper.

Notes

1. A cursory survey of recent textbooks shows that the diagram in question is not uncommon. The figure drawn approximates that in

Ronald Bodkin, *The Wage-Price-Productivity Nexus* (Philadelphia: University of Pennsylvania Press, 1966), p. 87. Don Patinkin draws one such curve but with a perfectly inelastic supply curve so that his procedure is free of the main criticism made below.

2. Oscar Lange, *Price Flexibility and Employment*, p. 14. Lange's *negative monetary effect*, which with varying output and real income is *not* identical to the Patinkin real-balance effect, has not received the study it appears to merit. In his *Value and Capital*, 2nd ed. (New York: Macmillan, 1966), additional note B, Professor Hicks refers briefly to the imperfect stability of the system in Lange-like cases.

3. Martin Bronfenbrenner and F. D. Holzman, "Survey of Inflation Theory," *American Economic Review*, 1963.

4. Patinkin, *Money, Interest, and Prices*, pp. 38, 41.

5. A money supply function can be injected at this point; there is no necessary theoretical—or concrete—reason for assuming its perfect inelasticity, as insisted upon in the usual models.

6. Cf. Keynes, *General Theory*, Chap. 3.

7. When only the aggregate *real* outlay in these sectors is intended, the common GNP symbols of C, I and G will be utilized. Government outlays on goods may for our purposes be subsumed within Z_i.

8. On the simplifying Kaldor-Kalecki-Joan Robinson hypothesis that wage-earners spend all and capitalists save all, (4) is reduced to just W (neglecting θ).

9. Leon Walras, *Elements of Pure Economics*, p. 169.

10. In (5b) while we detect the importance of the real wage in determining consumption intake, as emphasized in the "employment-dynamics" of Solow and Stiglitz, transfers, dissaving, and government outlays, as well as personal income taxes, cannot be ignored, even in "pure" models. See "Output, Employment, and Wages in the Short Run," *Quarterly Journal of Economics*, November 1968.

11. In a simplified W, R, θ model, with $Z = W + R$, we can write:

$$\frac{Z}{P_c}\left[c_w \frac{W}{Z} + c_r \frac{R}{Z} + \frac{\theta}{Z} \right] \lesseqqgtr Q'_c, \tag{6c}$$

$$[c_w \eta + c_r \pi + \theta'] \lesseqqgtr Z_c/Z. \tag{6d}$$

With $\eta = W/Z$, and $\pi = R/Z$, relation (6d) reveals that market clearing depends on consumption propensities, income distribution, and the relative size of the C-sector.

12. Otherwise, the term $(1/A)(dw/dQ)$ must be included. While

(7) follows from (2) the final bracket comes from combining terms in the first bracket.

13. MC, AC, M and A are used in a sense analogous to that in the theory of the firm. With a "composite" good the difficult expository complications of aggregation are evaded.

14. F. J. DeJong examined these relations many years ago. See "Supply Functions in Keynesian Economics," *Economic Journal*, March 1954.

15. For the θ outlays, given the I-sector employment, as Q_c advances in tandem with P_c, unemployment transfer incomes will fall. A curve path for θ should resemble (3) in Figure 13.3a.

16. The C-sector wage share will be at its peak, near unity.

17. For $c_c = (c_w W_c + c_r R_c)/Z_c$. While c_w may go up, as c_c is a weighted average the rise in R_c/Z_c will pull c_c down.

18. In sum, while the "real-balance" effect tends to preserve the negative direction of CaD°, for the C-sector, which is heavily dependent on wage earner purchases, its total influence might be regarded as minimal, at least with typical Western-economy ranges of price variation per annum.

19. I tried to make this point many years ago, with a notable lack of success. Cf. Gardner Ackley, *Macroeconomic Theory* (London: Macmillan and Co., 1961), p. 337n.

20. By introducing technical change, with higher productivity accompanying an enlargement of Q_c, the effect may be to turn the customary picture around: the CaS curve can fall to the right while the CaD° curve may rise to the right. Policies conceived in a static context thus may have to be reversed on a dynamic view. To sustain the consumer price level would entail higher money wages.

14 Cost Inflation and the State of Economic Theory: A Comment

Considering what Mrs. Joan Robinson has called the "crisis of economics," in which unrealism becomes piled on irrelevance, it may be another instance of unwarranted optimism to think that the article by Peter Wiles,[1] "born of shame" (p. 377), may push economists on track to appreciate the crucial significance of money wages in our now chronic inflation. Wiles speaks of the persistent inflation phenomena as a form of "Latin Americanization" of the western world.

Even as Wiles wrote, articles were being published scarcely mentioning money wages, with others in process, and circulated in mimeo, with the casual proviso that "we assume money wages constant."[2] It would be easy to compile an extensive modern bibliography on inflation which ignores money wages while claiming to illuminate the price problems of our times.[3]

Lest it be thought that the wage omission has been confined only to monetarists, let it be said that Keynesians (the American fraternity to be sure, not the Cambridge, England family) earlier came to a dead end on the same issue. In their well publicized symmetric models, where money wages were utterly neglected, an economy could suffer unduly from unemployment through deficient (real) demand or inflation through excess (real) demand: we could be on one side of the moon or the other. Unfortunately for this theory, much of the underdeveloped world has often been subject to *both* inflation *and* unemployment.[4] In the last few years the western world has suffered from the same twin blight, injecting the word "stagflation" into our vocabulary. Fiscal policy and tight money have constituted the standard "Keynesian" remedy to our inflation troubles—mixed with frequent counsel for living with inflation. Such action prescriptions have come almost full circle to merge with monetarist concepts.

In lieu of the symmetric theory, a greater fidelity to Keynes's own writing would have averted the Keynesian disaster. In the *General Theory*, Book V, Keynes had been very clear and emphatic in providing the necessary instruction on money wages as the critical inflationary agent.[5] While this is not the place to argue the point, it may be said that Keynes's hypothesis of a constant wage-unit was injected to eliminate (major) price level phenomena from employment theory. A rising wage-unit would impart an inflationary spin to the economy, barring productivity improvements or variations in user-costs.

Now Wiles, in his admirable and evocative essay, advances what is routinely described in macro-theory as a "cost-push" theory of pricemaking. Thus: "Absolute prices are now decided by the primary input, labor. It is wage decisions that determine the absolute prices of the products of labor" (pp. 386–387).

Whilst agreeing with the tenor of Wiles's article one can strengthen his argument by including the dominant part that money wages play on the demand side in price determination. Even in the United States, about 90 per cent of consumption purchases are made by wage and salary earners; in other countries the percentage runs even higher.

To outline the relations between unit labor costs and consumer prices, a simple mark-up price equation can serve for the supply side. Thus:

$$P_c = k_c w / A_c \qquad (1)$$

where P_c = consumer good price level

$\quad k_c$ = unit mark-up (or reciprocal of the wage share in the consumer sector)

$\quad w$ = average money wage (and salary)

$\quad A_c = Q_c/N_c$ = average product of labor, where Q_c and N_c = output and employment in the consumer sector.

According to (1), a rise in money wages in excess of labor productivity will lead firms generally to raise prices, given the near-constancy of k_c.

On the demand side, from the truism that consumer sector sales receipts are equal to consumer outlays, we have:

$$P_c Q_c = c_w wN + c_r R + \theta \qquad (2')$$

where: N = total employment

R = capitalist income (or non-wage and non-salary income)

θ = transfer outlays and dissavings

c_w, c_r = average propensities to consume out of wN and R.

Since $Q_c = A_c N_c$, we may divide $(2')$ through by Q_c to obtain

$$P_c = \frac{w}{A_c} \ (c_w + c_r R' + \theta') \frac{N}{N_c} \qquad (2)$$

where $R' = R/wN$ and $\theta' = \theta/wN$.

Starting wholly from demand considerations, equation (2) reveals the parametric significance of money wages for the consumer price level. In the full "demand = supply" adjustment we see from a comparison of the demand equation (2) with the supply equation (1) that the terms in the square brackets in (2) must equal k_c.[6]

Using the "grand generalization" of Mrs. Robinson, that "wage earners consume all, and that capitalists save all," and neglecting transfers and dissavings, then (2) simplifies to $P_c = (w/A_c)-[N/N_c]$.

Taking some sample approximate values for the United States, which are probably even less accurate for the United Kingdom, we would have: $c_w \approx 0.8$; $c_r \approx 0.4$; $R' \approx 1$; also in United States *Gross Business Product* the wage share is only a little more than half the total market receipts. Too, $\theta' \approx 0.1$ while N/N_c may approximate 1.5. Multiplying out, the value of the bracketed terms is about 2—approximately the mark-up factor in the United States economy.

As the mark-up in the United States (and elsewhere) has remained quite constant, the various bracketed terms in (2) can, at most, lead to minor wriggles in the consumer price level: they are not the stuff of which serious inflation, say in excess of 5 per cent even over a period as long as a decade, is made. It is to the relations of w to A_c that we must look in seeking to explain—and control—the price level.

Equation (2) is also noteworthy for it includes the consumption propensities (c_w and c_r), income distribution (R'), transfers (θ), and the employment–output structure (N/N_c). If pressed we would admit that these factors may lead to inflation. But the concession involves only logical completeness: the several elements do not carry the tinder for the typical inflationary fires that menace the advanced economies.

Wiles's argument can thus be strengthened by incorporating "demand-pull" elements as a simultaneous contributory cause of inflation. With "cost-push," the demand-pull originates in excessive money wage and salary advances.

The price level for the investment sector may, with Wiles, be interpreted in terms of wage-cost factors on the supply side. Demand phenomena are fed by bank loans, internal finance, and savings-flow diversions to entrepreneurial hands.

The analysis has been confined to a closed economy. Consideration of the open economy complicates the argument in details, while forcing concentration on elements over which domestic control is more elusive, and often less vital, from a stabilization standpoint.[7]

In his persuasive appeal to economists to comprehend the wage origins of inflation, Wiles might also have alluded to the signal lack of serious wage-restraint proposals which minimize bureaucratic forms of market intervention.[8]

Notes

1. *Economic Journal* (June 1973).

2. Cf. "Symposium on Friedman's Theoretical Framework," *Journal of Political Economy* (September/October 1972). In 140 journal pages devoted to monetary theory and inflation, one looks in vain for passages dealing with monetary policy under conditions of wage inflation.

3. The words "money wages" fail to appear in the index of Professor Friedman's prominent work. Cf. *The Optimum Quantity of Money and other Essays* (Chicago: Aldine Publishing Co., 1969).

4. My own protest against the Keynesian "theory" goes back to "Classical Keynesianism: A Plea for its Abandonment," in *Classical Keynesianism, Monetary Theory, and the Price Level* (Chilton, 1961).

5. Besides Keynes's Book V (chapters 20 and 21) which contain numerous, and luminous, remarks on the key importance of the wage-unit in inflation, Keynes observed: "For the purposes of the real world it is a great fault in the Quantity Theory that it does not distinguish between changes in prices which are a function of changes in output, and those which are a function of changes in the wage-unit." *General Theory*, p. 209.

6. I have developed the same theory somewhat differently, with essentially similar results, for an output variation. Wiles seems generally concerned with a given output level. Cf. "Rising Demand Curves In Price Level Theory," Chapter 13.

7. For the open economy the right-hand side of equation (2) would have to be supplemented by terms for the sales value of consumer goods exported minus consumer imports, divided by domestic consumer good output (in constant prices). Thus $(E_x - I_m)/Q_C$. An excess of consumable exports, obviously, is inflationary—the U.S. 1973 farm exports would be a case in point.

8. Cf. Chapter 16 below.

15 New Books on Keynes*

New books on Keynes? After so many uninformed Keynesian imposters both books instantly vault the subject proficiency test. This is not entirely facetious for as Galbraith, that courageous part-time Keynesian gadfly who has surmounted professionally his sins of uncanny perception, literateness, and enviable sales, remarked of the *General Theory* (hereafter *GT*): "All economists claim to have read it. Only a few have. The rest feel a secret guilt that they never will. Some if its influence derived from its being extensively incomprehensible."[1] Friedman, once capable of indiscriminately lashing Keynes to Keynesians, belatedly confessed that a "rereading" (apparently under the playful tease of Paul Davidson[2]) "has also reminded me what a great economist Keynes was."[3] On the path to redemption, Hicks dodges his *IS-LM* Keynesian progeny (with Hansen and Samuelson named in the paternity suit) in proclaiming Keynes's "wage-theorem" as of supreme importance for the price level.[4] The tidy Keynesian symmetrical model has collapsed for want of Keynes's "wage-unit" shoe: Hicks suggests Keynes's guilt by obscurity; I myself wonder how he could have been more luminous.[5]

So the fire lit by Keynes still rages after 40 years. Minsky and Moggridge, and the publication of Keynes's *Collected Writings*, should set off a new blaze, to the immense profit of economics and public policy. The half-Age of Sraffa will encounter an old friend on the research trail.

* A review of Hyman P. Minsky, *John Maynard Keynes*, Columbia Essays on the Great Economists. New York: Columbia University Press, 1975; and Donald E. Moggridge, *Keynes*, Fontana Modern Masters. (London: Fontana/Collins, 1976.)

Professor Minsky offers a thematic, often polemical, book as an undaunted warrior making constructive accommodation. Reflection has led him to shed a Keynesian blanket and to return to Keynes, to join a dissenting band who have often swum upstream to protest the Keynesianism fobbed off as Keynes: the overlap lay in the technical C, I, and L concepts, which Keynesians then purveyed in an *equilibrium real* system, managing for about a quarter-century spirited talk about inflation in a model bereft of a price level, treating inflation and unemployment as rivals, never bedfellows. Some high-brow mathematized confusion still prevails in assigning inflation to "excess-demand"-in a demand-deficient economy! In the Keynesian transmogrification of Keynes as an equilibrium theorist, Keynesianism mimicked Walrasianism, each balanced neatly on an equilibrium pin, transcribing Keynes *sans* contractual payments, without "spontaneous" money wages feeding into prices, absent uncertainty clouds and dervish investment functions. Of course, in the non-Keynes nonsense there was the $M = \overline{M}$ proviso as output ran from here to eternity unless the monetary authority, in some pique or unemployment despair, injected a ΔM shock to start a new and nice stable equilibrium.

Patinkin's prestigious account[6] emboldened a flock of imitators to translate Keynes's unemployment as simply a "dynamic" run of short-term errors in labor-hire decisions, even though Keynes was explicit that "daily" or short-term production decisions created little damage, that the equilibrium miscreant was *long-term* expectations, which eluded frequent check.[7] The labor-market imbalance theory imprisoned Keynes in the short-period *tâtonnement* zone of Walras, even though Keynes, a follower of Marshall, sought to pursue his analysis with the looser "static method." While Keynes struggled to shake the stationary syndrome, Keynesians keep driving him into a Walrasian pen.[8]

Minsky declares Keynes's revolution was "aborted" by "the neglected facets" in Keynes, which contain "a theory of the processes of a capitalist economy" (Preface). Lost horizons are: (1) decision-making under uncertainty, (2) the cyclical nature of the capitalist process, and (3) financial relations of an advanced capitalist economy. Minsky brings his considerable analytic and expository talents to these aspects, with an extraordinary awareness of topical events that elude eager analytic-model

beavers. To be sure, Minsky credits some congenial work by Joan
Robinson, G. L. S. Shackle, Nicholas Kaldor, Sidney Weintraub,
Paul Davidson, Robert Clower, and Axel Leijonhufvud: a handful of others might be added on waiving a 10-year qualifying
proviso.

Early, there is the delectable attribution to Gardner Ackley on
how Keynesianism "carried macroeconomics far beyond the high-
water mark of Keynes's own great contribution" (p. 3). Into a
dry hole? Minsky lumps Samuelson, Patinkin, Modigliani, and
Friedman as "more classical than Keynesian" for abiding a quantity theory of money (p. 4).

In many ways Minsky's book dovetails with that by Paul
Davidson, whose important work on money has suffered unsport-
ing modular Establishment silence in the society's mutual admiration conferences in ritual patching.[9] Yet while Davidson, and
Harrod too, seize on the *Treatise*, Minsky opts for the *GT*, where
the money spots are scattered and tucked away, imposing a pre-
mium on an investigatory sleuth for assimilating clues. I mostly
side with Minsky while praising the richer *Treatise* institutional
detail.

Minsky peremptorily scouts the old wives' tale that Keynes's
unemployment endures in wage rigidities. What a Humpty-
Dumpty word, "rigidities," to denote the perpetual motion of
money wage escalation! The eminent Keynesians, like their Vic-
torian ancestors, really think that wage cuts would eliminate
unemployment; it is like selling Cadillacs where surplus stocks
can always be depleted by slashing prices to 3 for 8 cents.

This model hokum has long qualified applicants for membership in the Society of Precious Keynesian models. Keynes wrote
his book to *protest* the doctrine. There was labor recalcitrance
and, in Keynes's world never inhabited by the modelers, imminent bankruptcy as lower money wages forced the price level
down to make contractual payments onerous. Now, through
model subtleties of real-balance effects, the old dogma rides
again in "pure" economics. Keynes's impurities, however, would
inflict a blow on investment and predict social distress and tur-
moil menacing the market economy even as the pure model
preaches real-balance salvation.

Debt-burdens, insolvency, credit-crunch, domino effects, shattered confidence, and suppressed real-investment, have seldom dissuaded Keynesian modelers that God, in His own good time, intended flexible-price voluntary full-employment equilibrium to prevail—regardless of how much calendar time it would take and how much misery it would condone. It is the underlying "fragile financial layering of claims" that constitutes Minsky's marvelous core, providing excellent, exciting, and intriguing reading. A moral cavil: as this is a balance sheet orientation, Minsky could have rectified the perils of originality that befell Kenneth Boulding's *Reconstruction* a quarter century back.[10]

Decision-making under uncertainty has been in before Minsky, for all willing to see, in Shackle, a dominant majority of one: it is also the strong-suit in Davidson's monetary theory. More must be done, of course, to integrate it and displace illusory "perfect certainty" and "fully-anticipated" paradigms.

Minsky's individuality is in his perception of inherently flawed decision-making in a concatenated cyclical setting, where each of the up-down states are transient, with each of vague amplitude and duration, while each serves to "transform the economy." Too, "the proximate cause of the transitory nature of each cyclical state is the instability of . . . portfolios and of financial interrelations" (p. 57). Aggravating, often dominating, the hazy real-investment (real-I) profit-planning in the oscillating context are the financial trepidations: finance and real-I decisions are tangled as spaghetti, for bankers participate in both expectational streams. It is cyclical fuzziness that bans the stability prize as the economy edges or bangs from one incomplete equilibrium state to another.

Minsky's work has long been exemplary on financial linkages and fragility. He also sketches a new investment theory, founded on a laudable stab to carve Keynes's borrower's and lender's risk in diagrams, for investment must have financing outside the "real-I" models. Quickly, Minsky is able to juxtapose the indispensable theory of financial webs once internal finance succumbs to external borrowing.[11]

Here, Minsky may violate his own distaste for equilibrium models in resorting to pyrotechnics of intersection in a plane diagram. The diagram is an awkward ally for, as Joan Robinson has tried to remind us, Keynes was always walking away from the blackboard and out into time, into a new day from one momentary curve-point to another curve, with "stable" functions sliding about. Minsky courts the danger of spawning another, albeit superior, equilibrium model for Keynes via a new illustrated investment sports section. The equilibrium bath is sanitized by reminders that "Keynesian [Keynes's] economics as the economics of disequilibrium is the economics of permanent disequilibrium" (p. 68). Some of us prefer, on Keynes's fulfilled "daily" output expectations, to adopt it as a "weak" equilibrium system, containing Marshall's equilibrating tendencies (as noted by Minsky), always on the go to another weak daily-plus equilibrium.

Minsky would also want to be judged on his amendment to Keynes's liquidity-preference theory. He writes:

$$M_1 + M_2 + M_3 - M_4 = L_1(Y) + L_2(r, P_k) + L_3(F) - L_4(NM)$$

The Ms involve Keynes's analytic pigeonholes rather than Friedman's measurement categories. L_1 is, of course, the "transactions-motive." L_2, the "speculative-motive" in which Minsky inserts the price level of investment goods. This is a merger, of sorts, with Keynes's post-GT finance-motive "coping-stone," to deflect the Ohlin-Robertson punch. Whether P_k is instead best entered (as reflecting the supply price of equipment to which Keynes attached much importance in extracting the marginal efficiency of capital) in L_1, as an expanded transactions aspect, need not detain us for all Ls must ultimately gather in a combined function. L_3 is the "precautionary-motive," underplayed by Keynes, but restored by Kahn, Harrod, and Davidson. Minsky appropriately ties L_3 to "outstanding financial commitments," especially for refinancing contingent maturing debts. L_4 denotes "near-monies" which, when plentiful and highly liquid, can axe the demand for cash.

Minsky might have included an M-term in L_2 (as I once did[12]) for, as in all the "fixed stock" problems of Marshall and Wicksteed, owners (of money) are also money-demanders, priming the liquidity schedule. More surprising, I do not recollect allusion to M and L interdependence, even though deep-think money-market strategists draw bloated inferences from every Fed sneeze.

Closing his Keynesian *défi*, with analytic skill and compassion, Minsky identifies with Keynes in deploring gross income inequalities. Joining Galbraith, Minsky leans to more nationalization despite the dwindling support of this populist academic stand: the Soviet, conservative fear-mongering, U.S. bureaucratic bungling, and the uninspiring U.K. record have dashed the legendary idealism.

D. E. Moggridge, from his riches as editor of Keynes's *Collected Writings,* has provided a biographical, interpretative, and expository book, delighting the reader with wise commentary. To Kings College "irregulars" (*pace* Sir Arthur Conan Doyle), whose lifetime preoccupation has been Keynes's work, the first impression of an up-date filler for the fresh economist harvest is dispelled by asides and glimpses from Keynes's correspondence. The book thus turns into a sure communicative gem. (At least it confirms *my* interpretative bias.)

The Prologue on early Keynes, Bloomsbury, G. E. Moore, the Civil Service exams, is mostly chit-chat: as a youthful golfer was Keynes a scrambler or spot shooter? "The Economist" conveys an exceptional gaze at Keynes on methodology, on premises, intuition, introspection, and a guiding faith in man's rationality if properly informed. Saturating all, the practical slant of economics, Keynes's wariness of turning "essentially a moral science" into "a pseudo–natural-science" (p. 26). "Premises, premises matter" in model selection.

The Marshallian heritage dominated Keynes's economics until the mid-1920s. Noting the *"Treatise*-troubles" in definitions and in the Fundamental (Price Level) Equations, Moggridge organizes a splendid *General Theory* chapter. One extract: "Rather than arising in asides, as in the *Treatise,* uncertainty dominated the *General Theory*" (p. 92). A succinct blow to 45-degree and *IS-LM* models!

Moggridge replicates Minsky's quote from Keynes, that with decision-making "being based on so flimsy a foundation, it [investment] is subject to sudden and violent changes" (p. 93). Too, money "is not neutral" (p. 93). Unlike Keynesians, Moggridge concludes that "the inclusion of Keynes's concerns . . . are highly destructive of the notion of equilibrium itself" (p. 160). An addendum can follow, however, that Marshall's or Keynes's equilibrium-method can survive.

Final pages amass much information on Keynes's ambient presence in the bureaucratic maze as a wartime "Economist Statesman." In summing up, Moggridge elects Austin Robinson's judgment that "Maynard Keynes was utterly unique" (p. 147). Recalled is Samuelson's faint obituary praise (at the dawn of the 45-degree heyday) that Keynes "left no mark on pure theory" (p. 156). Though I reject this dismissal, Keynes could rest comfortably on being drummed out of the pristine circle: Marx would be a more exciting cohort. Unfazed, pondering Keynes's giant shadow, Moggridge declares: "Some accomplishment for someone who 'left no mark on pure theory'" (p. 161).

Two small dissents: the book is not enhanced by the *IS-LM* Appendix despite Moggridge's tentative rendition. And Harrod's biography deserves more than the mild nod (p. 184). Fashions in revelatory standards are likely to overturn only parts of it.

"Two pyramids, two masses for the dead, are twice as good as one," so Keynes wrote in the memorable closing paragraph on the multiplier. Two fine books on Keynes should start a multiple chain reaction to put more Keynes in Keynesianism.

NOTES

1. J. K. Galbraith, *Money: Whence It Came, Where It Went* (Boston: Houghton Mifflin, 1975), p. 218.

2. P. Davidson, "A Monetary Theory of Nominal Income," *Journal of Political Economy,* 79 (March/April 1971), p. 325n.

3. M. Friedman, "Comments on the Critics," *Journal of Political Economy,* 80 (September/October 1972), p. 908.

4. J. Hicks, *The Crisis in Keynesian Economics* (New York: Basic Books, 1974), p. 59.

5. See Chapter 6 above.

6. D. Patinkin, *Money, Interest, and Prices,* 2nd ed. (New York: Harper and Row, 1965).

7. J. M. Keynes, *The General Theory of Employment, Interest, and Money* (New York: Harcourt, Brace, 1936), pp. 50–51.

8. On Keynes's methodology, see the illuminating article by J. A.

Kregel, "Economic Methodology in the Face of Uncertainty," *Economic Journal*, 86 (June 1976), pp. 209-225.

9. Davidson, *Money and the Real World* (London: Macmillan, 1972).

10. K. E. Boulding, *A Reconstruction of Economics* (New York: Wiley, 1950).

11. On the real-world importance of nonequilibrium *tâtonnements*, see the important article of Douglas Vickers, which deserves a wider audience, "Finance and False Trading in Non-tâtonnement Markets," *Australian Economic Papers*, 14 (December 1975), pp. 171-186.

12. S. Weintraub, *An Approach to the Theory of Income Distribution* (Philadelphia: Chilton, 1958).

16 A Tax-Based Incomes Policy

WITH HENRY C. WALLICH

In using the income tax mechanism to implement an anti-inflationary incomes policy this article aims: (1) to present a fairly detailed statement of the approach, (2) to extend the economic analysis underlying it, (3) to assess some troublesome technical matters, and (4) to demonstrate the advantages of an incomes policy relying on market forces over those that do violence to the market.[1]

The facts of our intractable inflation need not be recited. Complicating the price rise has been an unduly high rate of unemployment. The twin goals of price level stability and full employment have so far eluded conventional monetary and fiscal techniques. New measures commend themselves to counter the new experience of 1969–70 in which prices and unemployment rose simultaneously in contrast to past business cycles when their paths diverged.[2]

Rather than regard an incomes policy, such as we propose, as a substitute for monetary and fiscal policy, the proposal is conceived as a supplement to the familiar monetary-fiscal policies so that the economy might operate closer to full employment without the inflationary danger of excess demand and "overheating."

Fundamentally, an incomes policy in a wage-induced inflation involves mainly a redirection of the traditional emphasis. Both Monetarists and fiscalists argue that to control inflation aggregate demand must be depressed, and that the ensuing unemployment will dampen wage and price increases. These policies bring *in-*

direct pressures to bear on wages and prices.[3] An incomes policy projects a *direct* attack and can thus improve the short run trade-off between inflation and unemployment.

THE *TIP* PROPOSAL

We turn now to state the underlying principle of our tax-based incomes policy (hereafter *TIP*). Alternative proposals such as a wage-price "freeze," Kennedy guideposts, price and wage stabilization boards, or intervention in labor disputes will be by-passed. The shortcomings of these approaches are well known. The method we propose, instead of disrupting the market process, relies upon market forces, leaving business and labor free to make their own decisions.

The corporate income tax mechanism provides a ready lever for policing an incomes policy, with only nominal administrative costs and minor amendments (in principle) to prevailing tax laws.

In simplest terms, it is proposed to levy a surcharge on the corporate profits tax for firms granting wage increases in excess of some guidepost figure. If the wage guidepost were 5.5 per cent, and a wage increase of 7 per cent were granted, the corporate profits tax for the firm would rise above the present 48 per cent by some multiple of the 1.5 per cent excess. If the guidepost were 3.5 per cent, the excess would be 3.5 per cent and the multiple would be applied to that figure.

The added tax burden may be expected to stiffen the company's back in wage negotiations. The result would be a lower rate of wage increases, and a slowing of the rate of inflation.

In analyzing this form of incomes policy, we shall first discuss its general economic logic. Subsequently, we shall deal with a number of specific problems which relate mainly to the technique of tax administration but are nevertheless of great importance in evaluating the proposal.

Note that the proposal is asymmetrical in character. The tax is levied on and paid by the corporation while it is the advance of wages that is to be restrained. Thus one can argue that the proposal is broadly even-handed. Nonetheless, this claim needs to be supported by more detailed consideration.

Most forms of incomes policy address themselves to both wages and prices, or to wages, prices, and profits. It could be argued that under the present proposal, prices, too, should be controlled in some form. The reason why this is not done is that, on the historical evidence, the average markup of prices over unit labor costs has been remarkably constant. Expressed differently, the share of wages and salaries in the national income, or in gross business product, has been historically constant. If prices are in this form tied to wages, restraint of wage increases implies restraint of price increases. No separate control of prices is required. Furthermore, as we shall show in greater detail later on, the corporation paying the surcharge is unlikely to be able to shift it to the consumer in the form of higher prices. This circumstance, crucial to our proposal, likewise argues against the need for direct intervention in the price mechanism, which would nullify the principal advantage claimed for the *TIP*.

The simple wage-cost mark-up price level (*WCM*) formula illustrates the argument. We have: [4]

$$P = kw/A.$$

That is, the price level equals the index for the wage level multiplied by the markup factor, divided by average labor productivity.

Of all time series in economics that of k, the average markup, is most nearly constant, in the short run and the long run.[5] Annual fluctuations rarely exceed one or two index points. We can rely on k to remain firm—unless our economy is structurally altered almost beyond recognition. On this hypothesis we can surmise that the price level and unit labor costs will move in unison, or that for price level stability average wage-salary payments must be geared closely to average improvements in labor productivity. Over time productivity has risen by approximately 3 per cent per annum.

This means that, over time, prices have been closely tied to wages. Business, whether it has tried or not, has never effectively

raised its markup for any length of time. It follows that a measure slowing the rate of increase in wages will also slow the rate
of increase in prices. Our incomes policy proposal rests in part
on this proposition.

This view of the relation of wages and prices is also shared by
the designers of most of the large econometric models of the
American economy in use today. For the most part, these models
assume that prices are related to wages by a fixed markup. This
does not necessarily mean that all inflation must be regarded as
cost-push inflation. It does mean, however, that when inflation is
of the demand-pull type, business does not succeed in significantly or durably increasing profit margins. Wages quickly follow to keep the markup and the wage share constant. A demand-
pull inflation, in any event, is more amenable to the traditional
tools of monetary and fiscal policy. These work against aggregate
demand, and they thus restrain the source of the demand-pull inflation. They are less appropriate for a cost-push inflation. Hence
an incomes policy, the *TIP* or any other, is particularly appropriate to a cost-push inflation.

To conclude this comment on the absence of a price control
component, it should be noted that the effect of a proposal for a
surtax on profits is similar to that of a price freeze unaccompanied
by a wage freeze. If business was not able to raise prices, wage
increases would eat directly into profits, and management's resistance to wage increases would be stiffened. Precisely the same
effect is achieved under the *TIP*. However, the harmful effects
and administrative difficulties of a price freeze are avoided.

The tax surcharge, it is important to note, is a tax on the income of the corporation. It is not a tax on the excess payroll, nor
on excess labor income. This feature, too, is an essential aspect
of the *TIP*.

It might be argued that, if excessive wage demands on the part
of labor are largely responsible for inflation, a penalty tax should
be levied on the income of labor rather than of the corporation.
This could be done by means of a payroll tax, or by making excess wage increases nondeductible for income tax purposes, or
by taxing labor income directly. None of these techniques, how-

ever, would achieve the objective of restraining the corporation in the granting of wage increases.

The reason is that a wage tax or any similar tax can easily be shifted by the corporation. In the case of a payroll tax, which represents a direct increase in costs, this is obvious. Disallowance of the dollar amount of an excess wage increase for income tax purposes has the same effect of raising costs. A tax on labor income very likely would be included by labor in its wage demands and would thus be translated into an increase in costs. Any tax that can readily be shifted leaves the profit margin of the corporation unchanged. If the volume of production does not change, the dollar amount of profits and hence the rate of return on capital also will not change. There would be no stiffening of backbones from such a tax.

A tax on the income of a corporation is very much less likely to be shifted. Both economic theory and empirical research seem to confirm this, especially with respect to short-run tax changes. The reason is that profits per unit of sales vary widely among corporations. For a highly profitable firm, profits per unit of sales are high, and therefore corporate profits tax per unit of sales is high. The opposite is true for a relatively unprofitable firm. For a firm with zero profit, the tax per unit of sales is also zero. Further differences in the amount of profit and of tax per unit of sales result from different degrees of "leverage," that is, differences in the amount of debt in the capital structure of the corporation. A tax that affects cost per unit very differently among firms evidently is harder to shift than a tax that affects all firms equally.

It is sometimes argued that the degree of shifting of the corporate income tax depends upon the structure of an industry. Highly concentrated industries might find shifting easier than highly competitive industries. If this effect were pronounced, however, it would tend to make concentrated industries more profitable than competitive industries, that is the rate of return on capital would be higher in the former. There is no strong evidence that this is generally the case.

If the tax were shifted, the result would be to raise the level of prices. During the period in which the shifting takes place, the rate of inflation would therefore accelerate. This effect would probably be small, as long as the revenue from the surcharge was small. An average surcharge of 5 percentage points on the corporate income tax would amount to less than $2 billion at present. Spread over a *GNP* of $1 trillion, the effect on prices would be minimal. However, if the tax were indeed shifted in this manner, it would lose its restraining effect upon business behavior. If corporations can shift the tax, they will have little more reason to resist wage increases than they had before. The issue of tax shift-· ing, therefore, and the foregoing demonstration that large-scale shifting is unlikely, are important because a shifted tax constitutes no restraint at all.[6]

Partial shifting will reduce the wage restraint exerted by the tax without altogether eliminating it. More precisely, the firm's and the union's expectations of the degree of shifting will be decisive. Most students agree that more shifting will occur in the long run than in the short. Unless a firm expects to be paying a *TIP* tax continuously, it can hardly plan on long-run shifting. Its expectations of being able to shift in the short run will be relevant.

The foregoing analysis suggests one further comment on the distributional effect of the *TIP*. We started by stressing the historical evidence that the share of labor in the total product has been quite constant or at most has edged up slightly. A slower rate of wage increases is not likely to reduce that share. With price increases also slowing, labor's real wage gains will continue unchanged. Historically, these real gains have been equal to the rate of productivity growth.

Nothing in the *TIP* proposal is likely to alter this. As the intention is to hold wage gains (nearly) equal to the average productivity improvement, the wage share will tend to be maintained.

This would be the minimum share-prospect for labor. If the wage-cost aspect of price movements were brought under control it would be an easier matter thereafter to clarify our understanding of the impact of monopoly on price making without our vision being clouded, and any study hopelessly confounded, by the facts on wage movements. A more intelligent scrutiny of monopolistic practices could ultimately contribute to improving labor's income share.

So far we have established grounds for believing that the corporation will be sensitive to the *TIP*. If it cannot shift more than a small part of the surcharge, its rate of return will be reduced. We must now proceed to examine the response of the corporation to this changed condition, and also the response of the union.

In any bargaining situation, the two parties start at some distance from each other and end up together. This implies that one of the two or both change their initial position. They may do this because the initial position was just a bargaining stance, or because the ongoing negotiation, which may involve a strike, becomes increasingly costly to either or both of them.

This progress of a negotiation is shown systematically in Figure 16.1. It shows labor's wage claim curve, *U*, starting high and declining over time. The corporation's wage offer curve *E* starts low and rises. At the level and the point in time where the two curves intersect, the parties settle—point S_0 of the diagram.

Suppose a *TIP* is introduced, with a guidepost level, *G*. The company may be expected to respond to this by lowering to E^T that part of its curve which goes above *G*. In the diagram this is indicated by a horizontal stretch at the level of the guidepost, where the company for some days or weeks refuses to increase its offer.

If the union does not change its bargaining plan, the union curve will remain unchanged. In that case it will intersect with the revised company curve E^T at S_1, at a somewhat lower wage increase and after a somewhat longer negotiation or strike. This illustrates the effectiveness of *TIP* even on the unfavorable assumption that the union is quite unimpressed by the tax. If the union takes into account the reduced ability to pay of the corporation, it may lower its wage demand curve. This is indicated by the dotted line U^{T1}. In that case it is possible that the settlement will not only be substantially lower, but also will occur earlier in time than without *TIP*.

It is theoretically conceivable that a union may be totally impervious to any of the forces at work—the passage of time, the

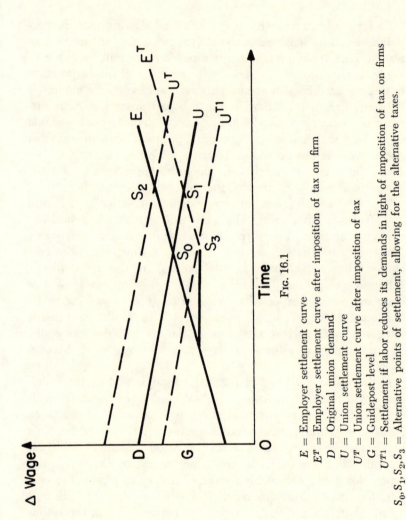

FIG. 16.1

E = Employer settlement curve
E^T = Employer settlement curve after imposition of tax on firm
D = Original union demand
U = Union settlement curve
U^T = Union settlement curve after imposition of tax
G = Guidepost level
U^{T1} = Settlement if labor reduces its demands in light of imposition of tax on firms
S_0, S_1, S_2, S_3 = Alternative points of settlement, allowing for the alternative taxes.

mounting costs of the strike, the reduced ability to pay of the corporation after *TIP* becomes effective. This could be expressed, in the diagram, by a horizontal line along which the union maintains its original demand of *D*. Some observers or negotiators on the business side appear to believe this to be the typical union attitude. Several considerations suggest that it is an erroneous appraisal. In the first place, if unions assume a completely intransigent position, employing a kind of labor Boulwarism, corporations would be ill-advised ever to accept a strike. They ought to settle immediately, knowing that to hold out will avail nothing. The fact is, of course, that corporations do accept strikes in the expectation of getting a lower settlement. Only in cases where a large union confronts a small employer and thus faces negligible costs from a strike is a-take-it-or-leave-it bargaining stance at all plausible.

In the second place, a union that fails to take into account the impact of *TIP* upon the corporation's ability to pay is demonstrably not maximizing benefits for its members. Suppose that the union asks for wage gains estimated to cost $10,000,000 at a certain level of output, with or without *TIP*. If the union believes that the company could pay, in addition to the $10,000,000, a *TIP* of, say, $3,000,000, it would not be maximizing its possible take if in the absence of a *TIP* it were to ask for only $10,000,000, or its hourly equivalent. Knowing that the company can pay $13,-000,000, that is the amount it should demand in the absence of *TIP*. A union that does not respond to a corporation's reduced ability to pay under *TIP* would not be doing a good job for its members.

Let us take one further look at the diagram in order to illustrate a point made earlier. We argued that if *TIP* took the form of a tax *on the income of labor,* this would cause the union to raise its demands and incidentally also cause the company to shift the increase in cost to the customer. The position of the union's wage demand curve is shown in the diagram on the dotted line U^T. It will be seen that that curve intersects with the corporation's unchanged offer curve at a higher settlement than before, as well as later in time. This is why a tax on the income of the union's members would not restrain inflation. A *TIP* in the form of a pay-roll tax would in all probability not induce the corporation to lower its wage offer curve substantially, since that tax could be shifted to the consumer.

AN ALTERNATE *TIP* ANALYSIS

The same result can be realized by examining the problem from another angle.

In Figure 16.2 profits are measured vertically while the percentage wage change is measured horizontally. Curve 1, for example, is an *opportunity* curve: it assumes that regardless of the wage change, the firm recoups the *same* volume of profits: its higher wage costs are translated into proportionately higher prices and, with sales unchanged, its profits are unaffected. Curve 2, on the other hand, reports lower profits with higher wage movements: the firm is unable to transmit its higher costs into prices.

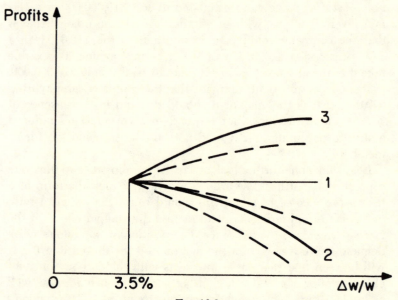

Fig. 16.2

Curve 3 represents the case in which either the firm has failed to maximize profits at lower wage costs, or that as wages and prices rise, its debt burden eases and its profits rise.

For all three cases the dashed lines indicate the impact of the *TIP* program: profits are reduced for wage movements in excess of 3.5 per cent per annum.

Viewing curves 1, 2, 3 as *opportunity* curves, profit indifference curves can be superimposed. (We refrain from executing this simple exercise.) With the firm dominated solely by profit objectives, the indifference curves are horizontal: in all cases, *TIP must* reduce the profit possibilities. Presumably, to maintain any level of profits—if the firm was not maximizing profits previously—there will be resistance to higher levels of wage increases.

If the firm is motivated by a "high wage" psychosis, the profit indifference contours will fall to the right. The general conclusions still follow: the maximum profit possibilities will be lower barring strange cases of *important* deviations from the maximum profit principle. But these cases of benevolence and philanthropic business behavior are not the stuff of sensible economic analysis; we may be permitted to neglect them in accord with common practice.

We conclude, therefore, that on (approximate) profit maximization analysis, the *TIP* proposal would lead firms to seek lower settlement terms. This force would tend to check the inflationary wage increase of recent years.

THE *TIP* TAX STRUCTURE

We turn now to the tax ingredients of the *TIP* proposal. For immediate purposes the statement will be primarily suggestive and tentative. Tables on the precise scale of tax progression would, at this time, have primarily an intuitive appeal.

A case can be made for a relatively low rate of *TIP* tax, say 1½ percentage points of corporate surcharge for each percentage point of excess wage increase. A 7.5 per cent wage increase, in the face of a 5.5 per cent guidepost, would then cost the corporation a 3 per cent surcharge over and above the regular corporate

rate. The reason for such a moderate tax might be that *TIP* is new and experimental, and that part of its merit might be the informational and educational effect upon business, labor, and the public. In the case of such a low tax, however, the control of inflation might very well require reliance upon additional forms of incomes policy.

A case for a heavier tax, say 3 or 4 percentage points of surcharge for every percentage point of excess wage increase, can also be defended. It would make *TIP* a powerful instrument. It might make superfluous the use of other forms of income policy, although not the use of proper monetary and fiscal restraint. In case of a high *TIP* rate, it might be well to put a substantial tax on any transgression of the wage guidepost, even if it were fractional.

Nevertheless, in no case should the tax be set so high as to completely erode the corporation's profit position. For instance, a very high excess wage settlement, say of 15 per cent, would completely wipe out the company's profit in case the tax rate is set high. Some kind of a tapering off or ceiling would have to be provided.

A SCHEMATIC VERSION

The main *TIP* choices appear in Figure 16.3. In curve B, *TIP* rates rise quickly for transgressions beyond a 3.5 per cent annual wage increment norm. The danger here is that if firms cannot hold the line, the tax penalty will become onerous; if the phenomenon is widespread, the general level of economic activity will be depressed as investment dries up.

Considering the novelty of the proposal and the obscurity on the fundamental matters involved stemming from the lack of operating experience with it, only relatively minor additions to the ordinary tax imposts would be feasible with levies confined within 5 to 10 percentage points of existing corporate income taxes. Such levies would parallel past experience; also they are unlikely to be inimical to high level activity even if firms acceded to excessive wage settlements. Curve A would thus be the im-

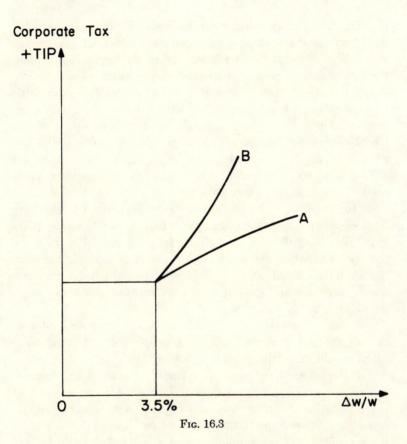

FIG. 16.3

mediate object of policy and should tend to foster a greater adamancy toward excessive settlements.

SETTING THE *TIP* GUIDEPOST

The setting of the guidepost is a separable issue. The principle of a wage guidepost is by now well understood, thanks to the efforts of the Council of Economic Advisers. The principle is that wage increases should be governed by nationwide productivity gains and not by the gains of a firm or an industry. If productivity gains of a firm or industry were made the basis of wage increases, different firms and industries would soon have widely different wage levels. This would lead to spillover effects, the high wages pulling the low wages up, and prices would rise in consequence.

Equal wage increases throughout the economy, for comparable types of labor, would be the rule if labor markets were fully competitive. There could then be no differentials on account of different productivity gains, else labor would move out of the low gaining industries into the high gaining industries. The guidepost simply seeks to accomplish by rule what in a competitive labor market would happen automatically.

As for the level of the guidepost, anything from (1) the pure level of productivity gains, ignoring inflation, to (2) productivity gains plus the full rate of inflation, is conceivable. For instance, with productivity gains at 3 per cent and inflation at 5 per cent, the guidepost could be set anywhere between 3 and 8 per cent. A case can be made for setting it low, in order quickly to bring down the rate of inflation.

An alternative case can be made for taking into account part of the inflation, perhaps half, which under the conditions indicated would make the guidepost 5.5 per cent.

A low guidepost very probably would, at least for awhile, be exceeded by many corporations and cause a large amount of revenue to be raised by the surcharge. This could be compensated by a lower rate of surcharge, or perhaps by lowering the basic profits tax. On the whole, there is much to be said for not making many corporations pay the surcharge and for not collecting a large amount of revenue. This would argue for a relatively high guidepost, which would of course come down as the rate of inflation itself came down.

HOW TO COMPUTE THE TAX

Two principles must be observed by any tax proposal that hopes to prosper at the hands of the American bureaucracy and the tax writing committees of the Congress. First, the tax must be entirely precise in all details, so that it can be audited by the Internal Revenue Service and if necessary taken to court. Any imprecision is bound to lead to conflict between IRS and the taxpayer, with an attendantly large number of law suits. The courts would then do the job that the legislator had failed to do.

Second, the tax must be reasonably equitable as among taxpayers, avoiding significant hardships or windfalls to particular firms or groups. Above all, there must be no opportunity for political opponents, whoever they may be, to construct horror cases.

The problem is to establish the exact amount of a wage increase. The amounts published at the time a contract is concluded are estimates and approximations. Hard numbers are needed for tax administration. This means, in the first place, that the tax cannot be computed until after the end of the company's fiscal year. If the year or years of the wage contract do not coincide with the fiscal year, averaging may be necessary. The wage data can be reasonably expected to be available from two sets of records: the tax records, which must show total wages, fringes and other deductions in arriving at taxable income, and the payroll records which the company needs to pay its employees and also to make up its tax return. The payroll records may indeed be rather widely dispersed among company offices, but they must have been available to the company's accountants for normal corporate purposes.

The wage increase can be computed on one of the following bases:

1. Total wages, salaries, bonuses, fringes, and related payments divided by the number of employees on a particular date would give the average "wage" per employee and its increase over the same figure of the previous year. It is open to the simplest kind of manipulation, however, by adding to the number of employees on the critical date.
2. Total wage and related payments divided by the daily average number of employees. This avoids the obvious difficulty of (1), but still raises the awkward question of how to define em-

ployees, consultants, and other nonemployees receiving fees
that are customarily entered as salaries. The most serious form
of legal tax avoidance possible under this method probably
would be a deliberate reduction in the number of weekly
hours.

3. Total wage and related payments divided by man-hours
worked, adjusted for overtime. This would eliminate some of
the difficulties under (1) and (2). It would still allow the employer, however, to change the labor force mix toward lower
skilled employees. Very high wage increases in each job specification and grade would go untouched by the tax if the
average skill level is reduced sufficiently. Effectiveness of the
tax could be severely reduced by such maneuvers.

4. Total wage and related payments in each job classification and
grade, divided by the number of man-hours worked in the
respective categories, and combined into a weighted index of
wage increases. This would give a fairly watertight specification of a wage increase. The data should be available on the
records indicated above. The difficulty of computation might
nevertheless be great for a large firm with numerous plants,
and with different local pay scales and job classifications all
shifting as the product mix and the geographical mix of the
company's output changes. These difficulties may have to be
faced, however, because tax writing committees may well reject any lesser standard of accuracy.

SOME ALLOCATIVE AND DYNAMIC ASPECTS

We now consider some allocative shifts in the capital-labor resource use that might be induced by the proposal. For whenever
a tax is introduced it will inevitably exert some repercussions on
factor input combinations. A *TIP* designed according to models
1–3 above will create an inducement to reduce the average level
of skill of the labor force. By firing a $10,000 man and hiring a
$5,000 man, the average wage can be reduced for tax purposes if
the numbers involved are large enough to influence the reported
figure.

This phenomenon, should it develop, would not necessarily detract from the proposal. A cut in costs, tending to reduce prices, should be welcome. As lower-priced employees are demanded, moreover, and their wages thereby lifted most rapidly, some damping of the shift-over will occur. Any tendency of the tax to encourage the use of less costly labor will contribute toward greater income equality. The greater balance in earnings, and the opening of more places for the (somewhat) less skilled, or for those lower in seniority, might be beneficial not only in terms of costs and prices, but in easing social tensions.

This would be particularly true at a time when, as at present, the supply of relatively unskilled labor is excessive. To the extent that an excess supply of low-skilled labor contributes to structural unemployment, strengthening the demand side of that market would improve resource allocation. It would help to lower the Phillips curve directly, in addition to the same effect that occurs indirectly when a successful incomes policy permits more expansive monetary and fiscal policies. Monetary and fiscal policies would insure that a changing structure of the demand for labor, should it become at all noticeable, would not lead to unemployment of the more highly skilled.

It will be noted that these tendencies toward downgrading the skill mix of the labor force would materialize only if the *TIP* is computed by methods (1), (2), and (3). Only they present opportunities to reduce the apparent magnitude of wage increases for tax purposes. In that case, a tendency might also arise to go slow on research and development and on the adoption of advanced technology. High technology is less easily combined with unskilled labor than with highly skilled.

An undesirable effect of this sort could be avoided by using computation method (4), which would prevent a rise in the proportion of skilled labor from showing up as an increase in average wage payments per man hour. Under methods (1), (2), and (3), this undesirable effect could under some conditions be avoided by an "averaging back" procedure over, say, three years. Suppose that, in year 1, the firm had an increase in its average wage payment per employee or per man hour of 8 per cent, owing to the introduction of more advanced equipment and a consequent increase in the proportion of highly skilled labor. The firm therefore pays a *TIP*. On the basis of method (4), the wage increase, let us suppose, would have been only 3.5 per cent. If the same rate of increase continues, the firm in the following two years will have weighted average wage increases of 3.5 per cent each. Suppose the guidepost is 5 per cent. The firm could then be allowed to average its wage increases for the three years, arriving at an average annual increase of 5 per cent, and claim a refund.

These consequences of *TIP* would largely disappear if a tax base somewhat like that described under (4) were adopted. In that case, employers could not escape the tax by reducing the skill level of the labor force. Neither would there be a check to innovational activity.

Could *TIP* be expected to create unemployment? If methods (1), (2), and (3) are employed, the demand for highly skilled labor would diminish relative to that for less skilled labor. This would not, however, imply a reduction in the aggregate demand for labor. On the contrary, the overall effect of a successful incomes policy, and therefore of *TIP*, should be to make possible a higher level of employment without increasing the rate of inflation. The Phillips curve—the tradeoff between inflation and unemployment—would be lowered. A lower level of unemployment would become consistent with a low or zero rate of inflation. This would, of course, be true also if method (4) were employed. The gains from a lower rate of unemployment would be substantial, quite aside from the noneconomic benefits. According to a familiar rule of thumb, known as Okun's Law, a reduction in unemployment by 1 percentage point yields an increase in *GNP* of 3 percentage points. Without attempting to guess the magnitude of the effect that *TIP* might have, it is worth noting that a 1 per cent reduction in unemployment would yield something like $30 billion additional *GNP*. It is hard to believe that adverse allocational or employment effects of *TIP*, should they occur, could approach this order of magnitude. Their occurrence is in any event unlikely for the reasons already stated.

Obviously, such comparisons are bound to be speculative.

Moreover, the gain in employment would not be attributable to *TIP* as such. Any successful incomes policy would have the same effect. The proper comparison, in evaluating the possible employment benefits of *TIP*, is not so much with the status quo, but with the results of an alternative incomes policy.

OTHER TECHNICAL PROBLEMS

The discussion so far has abstracted from all technical problems of tax administration except the crucial one of how to define a wage increase. Obviously there are a great many. We list a few, giving a summary indication of the issues involved.

1. *Coverage. TIP*, focusing on the corporate income tax, can be most easily applied to corporations. Application to unincorporated business or nonprofit institutions would create difficulties. On the other hand, it can reasonably be asked whether *TIP* should be applied even to the totality of corporations. Small firms, if they are unionized, usually confront a much larger union so that bargaining power is very unequal. In such a situation, the union might indeed be indifferent to the firm's profit position, because its demands would be guided by considerations extraneous to the particular negotiation. Freeing small firms from the paperwork of *TIP* would be a major administrative advantage. A good case can be made, therefore, for applying *TIP* only to large firms, say with profits of $1 million or some multiple thereof. Any cutoff point, to be sure, creates inequities and administrative difficulties. But such cutoffs are not unknown in corporate taxation.

   It is true also that low profits do not necessarily imply a small firm. For the effectiveness of *TIP*, however, exemption of a moderate number of large firms with low profits would not matter greatly. Low profits should by themselves exert a substantial restraint on wage increases. Exemption from *TIP* would avoid aggravating the problems under which firms in that situation already find themselves.

2. *New Firms or Defunct Firms.* Special provisions would be required for large firms that disappear or emerge as a result of

mergers and similar corporate reorganizations. Where ongoing enterprises are concerned, this should not present insuperable difficulties under any of the techniques 1–4. Where an enterprise stops operating altogether, or a new one is created, both the presumptive profit situation and the presumptive size of such enterprises suggest that coverage by *TIP* would not be important.

3. *Existing Contracts.* Whether existing long term "excessive" wage contracts should be honored or excluded from the *TIP* raises difficult legal and institutional questions. The inequities arising here, however, are those that would occur also under a price and wage freeze. Contracts entered into shortly before and in contemplation of the enactment of *TIP* could be included by making *TIP* retroactive to the date when it was first legislatively proposed.

4. *Public Utilities.* Since public utilities ordinarily are allowed, by their regulatory authorities, to earn some specific rate of return, the possibility of tax shifting clearly exists. It would probably be unwise to try to interfere with this well established procedure for the sake of making *TIP* fully effective with respect to utilities. However, the "regulatory lag" has often proved sufficiently long and costly to make utilities sensitive to changes in costs and income tax.

5. *The Transitional Period.* The problems of implementing *TIP* in any year resemble those of introducing any major alteration of tax laws. While these aspects create problems, precedents exist for dealing with them.

6. *Construction and Trucking.* These two industries lately have exhibited particularly pronounced upward wage trends. Many of the firms involved, moreover, are small and might be exempted from *TIP*. The effectiveness of *TIP* will be somewhat reduced if it cannot easily be applied to two industries where wage restraint is particularly urgently needed. The problems revealed by the construction industry, however, are so different from those of other industries that special measures may in any event be needed.

THE *TIP*: CONCLUSIONS

Analysis suggests that *TIP* should be able to make an important contribution to checking inflation. We do not regard it as necessarily more effective than any alternative incomes policy. It is simply less of a departure from reliance on free markets. Going beyond fiscal and monetary restraint to a *TIP* is less of a wrench than going to some form of direct intervention in wage and price setting.

The enactment of *TIP* will take time, perhaps something of the order of a year after it has first been seriously considered. If in the meantime inflation continues at a high rate, it may be necessary to move to another form of incomes policy that could be adapted almost instantly. Even then, however, *TIP* deserves consideration as a long run solution. One of the clearly demonstrated characteristics of other forms of incomes policy is that, even if they are effective initially, they tend to break apart in the course of time. The effectiveness of *TIP* should improve over time as administrative techniques are perfected and the market learns to respond to it.

NOTES

1. Our work was originally linked by Leonard Silk in articles in the *New York Times*, 1970; also, editorial, 1970. Earlier writings include: Henry Wallich, *Newsweek*, September 5, 1966, December 14, 1970; *New York Times*, December 16, 1970.

Sidney Weintraub, "An Incomes Policy to Stop Inflation," *Lloyds Bank Review*, January 1970, and a truncated statement on "A Proposal to Halt the Spiral of Wages and Prices," *New York Times*, 1970.

2. A. C. Pigou, *Industrial Fluctuations*, 2nd ed. (London: Macmillan and Co., 1929), p. 33. Pigou, among others, pointed out that prices or unemployment could serve as a cyclical measure for their movements were inverse. R. F. Harrod, similarly, argued that the empirical law was that prices and output moved in the *same* direction. This relation, therefore, was violated in late 1970. See *The Trade Cycle* (Oxford: the University Press, 1936), p. 39.

3. Chapter 1 above.

4. See *A General Theory of the Price Level* (Philadelphia: Chilton Book Co., 1959). Also, John Hotson, *International Comparisons*

of Money Velocity and Wage Mark-ups (New York: Augustus M. Kelley, 1968).

5. Cf. L. R. Klein and R. F. Kosobud, "Some Econometrics of Growth: Great Ratios of Economics," *Quarterly Journal of Economics* (May 1961).

6. For an argument that the corporate income tax is shifted, and an objection to it as an anti-inflation measure, see John Hotson, "Adverse Effects of Tax and Interest Hikes," *Canadian Economic Journal,* 1971.

Appendix 1

In Defense of Wage-Price
Guideposts . . . Plus

The wage-price guideposts provide a study in political as well as in economic power. For through them public policy has been assayed without formal legal sanction. This anomaly in our political life conforms better to British practice, where a word of intent by the ruling party can be as compelling as the force of law.[1] It is as if we tried to implement monetary policy without the institution of the Federal Reserve. Price-level control is being sought through an executive *request* for compliance on the part of labor and business.

In the past it would have been thought that vigilance against inflation was chiefly the preserve of the Federal Reserve authorities. Many in and outside of academic circles still think monetary policy is ample for the task. But theory and events are making the guidepost concept more creditable.

Postwar activity in this country has been marred by simultaneous price rises and unemployment. The 1957 recession, induced by tight money, revealed an awkward phenomenon: price levels kept edging up while output and employment moved down. Old doctrines of money control were rendered suspect in this instance. On the basis of two centuries of economic analysis it would have been thought that with restrained money supplies and lower output the price level should fall. But prices turned up. This outcome gave empirical confirmation to the concept of wage-and-cost-push inflation.

Many who were disturbed by the slow growth of the economy counseled that we learn to live with "creeping inflation" as a small price to pay for fuller employment. The thought was that an enterprise economy might have to compromise its objectives of full employment and price-level stability.[2]

THE ORIGINAL GUIDEPOSTS

At the close of the Annual Report of the Council of Economic Advisers in 1962 there appeared a six-page section entitled: *Guideposts for Noninflationary Wage and Price Behavior.*[3] In this a wage-income policy was born.

The original statement commences with:

> There are important segments of the economy where firms are large or employees well-organized, or both. In these sectors, private parties may exercise considerable discretion over the terms of wage bargains and price decisions. Thus, at least in the short run, there is considerable room for the exercise of private power and a parallel need for the assumption of private responsibility (p. 185).

As to new legislation:

> Mandatory controls in peacetime over the outcomes of wage negotiations and over individual price decisions are neither desirable in the American tradition nor practical in a diffuse and decentralized continental economy.

Later there comes the key concept of the guideposts:

> Productivity is a *guide* rather than a *rule* for appraising wage and price behavior for several reasons. First, there are a number of problems involved in measuring productivity change, and a number of alternative measures are available. Second, there is nothing immutable in fact or in justice about the distribution of the total product between labor and nonlabor incomes. Third, the pattern of wages and prices among industries is and should be responsive to forces other than changes in productivity (p. 186).

Still, it recommended:

> The general guide for noninflationary wage behavior is that the
> rate of increase in wage rates (including fringe benefits) in each
> industry be equal to the trend rate of over-all productivity in-
> crease. General acceptance of this guide would maintain stability
> of labor cost per unit of output for the economy as a whole—
> though not, of course, for individual industries (p. 189).

These are the salient guidepost pronouncements. Wags have
mocked them as "open mouth" operations, or a jawbone policy,
in contrast to the open market operations of the Federal Reserve.
But the guideposts can have teeth, as witness President Kennedy's
confrontation with the steel industry, or President Johnson's roll-
back of the aluminum price increase. Earlier success fizzled in
the New York transit settlement, in the airline strike, and in the
recent steel price boost (1966) where the presidential press
secretary observed laconically that the President lacked power to
control prices. Nonetheless, in a future struggle of wills the residue of presidential power might yet be displayed. Big industry
and big labor know this.

The guideposts must thus be considered as an important instrument of public policy even though the Executive Office has
temporized and equivocated in applying them and has been hazy
and indecisive in their enforcement. Still, one can often make the
same observation on monetary or fiscal policy.

PRICE STABILITY AND FULL EMPLOYMENT: TRADE-OFFS OR COMPATIBLE GOALS?

How stable should the price level be? Perhaps by limiting the
price rise to 1 or 0.5 per cent per annum, we would not be doing
badly. Some institutional perspective is required on this. For
other economies 5 or 10 per cent per annum, after chaotic price
rises of some hundreds of per cent, may be a reasonable objective.
In our economy the consumer price index rose by 23 per cent in
the 1950s. From 1960 through 1965 the rise was about 1 per cent

per annum. Since July of 1965 the rise has been 2.8 per cent. It may be as high as 3.5 per cent over the next year.

The recent price creep-up has raised the serious question of whether our economy can maintain near-full employment and a stable price level. Doubts arise from analysis and from the empirical results derived from the Phillips-curve relation which purports to show that larger wage rises accompany low unemployment, so that price levels become destabilized at high employment.

Let us take it that these are the facts for the essentially uncontrolled economy of the past. Those who merely read the quantitative history and declare that inflation is inevitable under full employment are the affluent society's modern heralds of the dismal science. Theirs is the gloomy view for, in effect, it concludes that we are helpless once we approach full employment. It is reminiscent of the dour predictions of Karl Marx, who insisted that a capitalistic economy survived only through procreating an "industrial reserve army" of unemployed so as to depress wages and bolster profits.[4]

There are also those who conjure the "trade offs"—the modern jargon for choices—between further moves to enlarge employment and to contain the price level. Arguing that fuller employment makes price-level increases inevitable, we must pick either *some* unemployment or *some* inflation. Either the divergent paths of full employment or of price-level stability must be traveled. More liberal expositors would argue for fuller employment; more conservative opinion would elect more unemployment to retain the price line.

THE GUIDEPOSTS AS AN OPPORTUNITY

It is in this context that the guideposts must be examined. For they aspire to be an instrument for attaining both full employment *and* price-level stability. They comprise our current version of a wages-income policy. Undoubtedly they will be modified over time. Their institutional nature may someday be formalized. An agency may be created to implement them. Some powers over wage bargains may be enacted. But aside from these administrative details—for these are what they are—the guideposts constitute our one serious effort to cope with the price-level aspect of full employment. They may yet make it possible to reconcile both full employment *and* a stable price level.

This is the theme to be developed. One of the distressing sights has been to watch the retreat of some Keynesians away from full-employment objectives in advocating tax measures to take some "steam" out of the economy, actually proposing to create unemployment by discouraging investment. Accustomed to unemployment, they are fretful now in the sight of the Promised Land. The *unemployment* policies they recommend would return them to the safer world that they do understand. By creating unemployment they can devise programs to eliminate it.

We are *nearing* full employment. But there is still a modest amount of slack in our economy; its absorption would offer hope to our cities, faced with juvenile delinquency and race riots of the unemployed and underemployed.[5] Support for the guideposts might render a contribution in these matters.

MONETARY AND FISCAL POLICY

While many minor measures, such as some speedup in tax collections, lower tariffs, and prohibitions on some exports, can undoubtedly be concocted to deal with the inflation problem in an economy with nearly full employment, the main instruments consist of (1) monetary policy, (2) fiscal policy, and (3) a wages-income policy.

Monetary policy is the time-honored method; the Federal Reserve has been pushing on this front rather strongly; interest rates are at a high for modern history. Undoubtedly, even tighter money can do more than depress the stock market and panic the bond market. Set on a really rigid course, it can dampen housing ventures and many long-lived investment projects; it can deflect us from full employment despite the high pace of government outlays. At present levels of interest rates monetary policy loses all sense of delicacy. Further moves can literally knock down the house.

Monetary policy can thus cool off the economy on the employment and the output front. But we may be skeptical of whether it really will maintain the price level. For if money wages rise in excess of productivity—and union leaders seem to be chafing at the guidepost bit—then we will witness a repetition of the 1957–1959 experience: unemployment will grow and price levels will also rise. Unemployment, to judge by experience here and abroad, is not clearly inconsistent with inflation. In short, monetary policy will not do on the inflation front unless union leaders are intimidated by unemployment experience. This is an illusory supposition. Every day they seem to be chanting "More."

Just as monetary policy operates through curbing investment, or by making housing and installment loans more onerous, fiscal policy has a more direct influence on take-home pay, or in discouraging investment through higher tax rates, or through cutting government demand.

Fiscal policy, like monetary policy, can undoubtedly depress demand and create unemployment. Only if it is argued that in so doing productivity can be increased, or that current levels of money wages can be maintained, can one be confident of its success on the price level. Insofar as monetary or fiscal policy impedes investment it will tend to repress a major positive factor in the long-trend improvement in productivity.

THE NEED FOR WAGE POLICY

The wages-income aspect of the guideposts remains the sole alternative for doing the job without obstructing the march toward fuller employment.

Essentially, the task of the guideposts is to maintain wage movements roughly in line with productivity improvements. Reference is, of course, to the broad average of labor productivity in producing the diversified output in the gross national product. Further, the wage movement, covering, say, a forthcoming year, must be equated to productivity movements over the same stretch of time. It is *future* productivity that must be considered. Studies of past productivity changes are thus relevant only insofar as they illuminate the future: it is thus always possible to question whether a past trend of ten or five or even two years is meaningful. A future projection rather than a historical disinterment of past facts is required.

THE EMPHASIS ON AVERAGE PHENOMENA

The important conformity is of average phenomena, in respect of both money wages and productivity. Structural relations are less crucial in the present context. Departures from the average in particular cases are tolerable so long as the average itself remains firm.

Formally, what is referred to is the wage-markup equation (*WCM*):

$$P = kw/A. \tag{1}$$

In practice, k has assumed an absolute value of just under 2, implying that for every one-cent increase in unit wage costs prices mount by nearly 2 cents. The reciprocal of k is simply the wage share, or the wage bill divided by the gross business product. It is well known that this has remained remarkably constant historically. It is this firmness which enables us to predict that if wages move in consonance with productivity, the price level will be maintained. After a slight downward trend in the 1950s the markup has recently tended to edge up a bit. But the price variation between 1962 and 1965, due to this factor alone, would have been about 0.7 per cent.[6]

Explanations for the stability of the markup factor are still obscure, though it is possible to offer convincing reasons why it will not change very much.[7] But why the wage share got stuck at its historic level is not easy to say. Interestingly, parallel phenomena can be found in many countries, in diverse stages of industrialization and with different degrees of governmental participation in economic life.

ECONOMY-WIDE PRODUCTIVITY

The concept of the average wage level has been belabored in these remarks. Of course, an average can conceal wide variations within its structure.

Clearly, if a group of 50,000 employees gain a wage hike of, say, 6 per cent, another group of 50,000 would have to be limited to 1 per cent in order to maintain the 3.5 per cent average movement (assuming that the initial wage rates of the two groups were identical). Recognizing this, public policy must pay particular attention to pay hikes for the largest labor groups in our economy.

What will not do, though the trial balloon was recently floated by the incumbent Secretary of Commerce, would be to permit wages to follow industry-wide productivity improvements. This would be wholly uneconomic and inequitable. Suppose that in one industry productivity advanced by the huge figure of 10 per cent per annum; with a wage rise of this magnitude unit labor costs would hold firm. The advantage to the economy of the higher productivity would be lost, for the institutional wage-push would erect an obstacle to a price reduction and an ensuing output enlargement. In another industry where productivity, and thus wages, failed to rise at all, unit labor costs, prices, and output would hold firm. There would be no reason for a modification of its output level either.

From an efficiency standpoint there should be a relative expansion of the first industry's output. For the productivity achievements reveal that we can increase its output more readily through technological developments.

The wage policy would be inequitable. A persistent trend of productivity improvements would mean that in the first industry money wages would double in less than 10 years. In the second industry they would stay constant. Yet almost the same abilities might be involved, with the sole difference being in the new technology and equipment. Inevitably, as workers sought to transfer from the one industry to the other this ill-conceived proposal would break down.

A proper policy would maintain the average wage movement

within the average improvement norm. Simultaneously it would seek to achieve a strong measure of equity between wage earners of similar skills. It must also aim to direct labor into industries, occupations, and geographical areas of most urgent need.

The analytic facets are clear in principle. Insofar as some wages have lagged in the wage upheavals of recent years, it signifies that society is obtaining some labor services on inequitable terms, and that some groups are failing to participate adequately in the technological advance that has taken place. Insofar as these groups can be identified, they would seem to be entitled to above-average increases, even though the outputs in which they are employed would be somewhat curtailed in relative terms.

DEPARTURES FROM THE PRODUCTIVITY NORM

That exceptions would be admitted into the general formula for wage increases would mean that those labor groups that have benefitted most in recent years would have to be restrained below the national norm.

This entire question of maximal and minimal increases deserves far more searching inquiry than has been publicly given to the issue by the Council of Economic Advisers and others. It is a hard question; there are so many diverse combinations of wage movements that can maintain the average constant. The Council must be ever mindful of equity aspects and the functional needs of the economy among occupations, industries, and geographical areas, while simultaneously serving to protect the price level. Policy implementation is difficult though the general principles are less recondite.[8]

WAGE DRIFT

"Wage drift," or the tendency of management to agree to the upgrading of labor so that those formerly in one hourly pay category are boosted to a higher wage bracket, seems to be a chief means of circumventing an agreement in which all occupations are limited to a wage move within the guideline norms.

Clearly the theory is concerned with the *average* wage level and its pace of change—not with hourly rates of pay or average wage movements for job classifications. Confusion has been rife on this; what must be borne in mind in each agreement is the previous *average* wage, for the industry or occupation, compared to the new average growth level. Otherwise, a spurious adherence to the guideposts can ignite a movement quite disproportionate to productivity phenomena.[9]

PRICE-WAGE TARGETS

In an economy that has been experiencing some inflation it may be desirable to aim for an average money wage increase below the expected productivity norm. With a projected improvement of 3.5 per cent, a wage move of 3 per cent may be the target. At other times we may want to overshoot the productivity mark to establish a rising price tendency. The art of policy depends so much on investment intentions and the past history of the economy. Presently, something may be said for a policy that endeavors to turn around the recent inflationary experience and induce a very moderate price-level deflation.

With a wage-income policy of the type outlined, after a decade the average wage structure would stand about 35 to 40 per cent higher, assuming a compound growth factor of about 3.5 per cent. Practically all wages would move up by at least 25 per cent. Some wage levels would stand about 50 per cent higher. An average wage of $5,000 would become about $6,500 after 10 years, and about $9,000 after 25 years. Pay envelopes would continue to swell but without upsetting the purchasing power of money over time. There seems much to commend in this policy. It should sate unionist desires for "more" without deranging the economic system. It would abort the unemployment wrought by monetary policy to stop an inflationary trend. It would be fair to pensioners and sundry semifixed-income groups in the economy. Guidepost policy thus can reconcile the interests of the various competing and conflicting pressure blocs.

WAGES AS DEMAND

Many will contend that what has been presented is simply a wage-push price-level thesis to the exclusion of demand elements. Yet this is a spurious contention.

It must be remembered *that wages are simultaneously demand as well as cost factors.* Though the WCM formula *appears* to stress only the cost aspect, really this is to misread the argument.

Wages are simultaneously costs to the employer and income to the recipient. As income they immediately determine the mass consumer purchasing power. As money wages go up, the sums for consumer outlays rise. It is no accident that when steel and automobile wages rise in Pittsburgh and Detroit, retail sales in the region also go up. One must occasion the other.

Nearly 90 per cent of consumer outlay in our economy emanates from wage earners.[10] Maybe a more detailed study would cut this figure a few points—or lift it a bit. But is it not obvious that in a mass production economy the mass of the output must be consumed by the mass of the populace, namely, the wage earners? It would be astonishing if this were not so; most of the food output, clothing, housing occupancy, the mass outlays on automobiles and consumer durables, on popular forms of entertainment, must be absorbed by the households of the 75 million gainfully employed workers.[11]

If it is correct that about 90 per cent of consumer output is purchased by wage and salary earners, then the familiar "consumption-function" is merely a euphemism for what is primarily a wage earner outlay-function.[12] The simple implication is that a rise in money wages will raise consumption outlays.

WAGE BILL AND TAX POLICY

All this is to assert the demand aspect of money wages in consumer markets. Consumption still constitutes some 70 per cent of the gross business product. Restraining wages is equivalent to exercising a strong rein over demand in this substantial sector of the economy.

The matter may be looked at in this way. Currently, wage and salary disbursements are running at about \$400 billion per annum. A 5 per cent increase would add \$20 billion to purchasing power. After taxes, perhaps about \$17 billion. Fiscal policy, by way of a tax rise, would have to aim at an overall personal income tax rise in excess of 25 per cent to dam up this sum and block it from consumer markets. Even then there would still be pressure on prices through the cost side.

Advocates of the fiscal weapon are thus the unrealistic ones. An ounce of wage-policy vigilance may outweigh pounds of cure through tax policy.

THE CONSUMER PRICE LEVEL

Analytically, an appreciation of the consumption-demand aspect of the average money wage can be reached in this way.

From the truism that sales to consumers are equal to purchases by consumers, we have:

$$P_c Q_c = cwN + c'F + c''\,'R + \theta. \qquad (2)$$

In this, P_c is the consumer price level and Q_c represents the volume of consumer outputs. The c terms denote the average consumption propensities of the various income groups. The w term is the average wage level, while N equals the number of employees, so that wN represents the total wage bill. The F term specifies rentier income. The R term consists of profit income. The θ term embraces expenditures by transfer recipients, pensioners, and dissaving.

Dividing by the wage bill (wN), and multiplying by N_c/N_c (for consumer goods employment), we have

$$P_c = \frac{w}{A_c}(c + c'E + \theta')\frac{N}{N_c}. \qquad (3)$$

The only new terms are A_c for average labor productivity in consumer goods and E to denote the sum of both rentier and profit incomes divided by the wage bill. The θ' term represents the transfer part of outlay as a portion of the wage bill. The ratio

N/N_c consists of the sum of total employment to consumer goods employment.

Estimating the size of terms to the right of the w_c/A_c relation yields the average price markup. The c term stands at about 0.9. The c' propensity may be about 0.5. The E term, of nonwage to wage income is about 1.0 or slightly less. The θ' term is about 0.08, meaning about 8 per cent of the wage bill.

On this basis, the terms in the parentheses add up to a value of about 1.5. Perhaps the ratio of N to N_c is about 1.5, meaning that consumer goods industries provide about ⅔ of the total employment. The magnitudes to the right of unit wage costs thus come to about 2.2.

What is interesting in this formulation of the problem is that the terms in the parentheses, which represent consumer behavior patterns as well as income division elements, are scarcely likely to show more than a small range of variation in the course of a year or two. Likewise, the ratio of total to consumer goods employment will seldom shift markedly over a similar period.[13] Neither set of terms is thus likely to give an important lift to the consumer price level.

Even in this formulation, which proceeds entirely from demand considerations, we are again led back to the importance of money wage changes to productivity improvements as the stuff out of which inflations are made.

IMPLICATIONS FOR MONETARY AND FISCAL POLICY

The formulation is not without its bearing on monetary and fiscal policy, given the importance of the consumer price level in our economy.

Monetary policy can affect investment; it can affect employment. Through both channels it can affect profits. Thus its impact can be on (N/N_c) and on R. But it would take a pretty good dose of monetary action to have an important bearing on these terms. The price of its impact would, to repeat, be unemployment.

Fiscal policy, through personal income tax, could affect the c-terms, computed after tax. But a heavy tax bite would be required to move them substantially. Corporate taxes could operate on the same variables as monetary policy, with the same dire employment consequences.

Note that monetary and fiscal policy strive to *lower* some of the elements of the equation. Wage policy would seek to control the *w* increase and so facilitate monetary–fiscal maneuvers without compelling their more serious toll by way of unemployment. Wage policy would thus permit the sensitive and delicate maneuvers of other stabilization instruments and free them of their bull in the china shop characteristics. The higher *w* rises the larger the necessary monetary and fiscal mix to restrain the price level. It is possible to doubt their effectiveness for important wage changes.

DISTRIBUTIONAL ASPECTS OF WAGE POLICY

Let us now turn to the distributional aspects of an *effective* guide-post policy.

If wages were geared to productivity, the price level should hold firm—if the markup factor remained constant. Historically, this has *tended* to happen. Hopefully, this would occur in the future unless some very new forces were at work in the economy. Only significant changes in the degree of monopoly power should alter this outcome. Casual observation furnishes scant basis to expect important changes in this phenomenon in the near future.

One could apply some of the newer theoretical developments to this matter. On the Mrs. Robinson–Kalecki–Kaldor hypothesis, namely, that wage earners spend their full income and that non-wage earners save their full earnings, it can be demonstrated that profits in the consumer goods industries depend uniquely on the wage bill in the capital goods industries. If wages and employment in capital goods hold firm, then profits in consumer goods industries will be unchanged. Even on abandoning the R-K-K oversimplification, consumer goods profits are vitally contingent upon the wage bill in the nonconsumer goods industries—to include government employment.[14]

The overall assumption of wage earner spending and nonwage

earner saving makes the profit total depend wholly upon the volume of investment, as Kaldor has shown. But an *implicit major assumption is that prices remain constant.*

Analysis thus confirms that if money wages do not rise unduly, the profit total will be well contained. We might pursue this conclusion further.

WAGES, PRICES, PROFITS

Even if unit wage costs remain constant, if the markup factor rises, the profit share can rise. This is clear in principle. Still, the evidence does not reveal any important changes in the profit share occurring through this channel.

What will happen to aggregate or absolute profits if wages and prices do rise? On Kaldor's simple but penetrating assumptions, if the volume of real investment remains constant, but the price level goes up, money investment magnitudes will be inflated. Higher money investment will compel money-profit totals also to be higher. This follows simply from his argument that profits are equal to investment.

Even dropping the extreme Kaldor assumptions, it can be shown that whenever the price level rises with a rise in unit wage costs, then the profit aggregate *must* be higher. For if the markup factor is constant, and the money wage bill grows with employment while output grows apace, inevitably the nonwage share must also rise in aggregate terms. For proof, consider the following:

$$R + F = PQ - wN. \qquad (4)$$

With $(\Delta P/P) = (\Delta w/w)$, and Q, N and F constant, then:

$$\Delta R = \frac{(R + F)}{w} \Delta w. \qquad (5)$$

The terms conform to previous usage.

Equation (5) should be pondered.[15] It attests to the potency of a money wage and price rise as a profit maker. Profits will be augmented even if wages and prices move up proportionately, so that real wages are unaffected. A faster price rise will mean still higher profits, and vice versa.

Thus, the profit total can be contained by a policy that succeeds in keeping the price level under restraint. An effective guidepost program should do this. There would be no general need to deal directly with profits so long as the price level follows a stable course while the investment aggregate does not grow unduly. If this view turns out to be mistaken, the corporate income tax would be the obvious instrument to cope with the problem insofar as political pressure compels action on this front.

ALLOCATIONAL ASPECTS OF WAGE POLICY

Allocational aspects of wage policy are also of concern. The contrast should be, however, to the allocational distortions of "boom and bust," to inflation and unemployment in the absence of wage policy.

On the general level there is no reason why adherence to guidepost rules should erect any obstacles to the proper allocation of the labor force. The growth industries coincide usually with the areas in which the union movement is strongest and in which wage levels rank among the highest. The chief impediment to procuring new labor in these industries is unlikely to be a limited near-future wage increase tailored to the national productivity average.

Generally, labor goes where jobs are open at the higher pay scales. In the past the limitation to the numbers in the more highly paying occupations resided in the restricted demand in those industries; the higher wages could be maintained by the observance of union pay scales. In conditions of underemployment it is probable that economists have overrated the allocational effects of the typical wage differentials.

Unions have been able to obtain the big gains in those industries participating most in the postwar production explosion. Further wage discrepancies, one could argue, scarcely serve any immediate allocational needs. So long as jobs in growth industries remain among the better paid, the allocational aspects of wage policy are, at the moment, a less critical factor in the formulation of public policy.

Some may question this view in particular applications. But this should not compromise the general policy. Allowance can always be made for special industry, occupational, or geographical situations where higher wages constitute the magic wand to attract the necessary work force. In a full-employment economy most industries will appear to be shorthanded. Where a differential can provide the remedy to attract labor we have a clear case for special treatment. On whether the policy would be threatened by severe labor shortages, we must wait and see, and then approve the adjustments in the light of the facts. But we shall never even make a start in understanding the problem if we permit wages to rise indiscriminately in all markets and in all job categories. This is the road to inflation and to the misuse of resources.

Analysis suggests that if the price level is held under control, with some industries lowering prices and other industries raising prices, with some expanding output relatively and others falling behind, we should be able to foster the kind of wage adjustments that the facts require.

The facts in Table A.1 are not without interest. This table shows the relative employment total by major industrial groupings. What is so astonishing is that despite the lopsided wage movement from 1950 to 1965, the distribution of the labor force was not vastly different in 1965 from what it was in 1950. It is doubtful that the wage movements that did occur were precisely those required as an allocational lever.

Of course it is possible to argue that the movements *were* precisely those required to maintain the allocational pattern! But it seems highly doubtful that if wages in construction, say, had been 10 per cent less, the labor allocational results would have been different. One can run down the list. Over most of this period there was significant unemployment so that, for the unemployed, a money wage rise was superfluous in enticing them to take jobs. A job vacancy was the essential element.

Undoubtedly, the allocational aspects of relative wage levels

TABLE A.1

Percentage Distribution of Full-time Equivalent Employees,
and Average Wage Increase, 1950–1965

	1950	1965	Wage Increase 1950–65
All industries	100.0	100.0	90%
Agriculture, forestry, and fisheries	4.6	2.6	51
Mining	1.9	1.0	97
Contract construction	4.9	5.1	97
Manufacturing, total	30.8	28.8	94
Wholesale and retail trade	18.5	17.3	79
Finance, insurance, and real estate	3.7	4.4	89
Transportation	5.4	3.7	102
Communications and public utilities	2.6	2.4	108
Services	12.5	15.3	93
Government	15.2	19.3	89

would assume greater significance in a full-employment economy. Until we note the pressures that full employment places on the respective labor markets, it is best that we take an open position on the problem. Maybe the personnel search will put the wage policy to a severe test. But there is enough flexibility in the concept of the average-wage move to allow structural variations to cope with the situation. Surely it is better to hold the general wage structure under some semblance of normalcy than to permit contest bidding for labor and spiraling wages and prices, without any guarantee that labor will thereby be directed into uses of highest social value.

THE CRUCIAL NATURE OF THE LABOR MARKET

It must be apprehended that the labor market is not quite like other markets. By its wage bargains the labor market sets the price-level dimensions for the economy. In a capitalistic system a large group of men are placed in the employ of a smaller group. As wage and salary incomes are paid, in the process the incomes comprise the production costs and the great base of demand in consumer markets. If we are to control spending, then we must do it at the source, in the wage bargain. Tax policy aims at taking away income *after* it has been obtained; this means locking the barn door after the horse has run out—though it may be possible, by creating enough unemployment, to cajole him back in again. Suppressing 2 per cent of the wage rise would surpass in effect even a very strong tax measure.

"OVERHEATING?"

The typical objection will undoubtedly be that the argument has been too casual on the matter of "overheating" in the economy, seeming to deny the problem not only currently but perhaps permanently.

Unfortunately, it is almost hopeless to try to estimate the magnitude of "excess demand" while wage increases exert their direct and indirect pressures on the price level. Holding the line on wages and prices, we can better decide whether there is some slack remaining in the economy or whether labor markets are fully taut. Despite the alarms and fragments of evidence the answer is not entirely obvious. Some were advocating demand-damping in the fall of 1965, when there was still ample unemployment. The current unemployment rate still remains at about 3.9 per cent; is this an indisputably low target? Adolescents without work experience are omitted in the unemployment count. The automobile industry is operating below peak. Housing is throttled below capacity. Other industries have a degree of elbow room. It thus may be that some voices have been too shrill too soon in pressing for a curb on the output advance.

With wage policy we should be able to discern whether some demand enlargement is still possible or whether an overextended demand should be nipped. Wage policy would thus impart a precision to fiscal and monetary maneuvers that is currently lacking. For consumer market binges, the personal income tax would be the direct lever so long as the wage level cannot be rolled back. Where capital goods are being bid up, a dose of monetary policy, a corporate income tax hike, and a curtailment of government capital expenditures would constitute the proper medicine.

The point is that overheating is obscured by the wage push. We may be near a point of overheating. Certainly we have not passed it. Those who counseled output restraint in the recent past because of the price-level trend have largely erred. Wage-cost facts have been hopelessly confounded with an inaccurate assessment of our productive capabilities.[16]

THE GUIDEPOSTS . . . PLUS

Most other countries of the free world, and surely the controlled economies, have resorted to a conscious wage policy. All have found it necessary, in smaller or greater degree. We are scarcely an exception, as our guideposts and myriad discussions of wage inflation affirm.

What kind of wage policy?

Despite the lack of punitive provisions, the guideposts were effective between 1962 and 1965. Some may allege that this was due to the unemployment, the excess capacity, and the quiescent labor movement. In 1966 and 1967 they have been punctured several times and in several places. More such phenomena may mar the future, as labor becomes restless in the midst of the employment boom.

What should the policy be in the near future?

The assumption is that military outlays will increase and the pressure on production facilities will be intensified. On this basis the following steps in a presidential program to revive the guidepost concept do not appear excessive:

1. The guidepost wage-productivity concept should be unequivocally affirmed.

2. The President should simultaneously pledge, and so inform the various business trade associations, that if prices continue to rise despite labor's adherence to the guideposts, he will press measures to increase the corporate income tax. Further, where administered price actions warrant attention, he will direct the

Justice Department to institute inquiry and bring all its powers to bear on the matter.

3. An executive agency should be established to assimilate all relevant data on wage, price, and productivity trends.[17]

Weekly reports on wage movements by industries and occupations should be published, with tentative interpretations of their implications for the average wage total and the price level. Important abrogations of guidepost policy should be spotlighted. Detailed monthly reports and occasional papers should be released for public information.

4. The Federal Mediation Service should be instructed to report on any negotiations in which the guideposts are in danger of being violated. The Executive Office should refuse to assist any settlements which deviate from these norms.

5. In wage negotiations in key industries where the guideposts must be especially observed, the President should publicize the important wage gains of the postwar era. He should remind all that in the major industries we are not dealing with an impoverished, underpaid, or underprivileged economic group.

The President must stress at all times the importance he attaches to his program. The aim of an average wage rise in the neighborhood of 35 to 40 per cent over the next decade is a reasonable one, well within our means of accomplishment. But it cannot be exceeded at the present time.

6. In the event that the guideposts are ignored, the possibility of cutting government purchases from the industries involved might be considered in order to deter business acquiescence in excessive union demands.

7. As a more decisive and censuring step, the withdrawal of National Labor Board recognition of unions which flout the national policy may be considered.

8. If these measures are unsuccessful, Congress may wish to authorize the President to set aside agreements which injure the national interest, as a temporary and emergency measure.

9. As a still more serious step, a four-month national wage and salary freeze might be considered if the inflation situation becomes more menacing.

To an unsophisticated mind unaware of all the nuances of the union movement and political power, none of the first five steps appear to jeopardize any basic freedom or depart in any way from our political and social mores. A serious statement from a determined executive in a time of military involvement should suffice. In other war periods far more extensive controls have been imposed on our economic structure. By previous standards the program is indeed moderate.

There may be disagreement on this assessment. But should we throw up our hands and say the problem is difficult, that little or nothing can be done? This is the way of the defeatist. Constructive voices will seek to devise better programs. There need be no attachment to the measures suggested. What is required is a beginning toward an equitable and feasible program.

Some will argue that to invoke the Office of the President in wage bargains is to demean this great office. But to say this is to become lost in the fog of resounding rhetoric. The Office of the President is already involved in the inflation issue. Successive administrations have constantly wrestled with wage problems, union organization drives, and strike disruptions. It is unrealistic to think that the Office of the President can reside in Olympian splendor aloof from the major economic controversies and the telling issue of price level containment or explosion. The argument that the President will be involved in each small conflict is unworthy. If the guidepost line can be enforced in big unions and big industries, the results will filter down and cut across the general occupational spectrum.

THE WILL AND THE WAY

If the program outlined—or a substitute—is ineffective or unacceptable, a more rigid set of wage controls may have to be imposed, at least over the period of military involvement. The need for any far-reaching program will be minimized as unions perceive that the President is determined and apprehend that their national survival depends on their acceptance of a code of public responsibility. Serious legislative changes may be unnecessary to gain their adherence to a program of restraint as an adjunct of power, influence—and affluence.

If these or alternate measures are dismissed, we will have to face up to a more severe program carrying overtones of public participation in wage agreements, as a third member of the collective bargaining panel, with a system of penalties for departure from the rules.[18] If the costs are too high and the noxious features too great, we must abandon any prospect of implementing a national wage policy. But the day on which we do that, we shall be conceding that full employment and a stable price level are inconsistent goals. We shall be declaring that our economic system must fail on the one front or the other. We shall be admitting that we do not have the will, the discipline, or the self-control to achieve both ends. Then we will inevitably revert to monetary policy with its toll of unemployment to discipline labor. We shall be proclaiming that Karl Marx was right in his assessment of capitalism's defects.

My guess is that we shall find a way to demonstrate that the Communist prophet was wrong. It should be possible, through a recognition of labor and business responsibility, and with a moderate extension of governmental power, to restrain the economy from an inflationary binge while making job opportunities full and universal. We know the ingredients of the program, and we are aware of the unsavory alternatives. Only the pessimists will choose inflation *or* unemployment, instead of a rational application of a necessary dose of wage and salary restraint.

Of course, the immediate crises may dissolve. The Vietnam fighting may cease. But need we always wait for military outlays to accomplish full employment? Can comfortable public officials and affluent intellectuals condone complacency when other men face the frustration of joblessness? Must we accept the view that unemployment for someone else is not an unmitigated evil? When unemployment is more generally regarded as immoral, and as an intolerable blemish on our democratic economic ways, we shall again have to consider our wage-income practices. The inflation–

full-employment duel will again have to be fought. After some tentative probes, I suspect that price stability and job opportunities will survive the final thrust.

NOTES

1. Interestingly enough, on the matter of wage and price control Britain finally instituted a mandatory wage-price freeze after several years of temporizing. *New York Times,* October 5, 1966.

2. The late Sumner Slichter was a leading exponent of this view. See his "Argument for 'Creeping' Inflation," *New York Times Magazine,* March 8, 1959.

3. A six-page space allotment has normally been given to the guide-posts in subsequent reports though there are some variations in the textual discussion.

4. It is true that Marx had *real* wages in mind. But those who would sacrifice employment to exert discipline over labor and the price level would invite his cynicism today. While for Marx the reduction in real wages protected capitalist profits, the effort to avert inflation through unemployment is directed to protecting rentier interests.

5. In the riots in San Francisco in late September 1966 the Mayor asked for federal assistance in finding jobs for the unemployed.

6. According to data of the Department of Commerce, between 1962 and 1965 the markup factor in gross national private product moved up from 1.92 to 1.93 (or 1.917 to 1.930). The price deflator for the same years rose from 104.7 to 108.9. Thus the markup factor rose by just under 0.7 per cent while the price movement amounted to just over 4 per cent. *Survey of Current Business,* July 1966, pp. 13, 30, 38.

7. See "The Constancy of the Wage Share," in my *Some Aspects of Wage Theory and Wage Policy* (Philadelphia: 1963).

8. A larger essay, "Toward a National Wage Policy," appears in *Wage Theory and Wage Policy.*

9. The Council of Economic Advisers has been less than explicit on this matter, noting the problem rather than suggesting a solution. The 1962 report states: "Such changes may either add to or subtract from the increment which is available for wage increases under the over-all productivity guide" (p. 190). Fortunately the statement is omitted in the 1966 report. Surely we must keep the average wage or salary under surveillance, and not the pay scale for a particular

job. The earlier report also seemed unconcerned about industry bargains in excess of the guideposts so long as the price of output was not raised. This could easily foster discriminatory treatment of labor by industry bargains rather than by economy-wide productivity relations. *Report* (1962), p. 190.

10. Cf. my estimates in "The Wage-Earner Outlay-Function," in *Wage Theory and Wage Policy*.

11. Results are much the same in other countries. For in those places that have a handful of millionaires, and a numerous and poor population, once we say that there is only a handful of the former, we must conclude that their aggregate consumption is not likely to be large, at least of the essentials of living, such as food and clothing. This is even the case in a country as poor as India, where despite the pitiful living standards most of the consumption will be by the poor— the wage-earning group.

12. Salaries have been injected into the previous remarks for the first time. A detailed examination of the exact dividing line between the concepts of salary and wage need not be undertaken here; one is scarcely distinguishable from the other. If we succeed in holding the line on wage movements we should be able to hold the salary line. If salaries move up sharply, policy may have to be directed to this sector of our wage structure. Better studies of salary- and wage-employee classifications are needed for the guidepost program.

13. In 1962 consumption outlays were about 63.4 per cent of the gross national product. They were in the same proportion in 1965. In the second quarter of 1966, the percentage was still 62.8 per cent despite the mounting military outlays. Taking employment to be in the same ratios as expenditures, the N/Nc ratio would rise from 1.58 to 1.59.

14. With the same assumptions of wage earners consuming and profit recipients saving, and government outlays balanced by taxes in both groups, the same general result follows. With a government deficit, profits are equal to the sum of investment plus the deficit, compared to the position of an untaxed but saved gross profit.

15. The sum of $(R + F)$ is about $300 billion, with w at about $5,000. On this basis, a $100 wage increase which raises prices proportionately can increase profits by about $6 billion.

16. Curiously, the overheating analysts have almost never recommended an extension of the work week. This should be the obvious measure to cope with temporary strains on our productive facilities.

17. A Price-Productivity-Income Office (PPI Office) has since been recommended by the Joint Economic Committee. See *Joint Economic Report*, 90th Cong., 2nd Sess., Report No. 73 (March 17, 1967), pp. 23–24.

18. The British Labour party seems to have this change in mind for its long-run wage policy. *New York Times*, October 6, 1966.

Appendix 2

An Incomes Policy to Stop Inflation

(Considering the topical references, the reader is reminded that this paper first appeared in Lloyds Bank Review, *January 1971.— ed.)*

Inflation in the United States continues substantially unabated; and in the United Kingdom, too, there are few signs of its slowing down. In America, all expectations are for continuing inflation through 1971 and 1972 with, at best, minor moderation. The value of money will continue to erode.

Whatever may have been true in the past, inflation today in the U.S. and in Britain is largely, if not entirely, "cost-push," induced by excessively high wage agreements. Monetary and fiscal policies have so far failed to bring rising costs and prices under control. Yet, because of the toll in unemployment, there are now more frequent pleas in the U.S. to loosen monetary policy. Monetary control has thus run its course.

Monetary policy works by denying funds to business, for investment, for construction, for housing. As the economy slows up and unemployment develops, the expectation is that pressure for excessive wage increases will be damped down. Clearly, this expectation has not been realized. Wage advances in the U.S. are averaging 9 per cent, while in Britain in the third quarter of the year the average wage settlement (for manual workers) was about 11 per cent, in both cases way above any current increase in productivity.

Fiscal policy involves expenditure restraint and tax increases. But inflation itself, the higher prices for goods the government buys, involves higher expenditure merely to stand still. New government programs require further expenditures. Even the economy-minded Nixon administration thus found itself facing higher outlays. On the tax front, with growing unemployment, the likelihood in America is that proposals for tax decreases, rather than increases, will become more commonplace.

The major fallacy of stringent tax measures to cope with inflation is that this attempts to capture the increases in wage incomes *after* they occur. The belief is that the absorption of income, *after* wages (and salaries) rise, will depress demand and thereby contain prices. Yet, no program recommended has ever been ample by this test. If taxes average 30 per cent of incomes, and incomes go up by 10 per cent, taxes would have to rise by over 20 per cent merely to hold incomes to their former net level. This sort of surtax has yet to be recommended! Further, while taxes *might* contain the demand side—if severe enough—they fail to deal with the effect on prices of higher labor costs. And costs *do* influence prices. This is the great deficiency of fiscal action or tax policy to counter inflation.

SUGGESTED REMEDIES

In the light of these shortcomings of monetary and fiscal policy, we can review some of the income policy proposals frequently recommended, before I outline an alternative plan that has the virtue of simplicity, while avoiding the major shortcomings of these other suggestions.

The first is a simple wage-price freeze, to endure for six months to a year. As a crash program, fired with initial enthusiasm, it might work. Yet, after a lapse of time, what then? Experience—as in Britain after 1966—has been a renewal of the preceding wage-price momentum that originally induced the "freeze." What is essential, therefore, is a durable program to assure price level stability over the long term. It is a policy for a decade that we seek, rather than one for the month or year.

Besides a freeze being too brief, and only a temporary palliative, its major disadvantage is that it also requires some policing mechanism to enforce it. This may immediately lose some potential adherents to an incomes policy, those sympathetic to a wages and prices program, but disenchanted with the prospect of a pervasive bureaucracy.

Establishing a control agency to supervise prices and all major wage contracts is the most direct solution; it is the stuff of wartime regulation, even in democracies. But this involves a new bureaucracy that may alter the economic system in ways which may turn out to be imprudent, inefficient, and interventionist. Its failures are likely to give other needed and potentially effective government programs a black eye.

Some have advised government to sit in as a participant on key collective bargaining negotiations in order to limit pay increases to norms that could be sustained by typical productivity improvements. The drawback here is that the approach is likely to lead to acrimony, as being one-sided. Employers could, in effect, relax and let the government hammer out settlement terms substantially below those of recent years. Inserting government as a bargaining agent is likely to thrust it into prominence as being hostile to labor. The policy would disintegrate under an administration eager to woo labor in an election year.

The guide-post plan under President Kennedy invoked the presidential office to dissuade unions from seeking undue advances and to deter business from making heedless price increases. The most dramatic incident was the President's confrontation with the steel industry, which then had to perform a humiliating retreat under threat of coercive investigation.

A "jaw-bone" policy, involving persuasion and reproach, derives its strength from an appeal to public morality. It obliges the President—or Prime Minister?—to "lay his prestige on the line" in numerous public controversies. As it dissipates his power, it is likely to be employed with caution before fading off into feebleness. More than name-calling must be directed to situations that arise persistently, rather than sporadically.

Suggestions for labor courts for arbitration can be brushed aside. We are dealing with an economic, not a legal, issue. What is wanted is not a place for lawyers to perform, but a proper resolution of the public interest on specific principle. A cumbersome bureaucracy may be a lesser evil than an undiscerning and dilatory judiciary.

INGREDIENTS OF A SOLUTION

These are the main approaches to an incomes policy recommended so far. All are found wanting. Let us consider the ingredients of a new and feasible approach.

Some people are convinced that the problem will not abate unless unions are either destroyed or so fragmented as to sap them of their bargaining power. This is an extreme attitude certain to generate heated and irrelevant debate. Unions are here to stay. There is no way of eliminating them in the present climate of democracy. Most people will view this as a good thing: well-run unions, and even some not so well-run, accomplish many important and worthwhile ends. They are the counterweight to the unbridled economic power of industry. They are the protectors, the big brothers, of their members. While their acts are often unreasonable, industrialists were not always the sweet souls of reason before unions developed their present power. Nobody can lament the transition from the age that gave credence to Karl Marx and led him to predict capitalism's demise. Unions have literally saved capitalism from its own crudities; it is no accident that American union leaders today are often greater champions of the enterprise system than some unreconciled capitalists flirting with totalitarian ventures that could prove their undoing.

STIFFENING RESISTANCE

Nevertheless, it is with the unhampered power of unions to secure excessive wage settlements that we must deal. Industrialists are too often too impotent to neutralize the ability of unions to impose inflationary settlements, which occur even to the detriment of other wage-earners, as all seek to protect their own position by counter-claims for wage increases. The upshot is that all are penalized by the ensuing general inflation. All run faster to stay pretty much in the same place.

The solution must consist of measures to stiffen the backbone of industrialists. Currently, industrialists are simply prone to yield rather than to endure costly strikes; the ritual involves a submission to union pressure before passing the bill on in the form of higher prices. We are caged in the jungle of inflation because others have been trapped there before. None can be blamed for the plight, yet everyone is culpable for the outcome.

Individual industrialists will be encouraged to resist unreasonable demands only when they are convinced that there will be resistance in other industries. Also, when each labor union understands that employers are no longer easy targets capable of passing on price increases to consumers, to rescue them from haphazard settlements, unions can be expected to act more moderately at the bargaining table. The hapless sitting-duck image of management officials must be erased before any plan can succeed as a defense against inflation.

Hence, we must change matters so that it is in their self-interest, for their own preservation, that industrialists will reject extravagant wage settlements. Penalties must be attached to abject surrender. Also, if defeat does come, it will be only partial; the terms of surrender *must not* be too onerous. Partial cave-ins and prudent compromise must thereby contain some safety-valve to avert a chain reaction and a business collapse; neither bankruptcy nor punitive levies should be engendered. But the price of submission must be made high enough to dissuade management from frequent surrender.

In substance, what is required is an application of the principle that if the strong (the unions) cannot be weakened, the weak (management) must be strengthened. In war, if the strength of the enemy is firm, then the condition of your own troops must be improved. In competitive sports generally, where you cannot govern the skill of your rival, you must raise your own. A similar principle must be applied to the bargaining table.

A REASONABLE WAGE PROGRAM

As one further preliminary matter, to allay any fears that the program is designed to eliminate unions or to thwart the legitimate aspirations of the working man, let us appraise its objectives.

The aim is increases in money wages at least equal, on the average, to the gains in productivity in the economy. In the past, these have tended to aproximate 3 per cent a year in America (about the same rate as in Britain for the increase in output per man-hour since the late 1950s). With little inflationary cost, an average increase of 3 per cent or so, or even of 4 to 5 per cent a year, could be granted without inviting an erosive inflation. Even a target figure of 5 per cent would be more rational than the 10 per cent and more figures of recent months that have exacerbated Britain's inflationary problem, and thus sapped the value of her money.

An average increase of 4 per cent would mean that in ten years the *typical wage income would mount by about 50 per cent*. All wage incomes would, on average, double in about 18 years. This is scarcely a program designed to grind labor to poverty or to confine workers to capitalistic misery. The goals are reasonable and realistic, attainable with only modest inflationary pressures: prices might mount gently, at a pace of 1 per cent a year. With slightly greater risk, an average annual gain of 5 per cent in wages could be promised. This would mean about 60 per cent per decade, with wages doubling every 14 years. Inflation, however, would build up to about a 2 per cent rate a year.

These are the wage objectives and the price level accompaniment. Only in slander and obfuscation could such a program be alleged to be inimical to the ordinary working man or to be antilabor generally. If achieved, it would protect labor and the economy from the sordid inflationary events of recent years.

A further gain of much significance to labor would be realized as a by-product. With the price level nearly steady, monetary and fiscal policy could drop their anti-inflationary stance. The economy could work closer to full employment. Unemployment would diminish. Needed public expenditures could be undertaken. The construction industry could be given the signal to build the new housing to make some dent toward reducing the urban housing blight and clearing the slums.

These are no small advantages of an average wage increase of 4 per cent to 5 per cent per annum—with prices rising only gently.

THE KEY TO COUNTERVAILING POWER

It is time now to get down to specifics and to outline the details of a program that satisfies the criteria described, not for the purpose of destroying the unions but for generating counter-pressures toward fostering what Galbraith has perceptively termed *countervailing power*. This must be localized within business firms, so that they stand fast against the more extreme inflationary exactions of unions.

Recent facts are abundantly clear. Unions have proposed, and businessmen have acquiesced, not of course to the initial more unreasonable demands of unions but to the ultimate, and equally unrealistic, settlement figures. As recompense, management has raised prices, so that the buyer has become the unwitting victim.

Management must be made to resist or be penalized for its retreat. Above all, it must not be sustained in craven settlements which then involve higher prices to protect its profit position.

AN EXCESS WAGE SETTLEMENT TAX

Government has a ready lever to perform the task with nominal administrative cost. Put simply, what can be done is to impose an extra corporate (or business) income tax on all firms that agree to settlements exceeding, say, 5 per cent on the average, as compared to their average figure for employee compensation in the previous year.

An illustration may help. Suppose that in 1970 the average wage (and salary) figure for a firm was £1,000. If the average wage and salary payment for the firm in 1971 exceeded £1,050 ($= 1.05 \times$ £1,000), it would be subject to an anti-inflation tax which would be superimposed on the tax base. If the corporate tax rate was 42½ per cent, and the average wage increment exceeded 5 per cent, but was less than 6 per cent higher than the previous year, then a 6 per cent added tax levy might be imposed (48½ per cent in all). For a wage increase between 6 per cent and 7 per cent over the previous year, an 8 per cent penalty rate could be applied, and so on.

The governing principle, therefore, involves *placing the full burden of policing anti-inflation wage increases upon the business firm.* Where they were supine in bargaining, the tax penalty would mount; they would have to be adamant in resisting union pressures. Unions would become cognizant of this; they would quickly perceive that they were no longer firing at ducks in a shooting gallery, knocking off firms that had paid in the past only by passing the burden on through higher prices.

It is unnecessary here to specify the exact details of the progression in the tax scale for firms that emerge as the worst offenders in ignoring the public interest in arresting inflation. Some will advocate lesser penalties, others may justify sterner levels. The main point remains; namely, that if the union structure is not to be altered, then the remedy consists of forcing employers to act in the public good in defending their private advantage. Employers must be the inflation fighters; they must no longer be permitted to act as agents in transmitting the price burden forward with profit immunity to themselves.

WHY THE PLAN WOULD WORK

Let us consider reasons why the plan should work, as well as anticipate some potential objections to it.

Unions would immediately realize that they could no longer toss on to the bargaining table a take-it or leave-it package, and hold out a strike threat which employers could avoid with small loss through price increases. Unions would apprehend that, because of the tax aspect, employers would be *bound* to resist. Long, drawn-out strikes for nominal gains are not consciously sought by unions. This unwelcome prospect would pull them down from the heights of unreason.

There would be an obvious reason for management to stand firm: the costs of excessive settlements would be lodged with shareholders. No management that was negligent in protecting the shareholder interest could survive for very long; its submissiveness would be publicized. Currently, shareholders accept inordinate settlements so long as most of the cost is passed on via prices. 'Why suffer needlessly,' is the prevailing attitude; this would quickly change.

The proposal should also commend itself to the ardent devotees of monetary and fiscal measures to curb inflation. For, in an atmosphere of excess wage gains, the proposal would accomplish an automatic increase in the corporate tax rate, thereby alleviating inflationary pressure through absorbing purchasing power. Thus, the recommendation entails a built-in anti-inflationary fiscal policy, from the tax side. The budget would thus benefit.

This adds another cutting edge to the proposal. On the monetary side, the lower net profits resulting from an injudicious settlement would tend to restrain borrowing and investment, reducing the demand for funds in the capital markets.

AUTOMATIC POLICING

It is in the policing of the program that the virtues of the plan outweigh those of any of the alternative proposals. At present, for social security programs and the like, firms must report the number of their full-time employees, and they also report their wage and salary bill. Dividing the latter total by the former will yield the average employee compensation. The final step involves comparing this figure with the amount for the previous year. If it was excessive, then the penalty rates would take effect.

No new form of government intervention would be involved; only the tax structure would be affected. No new bureaucracy would need to be created to police the program. Everything would be accomplished through the well-established tax procedures for filing returns, and checking their veracity. There would be no new complex procedures nor any harassment of business by yet another new arm of government.

SAFETY-VALVE ASPECT

The plan would not entirely prevent higher wage increases. But, where granted, the burden would be borne solely by the acquiescing firm. Unions would have to become more realistic, for firms would not be as vulnerable as in the past. If firms did yield to exorbitant demands, the penalties would involve only money. There would be no criminal charges, no bureaucratic harassment, none of the condemnation and moral disapprobation accompanying other price-wage programs.

The safety-valve feature of penalty taxes has even more in its favor. Where firms required especially skilled people they could still pay above-market wage or salary scales if necessary. While the practice would be somewhat more costly on the tax side, the firm's operations would not be unduly obstructed. Although the plan would benefit firms with little responsibility for the inflationary environment, the institutional impediment erected for small run-of-the-mill offenders would not be insurmountable.

The plan thus has the necessary flexibility. It cannot be contended in good conscience that an added tax on *some* firms would herald the end of capitalism. This is a stale refrain sung whenever new rules are promulgated or new tax rates imposed. Yet, the system has survived and flourished. It can support higher penalty rates on firms that are slack about inflation.

SALARIES

Common equity requires that salaries and executive pay be included in calculating the average employee compensation. It would be distinctly unfair to limit ordinary workmen, while executives were free to raise their own incomes freely on the pretext that their earnings were noninflationary. If incomes are to be restrained, it must be *all* incomes, including those of executives. The system would not be handicapped by this; considering that it would be only the corporate *average* that would be computed, larger individual merit increases would still be possible.

Legitimate issues arise with respect to stock options, retirement plans or other fringe benefits that executives have arrogated to themselves. But this is a separate theme that invites more detailed study. The point remains, that there is nothing in the present proposal that should in any way dilute the incentives of managers. There is enough variety in opportunity, status, interest of work, or the incontrovertible power aspects of being "boss" to assure a continuing flow of aspirants for executive posts.

THE BARGAINING ARENA

As another virtue of the proposal, collective bargaining would not be basically affected, although the more fantastic agreements of the past would probably no longer be seen. From the union standpoint, the inclusion of executive salaries in the average compensation figure would provide a little more margin for bargaining; wages could rise by a bit more than 5 per cent if executive salaries rose by less, without tax penalty to the firm.

This could also serve a healthy purpose in preventing indiscriminate pay rises to managers, while a firm was pleading poverty to the unions. A more wary eye would be placed on all business incomes, with the not unlaudable result of curbing rates of compensation to corporate executives vastly in excess of those of the President of the United States, or cabinet officers, or public officials, for tasks that are generally far less exacting.

To repeat, the corporation could continue to be magnanimous to employees or executives. But it would have to answer to the tax collector. The tax aspect would be like the American traffic policeman's whistle: look, advance with caution—or answer to the shareholders. In a small way, the corporation would be returned closer to its shareholders. This is an advantage, not a drawback. It may inculcate a greater sense of executive responsibility.

Collective bargaining would thus be retained under the proposal and it could proceed as before—almost. The annual ceiling of 5 per cent on average wage increases would not be absolute; more might be squeezed out occasionally, at executive expense or through the firm being made subject to higher taxes. But the extravagant settlements of the past would not often be repeated.

Unions could not really protest the deterrent program. Their status would be preserved. Their membership could be promised a doubling of pay almost every 15 years, and upwards of 50 per cent per decade. Unions today do not represent impoverished, undernourished, economically-deprived citizens. There is no intention to exploit their membership. But they would no longer be as free as before to injure other parts of society, including other wage-earners and their former members, the retired workers.

Undoubtedly, unions would make the usual noises in opposing the proposal. But these should fall on deaf ears, for it would place them in the anomalous position of opposing a *corporate income tax.* For the proposal is just that. Traditionally, unions have argued for higher corporate taxes in objecting to income taxes on lower-paid workers.

Like all of us, union members have a stake in the battle against inflation. The proposal recommended would permit them to carry on practically unhampered. It would serve their own long-run interests, in contrast to the futile current game of leap-frog in wages and prices, where excess wage gains end up mainly as an optical illusion while the value of money dwindles.

Unions would, of course, still retain their ultimate coercive weapon, the strike. Yet strike threats are carried out only if the projected gains are expected (over time) to outweigh the losses. While it might be some time before unions realized that the opportunities for success were not as rife as in the past, the understanding would come as businessmen knew that they could not agree as readily as before because of the unfavorable tax aspects. With greater business adamancy predictable, union demands would be more tempered and restrained. Temporarily, union leaders might continue their former tactics. But frequent strikes for limited wage improvements would not be resorted to as often as in the past, when the possibilities of large wage increases also constituted the prize at the end of a conflict. As the Nixon administration had expressed it, business must be "prepared to take it" to cut the settlement terms. "Taking it" on a few occasions, and then settling near the 5 per cent–6 per cent average annual increase level, would be likely to dissuade unions from frequent resort to their tactical strike weapon.

Business objections would probably be but a feeble echo of union complaints. Business, too, could persist in past practices. But there would be a cost, a tax bite. Otherwise, there would be "business as usual." The more demagogic might argue that the proposal attempts to restrain wages but not profits. This would be to misconstrue it entirely, perhaps intentionally. What we are concerned with is not a plan to remodel the market system but to render it effective by curbing its inflationary thrust. If prices can be contained, then profits cannot sky-rocket. One look at the stock market should be enough to reveal to the captious that profits have not been swollen in recent years. If experience were such that profits became unduly large the remedy would be the obvious one: to use the tax mechanism. But to discuss this aspect in the present context is to lay a smokescreen around the central issue of inflation.

THE SELF-EMPLOYED

Incomes of the self-employed, such as physicians, accountants, lawyers, small businessmen, and those of government employees, have gone unmentioned.

Briefly, we could expect that, if the mass of wage and salary incomes were contained, then it would not be possible for the self-employed group to secure incomes growing faster than the general average. There would be two strong reasons for this: first, in some cases the forces of competition would operate; the margins of substitution between employment and self-employment are often close in the small business sector; and, secondly, if incomes for the mass of employees failed to rise unduly, it would not be as easy for self-employed people, in the U.S. at least, to raise their prices (and incomes) at the same pace as in the recent past. Government employees, likewise, could simply be limited to the general wage rise to maintain competitive standards.

Thus, it is as if we put down a sturdy anchor for fastness and stability. If it ties the vast number of business incomes, of employees and executives, the income adjustments in the rest of the economy would be so held back as to bar the noxious drift to inflation.

We could proceed on this assumption. If it proved wrong with respect to some sectors of the economy, this could later be corrected. But we cannot shrink from taking the big step merely because it may be less than complete. A "do-nothing" program, or the present array of policies, entails more obvious and more serious omissions.

Another objection that may be put is the pejorative aphorism that "the power to tax is the power to destroy." While the phrase has merit it is regrettably incomplete: the power to tax is also a vehicle for making social, political, and economic life more tolerable. Ultimately, this is what taxation should be about, to accomplish worthwhile ends that would not otherwise materialize in the business sector without government policy. As the intended tax proposal aims to curb inflation, it is compatible with the greater freedom; it is destined to expand it, not inhibit it.

Whenever a stage is reached that warrants lower general

taxes, there is nothing in the program that jeopardizes such a move. Basic business tax rates could be lowered *so long as the anti-inflation penalty tax rate were retained*. If and when business and union conduct became more responsible with respect to inflation, even this feature could be dropped. But by then the tax would be likely to be a dead letter anyway.

CONCLUSION

There can, thus, be few serious objections to the anti-inflation proposal I have outlined. It has undiluted virtues. It *may* work, to take the most pessimistic assessment. On the basis of economic analysis, it should work. There are no serious costs involved; it does not shelter a new bureaucracy. It does not entail new data and business controls. Neither the scope nor the organizational structure of trade unions will be affected, although their ceiling in collective bargaining is likely to become more clearly defined. It does not embark on any radical paths in economic control. It is not incompatible with the traditions of a market economy and its greater freedoms.

Unless we adopt a simple remedy, such as that outlined above, we are likely to inherit the worst of both worlds, with inflation and unemployment increasing as the present inadequate policies are pursued. In desperation, we might ultimately be forced to adopt more extreme measures, of widespread controls, or face the more divisive steps involved in "cutting unions down to size." Failing either, we are likely to falter ignominiously in the struggle against inflation until the value of money is fatally eroded and large-scale currency reforms are undertaken—without resolving the fundamental underlying malady.

To reiterate, the policy is *not* anti-labor. It is *anti-inflation*. Opponents should not be permitted to obscure or distort our vision. It promises average wage increases for labor in the region of 60 per cent per decade, and 100 per cent in approximately 15 years. This is not the stuff that unions can represent as "an attack on labor's rights." It is destined to conserve them, and to enhance labor's esteem and self-respect in a non-inflationary economy.

The incomes policy suggested here can be expected to control the price level, for it has two sides to it: it limits the increase in unit costs which *push* prices upwards, and it governs the income purchasing power, which pulls prices higher. Later on, if it still happens that prices continue to rise, it will be time enough to look at the industries or special monopoly sectors—where these exist—that are upsetting the stability of the economy. Then we shall know that business is at fault. All the present evidence points to incomes, to excessive wage and salary gains and to their translation into costs as the dominating cause that requires immediate correction.

Appendix 3

Solow and Stiglitz on Employment and Distribution: *A New Romance with an Old Model?* *

I

Reading the recent contribution of Solow and Stiglitz, I gained the impression that I had seen much of it before—and in my own work (based on Keynes) a decade earlier.[1] While it would be surprising if two craftsmen as skilled as Solow and Stiglitz did not break new ground and elicit new insights, my own (biased!) view suggests that much of their argument can be fitted into my old framework. They also express their intention of introducing a monetary mechanism and of running their work "in terms of the money wage, price level, and employment."[2] This, too, was my earlier concern.[3]

In what follows, my main comments will focus on the overlap of basic concepts as viewed from a comparative statics or equilibrium standpoint.

* A helpful letter from Professor Solow led to some changes in this note, especially in the final section. I must thank Sir Roy Harrod, Professors Lawrence Klein, E. S. Phelps, and Almarin Phillips for comments on an earlier draft.

II

Solow and Stiglitz observe initially:

> It soon became clear to us that . . . in the marginal productivity theory the main function of the real-wage is to clear the labor market, while in the Cambridge theory the main function of the real-wage is to clear the commodity market.[4]

My own work proceeded without any suspicion of conflict between these theories. Rather than documenting this assertion, the same end will be served by considering their substantive conclusion, and then citing some parallels.[5]

Near the close of their paper they assess the "Cambridge theory" of Professors Kaldor and Robinson, later adopted by Mr. Pasinetti, that the profit (and wage) share depends on the investment-income ratio and on the savings propensities of the wage- and profit-earning classes. They remark:

> There is a sense in which the marginal-productivity theory can be said to hold at any supply-limited equilibrium, and the Cambridge theory can be said to hold at any demand-limited equilibrium.[6]

Of course, this is "disequilibrium" economics, akin to Marshall's celebrated scissors, when the blades are open. Then:

> If the economic system runs, or is run, in such a way as to keep it near the intersection of the aggregate supply and aggregate demand curves, then both theories can hold determinately and simultaneously.[7]

It follows that in equilibrium both theories are joined.

Since Kaldor's article appeared after my manuscript was completed, I was able to consider it only in an appendix to a chapter on "Distribution and Employment." [8] I had argued that the wage share depends, according to the marginal productivity theory, on the ratio of M/A, where M was the marginal, and A the average, product of labor.[9] Considering Kaldor's formula, I wrote:

> In equilibrium, where aggregate demand, D, equals aggregate supply, $(Z \equiv Y)$, it follows that $(R/Y) = (1 - M/A)$, so that formula (2) above must be equal to $(1 - M/A)$.[10]

The formula (2) referred to was Kaldor's, with the symbol R constituting profits. The next paragraph began as follows:

> Thus it is an incomplete view of the process to emphasize the investment volume and the consumption proclivities to the exclusion of productivity phenomena: equilibrium requires that both outlay and productivity conditions be satisfied. Emphasis on one set might be justified only if one were volatile and the other rigid.

Then, farther on:

> In part, this chapter was undertaken to redress the balance and insert the variations in consumption-outlay behavior arising through the distributive revision in an output advance as a determinant of the ultimate income partition. Stress still centered in productivity but recognition was extended to the fact that the income shift emanating on the supply side . . . had its impact on demand.

Other passages stressed the importance of productivity on income division, and of income division on demand, as both demand and supply elements mutually interacted to determine equilibrium employment, output composition, income distribution, and the array of prices at a stipulated money wage.

III

In introducing their model Solow and Stiglitz posit that their analysis is "limited strictly to the short run," where there is "a given inventory of capital goods." [11] This assumption governed my work.[12]

Their equation (1) is a statement of the production function, of $Y = F(N)$; following Keynes, I preferred to work in terms of an inverse employment function.[13]

Their equation (2) specifies Y_s as aggregate supply:

> Aggregate supply at any real-wage is the output corresponding to the employment at which the marginal product of labor equals the real-wage, and is, therefore, a decreasing function of the real-wage, because of diminishing returns.[14]

My work (prior to including monopoly) stipulated Price = Marginal Cost, with labor the one variable factor, and with money wages assumed constant in setting up the aggregate supply curve. Thus my aggregate supply function also rested on marginal productivity phenomena—"diminishing returns and all that," as Solow characterized it in his review.[15]

Their equation (3) involves "completely inelastic" supply. As this is a special unemployment case, it need not detain us here. The same is true of their equation (4), which involves "the simple linear adjustment process" when aggregate demand and supply are not in balance. Next, they make contact with Cambridge doctrine in their equation for aggregate demand. They write

$$Y^D = I + (1 - s_w)vN + (1 - s_p)(Y^D - vN). \qquad (5)$$

When terms are moved around, their equation (6) emerges:

$$Y^D = \frac{I}{s_p} + \frac{s_p - s_w}{s_p} vN. \qquad (6)$$

In (6), Y^D denotes aggregate demand, N is employment, v is the real-wage, and the s-terms are the respective average savings propensities of wage earners and profit recipients.

My aggregate demand function also included government outlay. The consumer outlay portion of the demand total descended from *Aggregate Supply Proceeds* to *Personal Disposable Income*, and included terms for wage earners, rentiers, profit recipients and corporate withholdings, transfer recipients, and dissavers. It also tried to portray the *changes* in income division as employment altered in the course of an employment-output advance. The argument is encumbered—and sometimes confused—by the effort to embody the price level changes as employment varies, so that the average consumption propensities show some flux on the path to equilibrium.[16]

The Solow-Stiglitz income partition seems so obvious now. Why the fuss?

But this blithe view misses the whole point, and essentially the thrust of the Cambridge doctrine. For it is in (5) that income distribution emerges as a macroeconomic determinant. Studies of "the" consumption function and "the" marginal propensity to consume, to the neglect of the split among wage earners, corporate withholdings, dividend recipients, rentiers, and transfer recipients, are equivocal and inconclusive; one needs only to ponder the illumination conferred by the Cambridge income bisection. Income division, as they have made us aware, affects employment and the output composition; in turn, the relative shares are affected by the employment-output outcome. Mutual determination is manifest in the equilibrium result.

Once it is perceived that the wage earner dominates the consumption side,[17] and that the wage is paramount in marginal cost on the production side, the interdependence of aggregate demand and aggregate supply acquires a new transparence: the wage bill, and thus the money wage, is a parametric variable in both the demand and supply functions. Can it then be seriously argued in inflation theory—applied to consumer markets at least—that demand-pull and cost-push constitute independent strands comprising separate theories? The present Solow-Stiglitz article still misses the crucial significance of the money wage, and thus the special niche that wage policy must occupy in inflation control. Perhaps their future work will accord to the money wage the prominence it deserves.

Their equation (7) entails a "momentary" nonequilibrium quantity of output. Equation (8) describes the movement of the price level. Thus

$$p'/p = g(Y^D/Y^S) + jw'/w. \qquad (8)$$

With respect to the second component on the right, involving money wage changes as a price level force, I need refer only to the preceding paragraph.[18] As to the $g(\cdot)$ portion they write:

we have made the pressure on the price level a function of the ratio of aggregate demand to aggregate supply.[19]

Either this is the same argument I made earlier, or so close to it that any difference is hard—for me—to disentangle. My own procedure was to compare aggregate demand quantities with aggregate supply quantities and observe the expansionary (or contraction) forces for employment, output, and prices.

For wage changes they write

$$w'/w = h(N/N^s) + kp'/p. \qquad (9)$$

The price term involves the real-wage aspects underlying the wage bargaining process; the only issue here is the empirical question on the precise size of k, and whether it is past or future price changes that shape the bargaining course. As to the $h(\cdot)$ part, the N^s symbol connotes the labor supply, which they decide to view as perfectly inelastic.[20] Following Dennis Robertson and A. C. Pigou, and a then recent study by Clarence Long, I had adopted the same view—over a limited stretch.[21] N refers to the actual employment level.

The $h(\cdot)$ component embodies the modern Phillips curve relations which have been studied so assiduously at M.I.T.

Well before these ideas became so popular—and undoubtedly many others had written in the same way far earlier—I wrote, concerning a rise in employment coming from a strengthening of investment demand, that "with the tightening of the [labor] market we can assume that events become propitious either for new wage demands by the unions or higher wage offers by entrepreneurs faced individually by smaller pockets of unemployment." [22] Also, that "it is the tightening of the labor market . . . which is regarded as causal in lifting the money wage floor."

This seems to come to the same thing as in Solow and Stiglitz, though they may contend that their wage change is "endogenous" while mine is "exogenous." But I doubt this, just as I am dubious of interpreting the Phillips curve as a line rather than a band of "likely" values.

IV

In sum, if one neglects the very suggestive disequilibrium aspect of their study, the basic Solow-Stiglitz equations *resemble* the functions I used years ago. I also included some theory of money wages, individual firms and industry aspects, monopoly and its price distortions in a nonintegrated system, nonmaximum profit markups, changes in money wages and price levels on interest rates and investment, and some expectational aspects. Earlier, and more clearly later, capital growth was analyzed. They defer some of these topics for future study.[23]

Nonetheless, one issue that may be sticky remains. They declare that they make "the pressure on the price level a function of the ratio of aggregate demand to aggregate supply," with aggregate demand "defined in (5) as the sustainable volume of real expenditures, given the going employment and real-wage."[24] I interpret this in a Walrasian sense, as meaning the demand quantity wanted to the supply quantity offered, given a money wage and the implicit price (level) to comprise the real-wage. This account conforms to my own procedure, adopted so that the same *prices* could be built into the aggregate demand *and* supply functions. They remark, however, that "one might argue that a better index of the pressure on prices is desired expenditure at the actual level of output." But they conclude that "this alternative formulation of demand pressure . . . makes no qualitative difference to the results."[25] While this must be so for the equilibrium outcome, there will be differences in the description of the problem when the functions are elaborated in explicit money wage and price terms.

That this is a deeper issue becomes apparent in their dynamics, developed in their major section on the mechanics of the model. In this phase of the study they seek to equate $Y^D = F(N)$, or aggregate demand to aggregate supply. Thus: "We must find, for

each real-wage, a level of employment which will yield an aggregate demand at that real-wage whose production will require the
same amount of employment." [26]

For Solow and Stiglitz, therefore, the real-wage is held firm (in
a parametric sense) and the search is on for the equilibrium employment: "The first step is to find, for each real-wage, the short-
run equilibrium level of employment." [27]

My procedure was to keep the employment level fixed, as a
resultant of the expected volume and distribution of market demand, given the money wage and the productivity features. At
the emergent *supply* prices the question posed was whether the
demand quantities wanted by *all* purchasers were excess or deficient compared to supply offerings. The theory of inventory can
fit in readily in this analysis, as filling the gap in conditions of
excess demand or absorbing the slack under circumstances of excess supply. [28] Expansory or contractionist forces could then be
noted.

If at each N-level the demand prices for each output quantity
were distinguished from the supply prices built into the aggregate
supply curve, then it could happen that for some employment
levels actual prices closer to demand bids and, at other times,
closer to supply offers would emerge: there would not be any
systematic way of interpreting the price level aspects of an employment advance consequent upon shifts in aggregate demand
due, say, to an investment upswing. A Walrasian scheme thus
seemed to have merit over a Marshallian outlook for this part of
the analysis.

It is in this respect that I have some difficulty with the Solow
and Stiglitz version of dynamics, inasmuch as it is usually rendered in real terms, involving the w/p real-wage ratio rather than
setting either as an absolute amount. My own preference—then
and now—is to pursue the logical consequences of a system in
which the absolute money wage is resolved immediately, and
then opened to allow for unemployment and transfer incomes,
rentier incomes, corporate withholdings, price policy, changes in
money supplies, investment variations, and so on. Of course, this

is Keynes's method, as I interpreted him, of working in terms of a constant wage unit.

At the moment, in the interests of brevity, a comparison of several conclusions which I regard as suspect may be deferred until Solow and Stiglitz have published a sequel to this article. Perhaps in the future they may find it useful to look at the problem on the hypothesis of a given money wage level—the wage unit thus fixed—and, with their powerful mathematical technique, reveal whether policy proposals depend on the change in point of view. I suspect that policy differences will develop, for what we decide to do depends on how we envisage the world.

Notes

1. Robert Solow and Joseph E. Stiglitz, "Output, Employment, and Wages." Reference is to my book, *Approach to the Theory of Income Distribution.*

2. *Op. cit.,* p. 559. I also applied the same structure to growth theory—as they propose to do. See *A Keynesian Theory of Employment Growth and Income Distribution* (Philadelphia: Chilton Book Co., 1967).

3. Solow reviewed my book, *Journal of Political Economy,* August 1959, 420–21. The present article indicates a substantial retreat from his earlier criticisms.

4. *Op. cit.,* p. 538.

5. While drawing heavily on Keynes, my own work proceeded independently of Mrs. Robinson or Nicholas Kaldor. No one can deny their priorities, in clarity and emphasis, along with M. Kalecki. If the Cambridge views had been available earlier I would undoubtedly have avoided many obscurities.

6. "Output, Employment, and Wages," p. 558.

7. *Ibid.*

8. The *Approach* was published in February 1958. I began work on it in the late 1940s.

9. This simple result was derived independently though it appears in A. L. Marty, "Diminishing Returns and the Relative Share of Labor," *Quarterly Journal,* 1953. Professor Marty was questioning Keynes's view that diminishing *marginal* productivity would lower the wage share. For recent use, see P. A. Samuelson and F. Modig-

liani, "The Pasinetti Paradox in Neoclassical and More General Models," *The Review of Economic Studies*, 1966, pp. 272, 279.

10. *Approach*, p. 106.

11. "Output, Employment, and Wages," p. 538.

12. See p. 24. The extension to a growing stock of equipment appears in *Employment Growth*.

13. This permitted me to retain the individual output functions for separate industries. I think that this retains awareness of the price-output *structure;* in my view Keynes's original concern with units still confronts Solow and Stiglitz, for an aggregate production function conveys output *and* employment homogeneity. The other way around, only labor homogeneity need be assumed.

14. "Output, Employment, and Wages," p. 539.

15. A word more on their equations (1–2). At the time I wrote, the 45° approach was the dominant brand of Keynesianism. Supply phenomena played no part in the argument; from my reading of Keynes I sought to repair this gap in the usual macroeconomic account of income theory. Now Solow and Stiglitz also strive to remedy this omission in the conventional theory of output and employment. One hopes that the function may henceforth appear more frequently in our textbooks; my own preference is for the money wage and price details to remain explicit elements in drawing the function, rather than to use simply their ratio as a "real" wage, as in the Solow-Stiglitz account.

Interestingly enough, Solow has for many years used an aggregate production function in his *growth* theory. On the other hand, output and employment theory has ordinarily emphasized only aggregate demand. My growth theory premises that both "blades" have to be incorporated into the argument.

16. *Approach*, pp. 30–39, 86–95. The income division aspects, as in the Solow-Stiglitz equation (5), are more neatly pronounced in my *Employment Growth*, Chap. 2, and *Wage Theory and Policy*, Chap. 1.

17. My estimates indicate that wage—and salary—employees account for nearly 90 per cent of the consumption purchases in the United States (*Wage Theory*, Chap. 1). In less affluent countries the figure may be higher. Yet so many discussions of "the" consumption function read as if the empirical propositions refer to wealthy English country squires in the past century, rather than mainly to wage earners with only a minor saving option.

For savings analysis, the identification of the corporation as the main vehicle of saving is long overdue even in simple models. Likewise, the influence of rentiers and dividend recipients in consumer markets deserves to be isolated from that of wage earners. Further, income shifts between rentiers and "profits" can occur even with a "constant" wage share. If we agree that most of the economist's analysis is concerned with the business sector, then the concept of (gross) business product rather than (gross?) national income should play a more prominent part in income models; on this basis the wage-rentier-corporate split would appear to be particularly apt.

My colleague Lawrence Klein informs me that he has made income-type separations in his econometric models for many years. While undoubtedly many others do the same, too many discussions in the past were less insistent on the importance of the wage earner on the consumption side. (It would not be difficult to document this point.)

18. My own writings on the money wage and the price level go back to 1940. Keynes, and Mrs. Robinson, argued this way even earlier.

19. "Output, Employment, and Wages," p. 544.

20. *Ibid.*

21. *Approach*, p. 120.

22. *Ibid.*, p. 127.

23. Numerous scattered remarks on the theory of money, which they announce for future inclusion, appear in my *Classical Keynesianism*, Chaps. 4–5. Also, *Employment Growth*, pp. 71–72.

24. "Output, Employment, and Wages," p. 544.

25. *Ibid.*

26. *Ibid.*, p. 545.

27. *Ibid.* The impact of government employees, the unemployed, fixed-income recipients, and dissavers will have to be spelled out in much more detail in a more realistic model.

28. The theory of inventory does not appear to be so formidable a problem on this basis.

Index